THE

TRIANGLE

American Encounters/Global Interactions

A series edited by Gilbert M. Joseph
and Emily S. Rosenberg

This series aims to stimulate critical perspectives and fresh interpretive frameworks for scholarship on the history of the imposing global presence of the United States. Its primary concerns include the deployment and contestation of power, the construction and deconstruction of cultural and political borders, the fluid meanings of intercultural encounters and the complex interplay between the global and the local. *American Encounters* seeks to strengthen dialogue and collaboration between historians of U.S. international relations and area studies specialists.

The series encourages scholarship based on multiarchival historical research. At the same time, it supports a recognition of the representational character of all stories about the past and promotes critical inquiry into issues of subjectivity and narrative. In the process, *American Encounters* strives to understand the context in which meanings related to nations, cultures, and political economy are continually produced, challenged, and reshaped.

THE

IMPOSSIBLE

TRIANGLE

MEXICO, SOVIET RUSSIA,
AND THE UNITED STATES IN
THE 1920S

DANIELA SPENSER

Foreword by Friedrich Katz

Duke University Press

Durham and London   1999

© 1999 Duke University Press
All rights reserved
Printed in the United States of America on
acid-free paper ♾
Typeset in Trump Mediaeval by
Keystone Typesetting, Inc.
Library of Congress Cataloging-in-Publication
Data appear on the last printed page of this book.

In memory of Vladimir Tosek,
who thought that one day
the entire planet would be the
homeland of Communism.
For Ruth Tosek,
who loved him for the strength of his faith.

In memory of Emma Rizo Campomanes,
Mexican humanist
who defended noble causes and justice.
For Daniel Yanes Grollova,
who inherited her ideals.

CONTENTS

FOREWORD

The Mexican Revolution of 1910–1920 was one of the few major twentieth-century revolutions that took place before the Russian Revolution and in contrast to others—such as the Chinese Revolution, which also began before the Bolsheviks took power in Russia—was never profoundly affected by the Russian Revolution. The reasons for this development are but one of the many significant and interesting problems Daniela Spenser seeks to explore in this book. She does so on the basis of a huge number of documents from archives of many nations, a large part of which have never been utilized before. To my knowledge she is the first to have systematically been able to access the diplomatic archives of the former Soviet Union. Many of the reports by Mexican diplomats in Moscow have never been studied before. Although the diplomatic files of the State Department have long been accessible, the same is not true of the intelligence files that the author utilizes with great ability.

Although this is diplomatic history, it is diplomatic history at its best. Daniela Spenser does not limit her analysis to the policies of governments but also studies the policies and attitudes of political parties and intellectual groups as well. She also examines public opinion by consulting a great many newspaper articles.

One of the most interesting contributions of this book as it examines U.S. policy toward Mexico in the 1920s is a systematic study of the attempts of significant segments of the U.S. press as well as the Republican administration of the period to demonize the Mexican government by calling it Bolshevik and by describing every nationalistic measure that the government took against foreign companies as inspired by Bolshevism. When both Ambassador Sheffield and Secretary of State Kellogg of the United States envisaged intervening in Mexico, they did so by describing the Mexican government as Bolshevik. This propaganda stopped once Dwight Morrow became ambassador to Mexico and succeeded in turning Mexico's policies toward a more conservative course. What did not stop was the attempt by the U.S. administration to put an end to diplomatic relations between the Soviet Union and Mexico, which were established in 1924 and finally broken six years later in 1930.

The history of Soviet-Mexican relations is one of the center points of Daniela Spenser's study. What emerges is that Soviet policy toward Mexico was characterized by a series of profound contradictions. The first contradiction could be found in the relatively low importance that Mexico had for the Soviet Union, on the one hand, and the first-rate quality and importance of Soviet diplomats sent there, on the other. Both Stanislav Pestkovsky and his successor, Alexandra Kollontai, were extremely prominent Russian revolutionaries who had played a major role in the revolution and had occupied high positions in the Soviet government. Spenser largely resolves this first contradiction when she emphasizes that both of these revolutionaries had been opponents of Stalin. Their appointment to Mexico may in part have been less a manifestation of Soviet interest in Mexico than an attempt by Stalin to consolidate his power at a time when that power was by no means yet absolute.

The second contradiction was between the conviction of some Soviet leaders that Mexico was ripe for revolution and the more pessimistic view of others such as Lenin that Mexico would never be an important center of world revolution. The Soviet policy varied from neglect to strong involvement in Mexican politics because of the belief that Mexico could become a focus of revolution.

The third contradiction of Soviet policy was manifested by Soviet diplomats who on the one hand stated that they were diplomats like all other diplomats, their main aim to establish normal relations between the two countries, but on the other hand actively intervened in Mexico's politics in order to encourage the Communist movement. These contradictions were tolerated by Mexican governments, though reluctantly so, as long as the Communist International and the Soviet Union viewed the Mexican government as a petty bourgeois government that had some anti-imperialist commitment. When the attitude of the Communist International abruptly switched its stance in 1928 after its Sixth World Congress and called for immediate revolution, those contradictions became much more acute and much more offensive to the Mexican government.

The popularity of Soviet diplomats also diminished with the changing of the guard. Many Mexicans sympathized with Pestkovsky because he pretended to behave less like a diplomat and more like a man seeking contact with the popular groups of society. After a diplomatic reception he would remove his smoking jacket and mingle with Mexican workers at union halls and other centers where popular classes congregated. Alexandra Kollontai became the icon of feminists in Mexico. Their successor, Alexandr Makar, was a different sort of man: a Stalinist apparatchik whose main interest was espionage and who never showed the kind of enthusiasm for Mexico that both Pestkovsky and Kollontai genuinely felt.

The third important aspect of this book is Daniela Spenser's analysis of the Mexican government's motivation for establishing relations with the Soviet Union in the face of harsh U.S. opposition. Although President Carranza did not establish formal relations with the Soviet Union, he showed an amazing degree of tolerance for the newly established Communist parties in Mexico. M. N. Roy, an Indian revolutionary who was one of the first organizers of the Mexican Communist Party, manifested a great degree of sympathy for Carranza in his memoirs. That sympathy is at first glance difficult to understand. Carranza fought with the greatest energy against the popular forces of the revolution. He engineered Zapata's assassination and repressed the general strike of workers in 1916, sentencing their leaders to death. Nevertheless, his policy was not so illogical or contradictory as it may seem. A convinced nationalist, Carranza always sought to play off other great powers against the United States. He wooed Germany and allowed its propagandists and spies to operate in Mexico with impunity during World War I. Once Germany collapsed, he may have been looking for other allies, and the newly created Soviet Union may have been such a potential ally. In addition, Carranza was always strong on making ideological concessions that were never matched by genuine social transformations. He acceded, though with reluctance, to the agrarian reforms proclaimed in the revolutionary Constitution of 1917, but he never implemented them. Allowing Communists to operate in Mexico as long as they were extremely weak was one way of gaining radical credentials at minimal cost.

When President Alvaro Obregón established diplomatic relations with the Soviet Union, he may have had similar motives in mind—all the more so because many of Mexico's radical intellectuals were fascinated at first by the Soviet experiment. It is interesting to speculate whether the same domestic considerations that drove Obregón and Plutarco Elías Calles to maintain relations with the Soviet Union drove the Mexican governments of the 1960s to maintain diplomatic relations with Cuba at a time when all other Latin American countries had broken them off under pressure from the United States. Obregón may also have hoped that in a situation where Mexico became unable to play off Europe against the United States because the United States had become the acknowledged preponderant power of the

American continent the Soviet Union might partially play such a role both politically and economically. It soon became clear to Mexican administrations that in economic terms the Soviet Union, itself a highly undeveloped country, had little to contribute to Mexico's economy. Politically, they resented the covert support given by the Soviet Union to the Mexican Communist Party.

The break in relations between Mexico and the Soviet Union that Daniela Spenser analyzes with great acuity was the result of a complex series of domestic and international factors. On the one hand, the Mexican government turned to the right and began unrelentingly to persecute the Communist Party. In addition, the Comintern's policy called for armed revolution in Mexico, and finally Calles and his successors began to woo the United States. The break in relations was also facilitated by the increasing disillusion of many radical intellectuals, such as Jesús Silva Herzog, with the transformations that Stalin was carrying out in the Soviet Union and the high price the Soviet people paid for them in bloodshed and the curtailment of freedom. No one who wishes to understand the complex situation Mexico faced after its armed revolution and the way successive Mexican governments dealt with it can afford to ignore this book.

FRIEDRICH KATZ

University of Chicago

ACKNOWLEDGMENTS

The research into this book was conducted while the Berlin Wall was falling, both physically and symbolically, and the countries of Eastern and Central Europe were recovering their freedom, which had hibernated for fifty years in a regime of never achieved socialism. I wrote this book after Mikhail Gorbachev's *perestroika* project had reached its end. It seemed that in terms of the history of revolutions and communism, the bell had tolled, but it was not so.

This project received generous support in Mexico as well as the United States. Several people contributed their opinions, criticisms, and doubts to help improve the manuscript in its different phases. I would like to thank Gilbert Joseph for his many years of support; Joe Tulchin for his friendship; and Charles Berquist, Lloyd Kramer, and Gerhard Weinberg for the cogent points they contributed. Several persons read parts or all of the manuscript and offered their valuable commentaries: Gil Joseph, Adolfo Gilly, Don Raleigh, Lewis Siegelbaum, Michael Hunt, Marie-Christine Kerr, John Chasteen, Sarah Chambers, and Jürgen Buchenau. With a generosity uncommon among academic specialists, Dan La Botz lent me his research materials, which allowed me to correct errors and fill gaps in my research. I would also like to thank Peter Gellert, who, in addition to his job as translator, scrutinized my unorthodox Leninism.

Institutional backing was essential to be able to conduct the research and write the text. I would like to thank the Center for Research and Higher Level Studies in Social Anthropology (CIESAS) in Mexico City for granting me all the time off, with or without salary, that I requested. Its directors—anthropologist Leonel Durán, Dr. Teresa Rojas, and Dr. Rafael Loyola—understood the peculiarities of my needs and did not place bureaucratic obstacles in the way of the long academic sojourn necessary to finish this work. I would also like to acknowledge that CIESAS defrayed in part the cost of the translation from Spanish into English.

I received generous financial aid from the University of North Carolina at Chapel Hill and the National Council of Science and Technology in Mexico, which allowed me to work in numerous archives in the United States, Great Britain, the Netherlands, Mexico, and Russia. While undertaking research in libraries and archives, I depended on the expertise of archivists and librarians: Dr. William Ilgen, Nadia Zeiper, and Rebecca Breazeale in the Davis Library at the University of North Carolina at Chapel Hill; the personnel at the International Institute for Social History in Amsterdam, the Netherlands, and at the Public Records Office in London; and specialists at the Colombia University library in New York and the Hoover Institution at Stanford University. At the Hoover Institution I became acquainted with Ella Wolfe, who at ninety years of age displayed extraordinary vitality and who shared with me her recollections of Mexico, which she had known during the 1920s.

In Mexico, I consulted the archives of the Center for the Study of the Labor and Socialist Movement, headed by Arnoldo Martínez Verdugo, and received help from the staff of the Diplomatic Archives at the Foreign Relations Ministry, from the General Archives of the Nation and the National Newspaper Library. In Moscow, Kyrill Anderson, director of the Russian Center for the Preservation and Study of Documents of Contemporary History, was of great assistance, as were his collaborators Svetlana Rozenthal, Eleanora Shakhnazarova, and researcher Yuri Tutochkin. I would also like to thank the staff at the Foreign Policy Archives of the Russian Federation for their help.

I had the good fortune of having friends in the places where the archives are located who offered me their hospitality. I would like to thank Vera, Ed, and Sasha Ebels in Amsterdam; Ruth Tosek in London; Adolfo Gilly in New York; John Burstein in Washington, D.C.; and Dagmar Dolan in Palo Alto. In Moscow, Rudolf Slánský, at that time ambassador of the Czech Republic, opened the doors of the Czech House oasis to me. Although only one name appears on the cover of this book, it was undeniably a collective effort.

INTRODUCTION

Mexico established diplomatic relations with the Soviet Union in 1924 because it shared the latter's ideal of raising the living standards of workers and peasants to dignified levels. In doing so, it expressed an attitude of solidarity with a country that, like Mexico, had struggled to put an end to centuries of exploitation. Like Soviet Russia after its revolution, Mexico was considered a pariah in the international community at the beginning of the 1920s. By establishing diplomatic relations with the Soviet Union, the new Mexican state reaffirmed its nationalist and revolutionary identity and sovereignty. Mexico recognized the legality of the Bolshevik Revolution despite its being vilified by its adversaries and even though the United States characterized the Soviets the same way it characterized the Mexican Revolution—as a threat to its national security.

Mexican nationalism was anti-imperialist in that it opposed foreign investors employing extraterritorial rights and invoking international law to perpetuate their interests. For certain groups, the Bolshevik Revolution appeared to fulfill their dreams and aspirations as a result of their experience with the government's inability to surmount opposition to revolutionary legislation. In addition to inspiring sectors of the workers and peasants movements, the revolution seemed to contain ideas that the radical elite in the Mexican government believed could be imitated or adapted to Mexican reality. Initially, this elite had hoped that the government would adopt radical measures and carry out the reforms being obstructed by domestic and foreign opponents. It believed that just as the new Soviet gov-

ernment gave power to the Russian workers and peasants through control
of factories and land, the Mexican government could delegate power to the
masses, redistributing wealth that was in private hands. During the first
part of the 1920s, the leftist elite believed that the government was committed to sharing power with those in whose name it claimed to govern.

In Mexico, the radical elite was committed to revolutionary change in
areas such as agrarian reform, the defense of workers' rights, education of
the masses, and international relations, and it believed that the Bolshevik
Revolution, which claimed to be worldwide in character, could facilitate
this arduous process. If for the United States, Soviet Russia was the inverse
image of its own economy and society, for the Mexican radical elite it
appeared to be the projection of the future revolution. This identification
with the ideals of the Bolshevik Revolution and the belief in the redeeming
power of its values and principles lasted the entire time the revolution
maintained its mythical attraction.

When more information concerning the Soviet Union reached Mexico,
and the intellectuals had the opportunity to visit the land of their dreams,
however, the myth and the attraction faded. Most woke up to the cruel,
discouraging reality that the Bolsheviks had little to teach the Mexicans.
This newly found consciousness was accompanied and in part stimulated
by the political changes occurring in the Soviet Union itself, the recurring
crisis in Mexico, and the difficulties it faced in resisting the political pressures and economic obstacles imposed by the United States.

The leftist elite represented the most progressive wing of the institu-
tionalized revolution. Although it rarely prevailed over the executive
branch's decisions, this elite wielded considerable weight—given its technical knowledge, educational levels, moral integrity, and, in the case of regional governors, possession of important popular backing. It was on this
group's initiative that relations were established with the Soviet Union,
although the group's motives were different from those of the government.
During the 1920s, the Mexican state was strengthened and mechanisms
were sought to legitimize its domination. Establishing relations with the
USSR was an act of autonomy vis-à-vis the powerful neighbor to the north
and at the same time served to demonstrate the government's capacity to
incorporate points of the radical elite's agenda as its own.

However, establishing contacts in and then recognizing Soviet Russia
was not an easy task. The images of the Bolshevik Revolution that the
Mexican and U.S. press projected to the public were ideologically biased. In

the United States, press reports tried to demonstrate that there were no differences between the 1917 Constitution and the Bolshevik program—the latter being viewed as the anathema of Western civilization. Already in 1918, the media employed distorted images of what was portrayed as Mexican Bolshevism, making its subversive ideas responsible for labor unrest and instability in Mexico. At the same time, these phenomena were viewed as a threat to U.S. security. In Mexico, the press took into account the dangers posed by anti-Mexican propaganda in the United States and tried to sell to its readers the idea that imitating Soviet policies was unviable. If to achieve its objective it had to resort to exaggerations and even present fabricated plots, the press—a medium characterized by the lack of trustworthy information—did not hesitate whatsoever to do so.

This ideological climate characterized Mexico when Lenin's emissary, Mikhail Borodin, arrived in the country to establish bilateral relations, which had been interrupted by the Bolshevik Revolution. It is true that President Venustiano Carranza sought to broaden the spectrum of Mexico's alliances in order to resist pressure from the United States and its European allies. However, he avoided any contact with the Soviet representative due to the tensions prevailing at the time between Moscow and Mexico's northern neighbor, a situation aggravated by the challenge being made to presidential power by Carranza's former political friends.

His successor, Alvaro Obregón, had more maneuvering room than Carranza once the former's government was recognized by the United States in 1923. Obregón's foreign policy objective was identical to Carranza's: to broaden Mexico's international relations to counteract the influence of the United States. Thus, with U.S. recognition under his belt, Obregón could openly pursue the negotiations with Soviet Russia that he had discreetly initiated in 1921. In 1924, several European countries recognized the Soviet government. Obregón felt that his international prestige would be bolstered if Mexico did the same. In addition, after the Bucareli accords with the United States were signed, recognition of Soviet Russia would counteract the accusation leveled at the time against him that his administration had lost its revolutionary bearings.

When Plutarco Elías Calles became Mexico's president in 1924, he inherited Obregón's achievements, both in domestic policies and foreign affairs. Although Calles had a more radical reputation than his predecessor, it was under his administration that relations with the Soviet Union soured all of a sudden, mostly due to the Soviet ambassador's participation in activities of the Mexican Communist Party and his support in organizing the leading labor conflict in the 1920s, the railworkers strike. In addition, the ambassador assumed the role of intermediary between the railworkers strike committee and Moscow to obtain Soviet economic aid for Mexican workers. Calles was aware of the Soviet ambassador's activities, but did not break diplomatic relations with the USSR. To have done so in 1927, when relations with the United States were at their lowest ebb, would have given the Americans exactly what they wanted. Mexico did not sever ties with the Soviet Union until 1930, after the former's relations with the United States improved, and the break could not be viewed as the result of U.S. pressure.

The United States did have an unquestionable impact on the course and pace of the Mexican Revolution during the 1920s and did indirectly contribute to the break in relations between Mexico and the USSR. Already in 1918, and during most of the 1920s, the line that the Mexican reforms did not differ from Soviet confiscation policies was taken up by the press and politicians within Mexico, both of whom were equally opposed to the constitutional reforms. No less influential on the evolution of relations between Mexico and the USSR were the attempts of different individuals to provide disinformation to the U.S. State Department concerning Mexican radicalism: to the country that viewed itself as the only home of democracy and liberty in the region, Mexico began to appear as the breeding ground for hemispheric subversion. Although it is not possible to determine the exact impact of such disinformation on U.S. foreign policy, circumstantial evidence leads to the conclusion that the portrait of Mexico as a country in the grip of Bolshevism created a climate of uncertainty in the political elite and motivated more than one businessman to seek countries less inclined to radical changes for investment purposes. In addition to the disinformation about Mexico being played up by the press and by U.S. espionage agencies, alleged Soviet-inspired plots to destabilize the Mexican government were invented. In most cases their authors could not be precisely identified. The uncertainty that the nebulous origin and unknown magnitude of the plots created in Mexican political circles increased their danger.

Generally, the Mexican government accepted the veracity of the fabricated documents without question and acted in accordance with the threat supposedly posed to the country's stability. It was particularly after the division of the governmental elite following Obregón's death in 1928 that the government became more sensitive to tales of subversive plans designed by the USSR and less capable of discerning the truth behind the fabricated accounts. U.S. interest groups, which for so long had tried to pressure Mexican authorities to abandon the reform program, could now exploit their vulnerability. However, the plots that illustrated in vivid detail the Communist plans to subvert Mexico would not have had the desired effect on the Mexican government had they not proven to be true. After the change in 1928 in Soviet foreign policy, which went from seeking coexistence with the capitalist world to overt hostility toward the capitalist system, the USSR did not hide its attitude toward governments that, as in the case of Mexico, were considered puppets of the imperialist powers.

The Soviet government understood neither the character and depth of Mexico's nationalism nor the process of construction of the Mexican state. It also did not appreciate the costly measures various administrations had to employ to resist the attacks made by both the domestic opposition and the interventionist powers against Mexican reform policies. Soviet ideologues considered Mexico a mere pawn in the interimperialist rivalry between Great Britain and the United States in Latin America. Although Soviet analysts recognized the significance of the agrarian reform and the anticlerical struggle, in the final analysis they viewed them as the failed attempts of a vacillating petty bourgeoisie in the face of all-powerful imperialism. From 1928 on, when the interpretation of history in the Soviet Union had to fit into the teleological vision of its ideologues, the Mexican government ceased to be of value to the Soviets and thus deserved nothing except to be overthrown.

My policy regarding Russia is very similar
to my Mexican policy. I believe in letting
them work out their own salvation, even
though they wallow in anarchy for a while.

—Woodrow Wilson (1918), in Link,
*Woodrow Wilson and the
Revolutionary World*

What distinguished bolshevism was the
subordination of the subjective goal, the defense of the interests of the popular masses,
to the laws of revolution as an objectively
conditioned process.

—Leon Trotsky, *The History
of the Russian Revolution*

I don't know what socialism is, but I am a
Bolshevik, like all patriotic Mexicans. The
Yankees do not like the Bolsheviks; they are
our enemies; therefore, the Bolsheviks
must be our friends, and we must be their
friends. We are all Bolsheviks.

—Aguascalientes military
commander (1919), in Roy, *Memoirs*

Part One

THE ENCOUNTER

OF TWO

REVOLUTIONS,

1917–1924

Chapter 1

THE UNITED STATES
IN SEARCH OF ITS
MEXICAN POLICY

The Bolshevik Revolution "shook the world" for ten days, in the words of John Reed, and immediately the Soviet experiment lent itself to the most varied interpretations. Politicians and different groups in the United States, already hostile to revolutions, extended their perceptions and misunderstandings of the Bolshevik Revolution to the Mexican Revolution. Their interpretations fed the hypothesis that the two revolutions were ideologically related. The foreign policy Washington applied to one should also be applied to the other. Even when similarities between the two revolutions were not clearly perceptible, those interested in presenting Mexico as a threat to the national security of the United States had no qualms in inventing such similarities, given the anti-Bolshevik ideological climate that dominated the 1920s.

From World War I on, and in particular after the Bolshevik Revolution broke out, the ideologues of the status quo within the U.S. government and business community considered the aspirations of weaker countries to control their own destiny as Bolshevik inspirations that would harm their respective interests. The Bolshevik Revolution had awakened fears that the "American way of life" could be destroyed. Bolshevism was invested by its adversaries with images of the destruction of symbols of civilization, the workers taking power, fires and killings—in short, as a world turned upside down. In the United States, some government politicians, representatives of business groups, and the communications media presented Communism as a strange and un-American ideology whose aim was to destroy freedom, property, and Christianity.[1]

Along with the belief that Bolshevism had launched an inexorable crusade the length and breadth of the world, the fear of an anti-American conspiracy also arose. In creating such a distorted perception of reality, paranoia gripped U.S. politics, particularly after genuine social conflicts emerged at the end of World War I, followed by an economic depression. In addition, the Bolshevik Revolution and the U.S. reaction had a significant impact among the intelligentsia. Besides stepping up surveillance, espionage agencies did not hesitate to invent evidence of a Russian-inspired, anti-American conspiracy, even if they lacked proof.[2]

With increasing certainty, the United States evaluated the Mexican Revolution's policies as Communist-inspired. Even though Mexican economic nationalism predated the Bolshevik Revolution, the fear of Soviet subversion prevented Americans from understanding that the Mexican revolutionary process had domestic roots. Thus, during part of the 1920s, U.S. businessmen and government officials viewed Mexico through anticommunist glasses. The Monroe Doctrine justified their interference in Mexican internal affairs; not only foreign countries but also European ideologies should be attacked and excluded from the Western Hemisphere.[3]

Toward the Red Scare

Even though the United States was economically strengthened as a result of World War I, it was not sufficiently confident that it was strong enough to preserve and increase its importance in the world. It also felt threatened from within. Democratic president Woodrow Wilson had strengthened ties between the labor unions and the government during the war to counterbalance radical anticapitalist movements. However, when the war-induced economic bonanza dissipated by around 1920 and workers began to see their salaries, union rights, and industrial democracy—understood as the workers' right to influence and control workplace conditions—decline, labor-government relations also began to sour. In addition, after the war, the Democrats ceased courting workers' votes and management no longer needed workers' labor power as previously dictated by wartime conditions. The wage freeze and the agreement to suspend strikes, which labor had respected during the war, remained in force even though prices rose on basic necessities. As a result, beginning in 1919 workers responded with nationwide strikes on a scale never witnessed before by Americans, in the process sparking concern among the public of a renewed radicalism. For their part, business leaders labeled unions as subversive and un-American organizations, and launched a campaign to wipe out the unions and to be able to freely hire wage labor.[4] The social peace experienced during the war years faded away.

Before the war, most Americans felt trade unionists and socialists had their place in society. However, opposition by the Wobblies (members of the anarcho-syndicalist Industrial Workers of the World [IWW]) and by socialists to the war and the government, and later their support for the Bolshevik Revolution, changed many people's opinion. The American left wing's apparent inspiration by the Soviet example provoked fears of imminent social upheavals, precisely at a time when the press was quoting leaders of the Communist International concerning the existence of favorable perspectives for world revolution, and when trade union and socialist leader Eugene Debs was proclaiming from his prison cell that from the crown of his head to the soles of his feet he was proud to be a Bolshevik. When the prosperity and exaggerated patriotism of the war period waned and gave way to economic depression and labor conflicts, Americans began to fear that the Bolshevik "disease," which had already reached Germany and Hungary, would soon spread to the United States as well.[5]

In the wake of the red scare, socialists were jailed and their newspapers banned. Patriotic organizations routinely broke up socialist rallies. When bombs went off in June 1919 in several cities across the country, fears that Bolshevism had spread to the United States intensified. In New York, state senator Clayton R. Lusk's committee investigated radical influence in the labor movement and concluded that radicals had penetrated the United States from several areas, including Mexico. To dampen such fears of Bolshevik expansion and to deal a blow to radicalism, Attorney General Mitchell Palmer created the General Intelligence Division of the Justice Department, and the government enacted antisedition laws to complement antilabor legislation, thus restricting freedom of expression.[6]

American Federation of Labor (AFL) leader Samuel Gompers was concerned with the erroneous association of industrial conflicts and labor unrest with Bolshevism. During the war, he had managed to convince the union movement to accept U.S. participation in the European war, and now he looked askance as management and the political elite put the AFL's demands, strictly trade unionist in character, in the same boat as socialist and Wobbly activities. From then on, Gompers attacked the Bolsheviks, intensified his struggle against the left, and supported only those strikes that raised strictly trade union demands. His anti-Communist declarations in AFL conventions went hand-in-hand with his demands for wage increases and a reduction in the workday.

Gompers was concerned with the possibility that the Mexican Revolution would follow the same course as the Bolshevik Revolution unless the United States did something to alleviate the social and economic depression in Mexico. His fear of Bolshevism made him a persistent champion of anti-Communism in Mexico as well. For Gompers, as well as for labor leaders William Green and John L. Lewis, who headed the union movement within the structure of the capitalist system that the Communists sought to destroy, the Soviet government was an enemy who had to be fought and defeated. For good reason, Secretary of State Henry L. Stimson in 1931 described the country's largest trade union confederation as "our main barrier against communism."[7]

By 1921, the fear of the red scare faded from newspaper headlines, but antiradicalism had impregnated the government, business organizations, the AFL, and especially public opinion. The fear of an invisible enemy within U.S. society remained, even though the left ceased to be a powerful mass movement. The once-strong Socialist Party of America divided in three, and the IWW continued to exist, but as a legend of the past. For most Americans, however, the socialists and Communists did not have to participate in street demonstrations or declare strikes to be viewed as a threat. It was enough that European immigrants continued to arrive in U.S. cities to create the fear in many Americans that they were bringing foreign ideologies along with them.[8]

Getting to Know the Bolsheviks

Governments and the public had only a vague notion concerning the true objectives of the Bolsheviks and about what was occurring in Soviet Russia after October 1917. The news arriving from Russia was confusing, contradictory, fragmentary, and sensationalist—to a large degree reflecting the way it was churned out. To begin with, following the revolution most of the news agencies and newspapers had to evacuate the Soviet capital. From then on, they received news of Russia from neighboring countries such as Latvia. In fact, foreign correspondents could not return to the Soviet Union

until 1921, when they returned together with the American Relief Administration, a charitable organization working to alleviate the famine lashing
the Volga region.

Second, although there were journalists with considerable experience in
reporting from Russia before the revolution, the revolutionary cataclysm
took them by surprise and left them ill-prepared to write competent reports
on what was occurring after the Bolsheviks seized state power. Before his
sudden and premature death in Russia in 1920, John Reed wrote perhaps the
most complete investigative reports on the events that transpired as a result of the revolution. However, because he sent his articles to the New
York socialist newspaper, *The Call,* leading newspapers and magazines did
not pick them up. At any rate, Reed had earned the reputation of being a
radical when he was a reporter during the Mexican Revolution.[9]

Third, at least during the first year of the revolution, the European and
U.S. governments maintained their illusions that the anti-Bolshevik opposition would grow enough to replace the Communists or that the Bolsheviks would not have the capacity to remain in power. It was this illusion,
more than trustworthy news accounts, that inspired speculative headlines
and sensationalist reports in the press. Predisposed against the Bolsheviks,
whom they considered "enemies of God and mankind," and not understanding the Soviet scene very well, the journalists tended to believe any
rumor and accept it as good coin.[10]

Walter Lippmann and Charles Merz, prestigious journalists from the
magazine *New Republic,* examined the reports published by the *New York
Times* between 1917 and 1920 and concluded that in "each and every one of
the essential problems dealt with, the end result of the news was almost
always misleading." The *New York Times* reported more than ninety-five
times that the Bolshevik government was at the point of collapsing. Lippmann and Merz accused the *New York Times* of citing events and atrocities
that never occurred, and charged journalists with reporting hearsay and
even with inventing incidents.[11]

During the 1920s, the quality and reliability of news concerning the
Soviet Union improved. In addition, the first Soviet dissidents began to
emigrate and were able to provide more detailed information about daily
life in the USSR. However, during this same period, a new style of "news"
and "documentation" emerged: anti-Bolshevik detective and intelligence
agencies were involved in the fabrication and sale of evidence to prove that
the Soviet state was expanding and interfering beyond its borders; in this

way, they were able to spark consternation among governments and in public opinion.[12]

Taking a Position toward the Bolsheviks

Within the U.S. government, different and contrary opinions arose concerning which policy should be applied to confront the supposed Bolshevik threat during the first years of the revolution. Even though President Wilson did not consider the Soviet government to be democratic, at the same time he did not favor its defeat as a precondition for renewing cooperation between the two countries. In contrast with Wilson, Secretary of State Robert Lansing, a rabid antisocialist, refused to negotiate or approve any contact with the Russians. He felt that "Bolshevism is the most hideous and monstrous thing that the human mind has ever conceived."[13] In the Commerce Department, Herbert Hoover proposed a material aid plan to the Russians with the hope that the abundant U.S. assistance would erode the population's confidence in the Bolshevik government. Secretary of War Newton D. Baker, who had opposed the armed intervention in Soviet Russia, wrote the president in 1918: "I do not know that I rightly understand Bolshevism. So much of it as I do understand, I don't like, but I have the feeling that if the Russians do like it, they are entitled to it."[14]

Evidently, the U.S. government was perplexed by events taking place in Soviet Russia. In order to understand these events better before adopting a definitive position toward the Bolshevik government, in February 1919 the Senate created a committee to undertake a corresponding study. The committee sought testimony from businessmen and bankers who had visited Russia before the revolution and witnessed the first months of the revolutionary period. Also called for testimony were John Reed and his wife, Louise Bryant; Raymond Robins, who headed the American Red Cross mission to Russia after the fall of Czar Nicholas II and who remained there until 1918; and U.S. ambassador to Russia David R. Francis.[15]

The committee rejected Reed and Bryant's laudatory testimony, and the views that dominated the proceedings condemned the Soviet government as a "despotic disenfranchisement" of its opponents. The reason the committee adduced for such views was the widely believed rumor that in Soviet Russia women had been "nationalized," and that chaos, anarchism, and immorality were rampant. The committee talked about Lenin and Trotsky with some deference. Lenin, it said, was treated with "fanatical respect" by his followers, whereas Trotsky, for all his disagreeable personal traits, was described before the committee by an exuberant American as "the greatest Jew since Christ." However, both men should, the committee believed, be distrusted because of their determination "to carry Bolshevism, by fair means or foul, into the four corners of Europe." In sum, the committee concluded that Soviet Russia had become "a menace to the whole world."[16]

The State Department also adopted this position, and members of its intelligence service became increasingly uneasy about the international activities of Soviet-inspired Communist parties. Stemming from a subjective disbelief that anyone should prefer the Soviet to the American way of life, their nervousness prompted policies that undermined the United States' professed faith in self-determination. Furthermore, the secrecy of Communist operations in revolution-prone countries encouraged the belief that Russia used hidden, unfair methods to gain influence.

Secretary Lansing led the way in the department's becoming more and more intransigent toward the Bolshevik regime. The separate peace treaty signed between Soviet Russia and Germany in March 1918 had further stimulated the prejudice against the Soviet system on the part of Lansing and the department's intelligence service. To the foundation of the Communist International in March 1919—at which Lenin declared, "Soon we shall see the victory of communism throughout the world; we shall see the foundations of the World Federative Republic of Soviets"—the State Department reacted by reinforcing its collaboration with the domestically oriented Department of Justice Bureau of Investigation. The socialist challenge and the U.S. concern about the spread of Bolshevism in undemocratic countries as well as in the United States made opponents of Bolshevism tar even British social democracy with the brush of Bolshevism.[17] In fact, Lansing turned the State Department into the bulwark of hard-line anti-Bolshevism.

Like U.S. policymakers, business leaders opposed the Soviet regime, calling Lenin's experiment a "monstrosity" and "a blot on the civilization" of the twentieth century. Class conflict, Bolshevik autocracy, official atheism, and international revolution clashed head-on with their beliefs in capitalist enterprise, democracy, Christian civilization, and loyalty. Liberal opinion, advocating recognition of the Bolshevik government, was drowned out by the conservative majority in the media and in Congress, which influenced the course of U.S. foreign policy.[18] The government, astonished that anyone could prefer the Soviet over the U.S. system, followed policies that contradicted its declared faith in self-determination of nations.

Confronting Mexican Economic Nationalism

In addition to being associated with anything and everything conceived as antagonistic to American traditional values, Bolshevism was characterized as a theory opposed to world economic and political stability in the postwar period. It was considered utopian, but was mainly viewed as a contagious disease.[19] When the U.S. government, businessmen, and the AFL faced Mexican economic nationalism, both separately and together, they tried to prevent that country's constitutional reforms from being implemented because they believed that, like Communism, such measures questioned the inviolability of business contracts and prevented the free expansion of U.S. capital. In the opinion of the U.S. government and companies affected by the 1917 Constitution, Mexican economic nationalism defied the precepts of liberal capitalism, provoking chaos and subversion within the country. If Mexicans aspired to build a republican government and achieve higher economic standards, they would be incapable of doing so without U.S. tutelage, leadership, and capital.[20]

During World War I, the U.S. government itself had assumed an active role in directing the economy. However, after the war political and business leaders felt such policies had negative effects on industrial progress because they encroached upon individual initiative, rights, and freedom. They viewed the Mexican government's desire to control its country's natural resources and foreign concerns, as well as its subordination of private property to society's needs, from the same vantage point. They interpreted constitutionalism as the Mexican government's desire to eliminate the presence of foreign capital and capitalists.[21]

In 1918, investors created the International Committee of Bankers to defend their interests in Mexico and to prevent President Carranza from having access to credits in the United States and Europe. Not content with such measures, throughout 1918 and 1919 businessmen and their representatives approached the Wilson administration with proposals designed to punish the rebel country and restore a government more in tune with U.S. interests. Henry Lane Wilson—former ambassador to Mexico and in 1918 an influential lawyer who was instrumental in bringing Victoriano Huerta to the presidential palace by a coup d'etat in 1913—proposed to get rid of the "arrogantly and blindly anti-American" government of Venustiano Carranza by

> installing in Mexico City a pro-American Government under General
> Félix Díaz or some other well known pro-American leader with a large

following among the people. The overthrow of the present anti-American government can be accomplished without the sacrifice of American lives and surely we would be justified by every consideration of
national and world concern, in aiding in the constitution there of a
government which will make Mexico an undesirable place for German
activities and which will join hands with us in the present critical
moments.[22]

Although in 1914 Wilson was in agreement with overthrowing Huerta
and in 1916 with pursuing Pancho Villa after the insurgent's incursion into
Columbus, in 1918 he would not entertain such drastic measures. The
State Department could send diplomatic protest notes to the Mexican government to remind the latter of "our requirements," but nothing more. The
president's position was to allow Mexicans to resolve their own problems,
even though they would "wallow in anarchy for a while."[23] If the Mexicans
could not resolve their problems and the conflict between the two countries were to escalate into war, the Democratic president would prefer to
leave the problem to the Republicans, who, according to all indications,
were going to win the 1923 elections.[24] In reality, he had his hands full with
European affairs and Bolshevik Russia, so he let the State Department, in
conjunction with big business, use its own methods to deal with Mexico.

Throughout 1919, Secretary of State Lansing, his undersecretary, Ambassador Henry Fletcher, and Secretary of the Interior Frank Lane orchestrated
a campaign to send threatening letters to the Mexican government with the
aim of forcing an annulment of Article 27 of the 1917 Constitution as a
condition for guaranteeing peaceful coexistence between the two countries; otherwise, they warned, "the government of the United States may be
compelled to adopt a radical change in its policy with regard to Mexico."
Lane, Lansing, and Fletcher let it be understood that the warnings would be
followed by an intervention.[25]

Although the State Department sent only insinuations to the Mexican
government, Senator Albert Fall of New Mexico plotted to make President
Wilson break relations with the southern neighbor. Fall, himself a small
businessman with interests in Mexico, felt that the United States should
install an alternative government willing to repudiate the 1917 Constitution. The New Mexico senator defended the inviolability of U.S. property
south of the border. Fearful that the Mexican "disease" would spread to the
rest of Latin America, he tried to twist Wilson's arm, describing Carranza's

administration as radical and linked to "subversive elements" in the United States.[26]

Nor were the petroleum companies satisfied when President Wilson patronized the Mexicans and adopted a policy of no more than "watchful waiting." By the end of 1918 these companies formed a protective organization, the Association of Producers of Petroleum in Mexico. To strengthen their position, the companies mobilized other investors in Mexico, and in December founded the National Association for the Protection of American Rights in Mexico. Their goal was to rouse public indignation over what they termed the confiscation of U.S. property in Mexico and to incite public support for the U.S. government in taking whatever steps were necessary to secure protection for U.S. lives and properties in Mexico. With a former manager of the Associated Press heading their propaganda machine, the association produced publicity materials for dissemination throughout the United States and beyond its border.[27]

Raising the Bogy of Bolshevism

On a more scandalous yet preposterous level, business leaders and the communications media began to raise the specter of Bolshevism in Mexico, with its supposed ramifications in the United States. "Confiscation of private property" was the legal phrase employed by businessmen with interests in Mexico and by their supporters within and outside of government to define Mexican economic policy. In addition to being synonymous with confiscation of property, the term *Bolshevism* was used as a metaphor to denote an amalgam of psychological and cultural characteristics supposedly inherent in the gullible Mexicans whom Communist agents were exploiting for their own ends.

The prestigious *New York Times* headed the campaign. Front-page articles described how dozens of Russian radicals were descending on Mexico, attracted by the "ultramodern" provisions contained in the new constitution. William Gates, a tireless propagandist hostile to Carranza, wrote various articles on the question in the widely read magazine *World's Work*. According to one of his fantasies, constitutional Article 27, written in Mexico, was later translated into Russian to "help Lenin." Without naming them, Gates claimed that he knew people who, having reached Russia, "were surprised to find already there a complete information among Bolshevist circles of this Mexican anti-capitalist legislation."[28] The campaign carried out in the United States to discredit Mexican nationalism targeted

President Carranza and Mexican radical labor. The crusade's goal against Carranza sought to undermine his political standing in the country in the hope that once he was gone, the Constitution could be eliminated.[29]

U.S. diplomats added their own rumors to those disseminating that Mexico was becoming the beach-head of socialism in Latin America. From Nogales, Sonora, Consul Francis Dyer wired: "The dissemination of socialist and bolshevist propaganda in this city is becoming bolder and more public."[30] The U.S. consul in Yucatán said that this southeast state governed by admitted socialist Carrillo Puerto was a bad example for the rest of Mexico's workers and peasants, whose "simple minds were filled with doctrines and ideas which their previous condition made it impossible for them to understand."[31] Boaz Long of the State Department Division of Latin American Affairs said that a Bolshevik regime such as Carranza's should be treated by the United States in the same way Russia was treated at the time: with military intervention.[32]

Meanwhile, Senator Fall tried to tarnish Mexico's image before the Senate Foreign Affairs Committee. At the end of 1919, he presented a report accompanied by an extensive dossier documenting the supposed collusion between the Mexican government and U.S. radicals. In addition to defending oil interests, Fall sought to neutralize the efforts of the Anti-Imperialist League of Free Nations Association, founded by a group of U.S. liberals interested in promoting peace following the world war. One of the league's objectives was to denounce before the U.S. public the conspiratorial actions by oil companies against Mexico. Its publications sought to demonstrate that the Mexicans were within their rights in opposing decades of U.S. exploitation.[33]

However, all the efforts expended during 1918 and 1919 in building up the image of a Mexican red scare did not provoke the expected diplomatic confrontation between Mexico and the United States, although it did weaken Carranza's position. Secretary of State Lansing, Ambassador Fletcher, Director Long of the State Department Division on Latin American Affairs, and the Association for the Protection of American Rights in Mexico may have failed in their attempts to convince President Wilson to break relations with Mexico, but they did succeed in pressuring Carranza into not applying Article 27 retroactively. The pressures from abroad also succeeded in preventing enforcement of a law approved by Carranza in February 1918 that stipulated that the oil companies were required to apply for a concession to drill new wells. The Texas Company drilled three such wells, but ignored the law in the process. Carranza also failed to force the oil companies to pay a tax decreed by the government. Without resorting to drastic measures against the oil companies, the Mexican president employed other strategies to threaten them. For a time, he attempted to attract German capital to the Mexican oil industry and invited domestic investors to purchase land the foreign companies were already exploiting.[34]

Even though Carranza returned some hacienda lands to their former owners, brutally persecuted the Yucatán socialists, and set a trap for and assassinated the peasant leader Emiliano Zapata, relations between the oil companies and the host country continued to be strained at the end of 1919 and the beginning of 1920. The red scare was at its zenith in the United States and the press viewed workers' strikes as Bolshevik conspiracies. In the same vain, the *New York Times* characterized the 1919 oil workers' strike as a Communist plot.[35] According to the State Department, the time had arrived to step up surveillance activities in Mexico.

Surveilling Mexico

The Department of Justice's Bureau of Investigation (later known as the Federal Bureau of Investigation [FBI]) had been very active in Mexico since it was established in 1908. In 1919, the U.S. government strengthened its espionage network in Mexico, sending an agent there from the Military Intelligence Division (MID), also known as G-2. Military intelligence activities were subordinated to the State Department and geographically divided according to the latter's organizational plan. In addition to the bureau and the G-2, the Office of Naval Intelligence (ONI) of the Department of the Navy also sent an attaché to Mexico. As in the case of the other agencies, the ONI was coordinated by the State Department.[36]

It was the policy of military intelligence to share information with the bureau and its General Intelligence Division. The latter was in charge of keeping tabs on those considered radicals within and outside the United States. In addition to espionage, the MID promoted the image of a peace-loving United States at a time when Washington had a well-deserved reputation to the contrary.

By 1920, the Bureau of Investigation also provided a counterespionage service for the State Department, becoming the eyes and ears of Washington. The bureau had one of its most effective agents in Mexico, the legendary Emilio Kosterlitzky. Russian by birth, Kosterlitzky was originally known as the iron fist of Porfirio Díaz. During the Porfiriato, he served as chief intelligence officer in northern Mexico and was publicly known for having put down the Cananea strike in 1906. In 1917, Kosterlitzky became an agent of the Bureau of Investigation, in charge of surveillance at the border to prevent joint actions by Mexican and U.S. leftists. The Mexican government was fully aware of Kosterlitzky and knew that his activities formed part of a vast U.S. operation to "undermine the present Mexican regime."[37]

The different espionage agencies transmitted a considerable amount of unreliable information to their home offices in Washington. Sometimes they did not detect events that could have been incriminating to the Mexican government. For example, when Lenin's emissary, Mikhail Borodin, arrived in New York in the spring of 1919 in order to seek recognition of Soviet Russia by the Mexican government and to attempt to create national sections of the Communist International in the New World, Bureau of Investigation agent Jacob Spolansky uncovered his true identity and together with other agents trailed him during his stay in the United States. Borodin, who was no novice in the art of eluding the police, slipped away from Spolansky and crossed the border into Mexico in July or August 1919. It seems the agents lost sight of Borodin, and the spies in Mexico never detected his presence. With the same skill, Borodin disappeared from Mexico at the end of 1919, but one of the military spies did not report on his subversive activities until almost a year later.[38]

Perhaps the biggest coup for military intelligence was the espionage work done for them by José Allen, a mechanic in a weapons and munitions plant and general secretary of the Mexican Communist Party. At least during 1920, Allen regularly sent reports to the U.S. embassy concerning the internal situation within labor organizations, personal conflicts between leaders in the Communist hierarchy, and relations of mutual support between the labor movement and the government.[39] Another informant was Martin Krainin, who approached the U.S. embassy in 1920 and for an exorbitant sum of money offered to provide names and political information on Communist activists he had known. Colonel Campbell, from the military attaché office in the embassy, did not reject the proposal, but negotiated a price acceptable to both sides. He did not believe, however, what Krainin reported about himself, or that his name was really even Krainin; the information Krainin provided did coincide with data the embassy already had, though, and threw new light on the activities of important Mexican and foreign activists.[40]

But on the whole U.S. espionage agents lacked key elements needed to understand the Mexican scene; their offices tended to produce and transmit more fantasies than factual information. As in the case of the U.S. government, the intelligence agents failed to distinguish between trade unionists and Communists, between Bolshevism and constitutional reforms.[41] Yet their advice to Washington to modify the course of its Mexico policy and to restore the undeniable U.S. preponderance in the country generally fell on fertile ground.[42]

Searching for a Policy

At the beginning of the 1920s, anti-Communist paranoia and the anti-Mexican campaign conducted in the United States throughout 1918 and 1919, to which espionage agencies' reports had contributed, provoked a climate of alarm in the State Department. The uncertainty regarding who would fill Mexico's presidency in the upcoming elections sparked considerable concern. This uncertainty and the impossibility of direct intervention in the elections explain the State Department's inclination to believe rumors that filtered up from Mexico: "Department informed one Pismer arrived in Mexico January 1. (He is) suspected of being a Bolshevik agent. Thirty Russians also reported in Mexico as being Bolshevik propagandists. Please investigate and advise by wire."[43]

Americans' nervousness was blatant and was noted as such by one British diplomat, who explained the former's state of mind: "The State Department spends a good deal of secret service money in watching developments. A short time ago, a story came to the Embassy from a good source indicating that the State Department was supporting Felix Díaz. In talking to me, Mr. Fletcher generally shows a personal preference for González. But the United States is really as barren of a real policy as ever, and will continue so until President Wilson either ends or mends."[44]

However, at the beginning of 1920 Wilson did little to resolve the thorny relations between Mexico and the United States. As a result, in February 1920 Ambassador Fletcher and Consul General Chamberlain resigned "as a protest against the attitude of President Wilson toward the mistakes of this government." According to the British diplomat, Fletcher "has taken a stand with many members of the Washington Congress that a way must be found to set the Mexican house in order and to restore the sacrificed prestige of the United States." In a confidential exchange with the British, Fletcher said that "the only policy appropriate to the Mexican situation was one of force which would exact respect for international rights and foreign institutions."[45]

In May 1920, the opportunity arrived that the hawks in the U.S. government had been waiting for—a chance to break diplomatic relations with Mexico: the Carranza government was overthrown by the Agua Prieta movement, led by General Obregón, and when fleeing the capital, the president was assassinated. In August 1920, Bainbridge Colby, who replaced Lansing as secretary of state, decided that U.S. foreign policy toward Soviet Russia would also be applicable to Mexico. The reestablishment of diplomatic relations with either of the two countries could not be considered as long as their governments were based "upon the negation of every principle of honor and good faith and every usage and convention underlying the whole structure of international law."[46] In addition, a New York investigating committee into Communist infiltration in the United States informed Congress that Mexico had become a threat not only because it was one of the points from which Communists infiltrated the United States, but because Mexican radicalism had already taken hold of the government, which moreover had sponsored the labor movement.[47]

In the second half of 1920, Wilson attempted to improve relations between the United States and Mexico by sending to Mexico his wartime propagandist, George Creel, and his nominee to replace Fletcher as ambassador, Henry Morgenthau, one of the politicians who favored unconditional recognition of the Mexican government as a way to strengthen its basis in constitutional law. However, in a bid to prevent recognition, Republican senators Henry Cabot Lodge and Albert Fall blocked Morgenthau's nomination. Fall insisted that the United States could not cooperate with Mexico as long as it did not "interpret the Monroe Doctrine as have most of the other Latin American nations." If Mexican economic nationalism remained unchecked, other Latin American countries could follow its example.[48]

This position was adopted at the beginning of March 1921 by the Harding administration, in which Fall was designated secretary of the interior, albeit not for a long period of time. After severing its European alliances, the Republican administration feared being isolated in the Western Hemisphere if other Latin American countries followed the Mexican example.

Big Business Wins Out over Small

The Harding administration made recognition of Obregón's government conditional on an agreement to establish a mixed commission that would appraise the losses suffered by foreigners during the Mexican revolution. In addition, Washington demanded that constitutional Article 27 not be applied retroactively, that payments be renewed on the foreign debt, and that the offices the revolutionary government had established in Latin America to spread information on developments in Mexico be closed. According to the untiring and belligerent Fall, this precondition was necessary because "the Mexicans were acting in bad faith, and we could not do business with them except through hard and fast, and formal agreements." Fall believed a prior agreement was imperative in order to avoid a Mexican appeal for Latin American solidarity.[49]

The oil companies dictated U.S. policy toward Latin America, and in Mexico they continued to demand the annulment of Article 27 as a guarantee of the inviolability of their properties. In June 1921 the Mexican government increased the tax on oil exports in order to boost its income and to be able to pay its foreign debt. The oil companies responded by suspending crude shipments. During the next two months, some twenty thousand workers were left jobless. In August, the government reduced the originally stipulated tax and thus was able to reach agreement with the companies.[50]

Whereas the State Department stood behind the oil magnates, thereby preventing an improvement in bilateral relations, the Commerce Department sought better relations in light of European competition. According to the Commerce Department, the figures spoke for themselves: the trade balance between Mexico and the United States between 1915 and 1920 had jumped 93 percent. The Commerce Department, as well as many businessmen and bankers, viewed Mexico as a world treasure chest and felt that no other country could provide so many commercial opportunities for the United States.[51]

It was this type of businessman who sought new opportunities in Mexico as a result of encouraging economic expectations and despite the prevailing political uncertainty. A firm that catered to the interests of businessmen, bankers, and small and medium-size investors was the Babson Statistical Organization of Massachusetts, which specialized in providing economic and political analysis and projections to clients who already had investments in Mexico and to those who were just studying the terrain. In 1921, for example, Babson warned its clients that even though conditions had improved in Mexico, Obregón had still failed to guarantee protection of U.S. lives and properties. It urged investors to proceed with caution and to "not leave unnecessarily large balances in Mexican banks," but to consider running moderate risks to retain clients and not lose their foothold in Mexico because "the time is coming when Mexico will be one of our richest foreign markets." Statistics backed Babson's optimism; despite the political difficulties between the two countries, U.S. exports to Mexico were on the rise.[52]

Among the businessmen with confidence in Mexico and with the conviction that only by backing Obregón would U.S. interests be protected was the magnate John Hays Hammond. As a mining engineer with many years of experience in managing businesses in Mexico and since 1916 owner of the Mexican Sealord Oil Company, Hammond went before the Senate Foreign Relations Committee early in 1921 to defend a strategy of expanding business with Mexico.[53] Other small-scale manufacturers and businessmen were willing to accept the new Mexican legislation and were opposed to large companies' interference in Mexico's internal affairs and their lobbying efforts to obtain U.S. government support for their business ventures.

The businessmen who supported U.S. recognition of Obregón's government with the aim of facilitating the expansion of commercial relations between the two countries felt that a poor Mexico, dominated by the United States, would have an adverse effect on their own interests. When the Mexican government became unable to provide employment to the workers, they would emigrate to the United States, taking away jobs from Americans. On the other hand, a prosperous Mexico would provide jobs to Mexicans and a market for U.S. products.[54]

However, the interests of big business prevailed over those of smaller companies. The State Department's policy of nonrecognition weighed more than the Commerce Department's stance combined with the opinion of prominent personalities—such as Henry Ford, William Randolph Hearst, and Samuel Gompers—of the chambers of commerce in the border states, and of border state governors, who wanted to expand relations with Mexico. The collusion between the large companies—trapped in the ideology of an unlimited frontier and an open door for their business ventures—and the State Department prevailed over the common sense of businessmen willing to accept the new winds blowing up from south of the border and Eastern Europe.

Manufacturing a Red Plot

Secretary of State Charles Evans Hughes periodically received suggestions on how to resolve the Mexican quandary. Irresponsible political schemers lost no opportunity to propose ousting the Mexican government. Judge F. J. Kearful, former counsel for the Fall committee, recommended establishing a protectorate over Mexico. Obregón's adversary, Manuel Calero, approached the secretary of state to obtain backing for a planned insurrection, or at least a pledge not to prevent it. U.S. businessman William F. Buckley and his partners hatched a plan to seize Baja California.[55] Hughes rejected each and every one of these proposals.

Another project presented to Hughes in 1921 was proposed by Henry Marsh, a well-to-do New Yorker with some interests in Mexico, and Colonel Arthur Woods, former chief of police in New York and nephew by marriage of banking magnate J. Pierpont Morgan. Woods was interested in investing in the Mexican lumber industry. Both men had participated in the persecution and organized elimination of persons and movements accused of radicalism during the months of the anti-red and antiforeign hysteria.[56] The two believed that Communism was at the root of the Mexican problem. It was just a question of proving it.

In February 1921, Marsh and Woods hired Jacob Nosovitsky to travel to Mexico and obtain the necessary evidence. Nosovitsky was the right man for the job. Born in Kiev, Ukraine, he had been a member of the Bolshevik Party before the revolution, but he left its ranks disillusioned and emigrated from Russia. In 1919 he offered his services to the U.S. Justice Department to "help the government's fight against communism." His first task in the United States was to win the confidence of Soviet representatives and infiltrate the Communist movement. Nosovitsky won the trust both of the Soviets and of his superiors in the Justice Department.

Marsh and Woods conveyed their concern to Nosovitsky over the danger posed to the United States by the "powerful communist movement in Mexico." In addition, "Mr. Marsh said he had heard that members of President Obregón's cabinet were Communists,"[57] but needed evidence to prove it. Marsh and Woods offered Nosovitsky twenty-five thousand dollars for the job.

When Nosovitsky arrived in Mexico, thanks to his reputation as a party comrade he won the trust of Linn Gale, who headed up one of the two groups that in 1921 identified themselves as communist parties. Gale's organization—the Communist Party of Mexico—was even less visible than the Mexican Communist Party, headed by José Allen. Nosovitsky was shocked by the discrepancy between the threatening situation painted by Marsh and Woods and the reality on the ground: "Frankly, the Mexican communist movement was a joke." Nosovitsky found neither the expected huge anticapitalist sentiment nor an organization that resembled a soviet. On the other hand, he did find Gale, who—not suspecting that his new-found acquaintance was an agent for U.S. intelligence—in good faith be-came an accomplice to a plan hatched by Nosovitsky. The two wrote a letter to the chairman of the Communist International, Grigori Zinoviev, in which they described Mexico as a stronghold of Communism in the Western Hemisphere; the document was, in Nosovitsky's words, "some-thing for the eyes of my New York employers rather than a true report for Zinoviev." Nosovitsky promised Gale that he would personally take the message to Moscow. The letter provided vivid details of the constant ad-vances of the party among the masses to soon establish "the dictatorship of the proletariat and the communist state." The most compromising section of the apocryphal letter referred to "the presence of several real comrades in the government of Obregón." The letter concluded with the boast that without fear of being wrong, "in no country in the world are the prospects of an early Communist revolution more certain than here in Mexico . . . It is certain that the flames of revolt kindled in Mexico will creep all over Latin America, and perhaps serve to light the fire in the United States as well."[58]

Nosovitsky and Gale attended the convention of the Regional Confedera-tion of Mexican Workers' (CROM) Labor Party in Pachuca, Hidalgo, in April 1921 to try to convince the Cromistas to join the Communist Interna-tional. It is not known whether Nosovitsky invited a U.S. military intel-ligence agent to the convention, but one was present. From an article by Nosovitsky and a report by the MID agent, we know that the former did not convince the CROM to affiliate itself to the Communist International. Had he succeeded, it would have had the effect of proving to the U.S. govern-ment that Moscow controlled the Mexican Labor Party, which included such important people as Luis Morones; Celestino Gasca, governor of the Federal District; Antonio Villarreal, agriculture minister; Adolfo de la Huerta, finance minister, and Plutarco Elías Calles, then head of the cabi-net.[59] Because Nosovitsky did not manage to convince the Labor Party delegates, he fabricated a resolution by which the Moronistas affiliated their party to the Comintern. With the two false documents, Nosovitsky returned to the United States.

In New York Nosovitsky submitted the two bogus documents to Marsh. When Marsh read them, he said he "needed some additional document of a much stronger nature to prove conclusively that there was in Mexico a strong body of communists capable of overthrowing the government and establishing a Soviet form of government." At this point, Nosovitsky forged another document, authenticating it with an official rubber stamp he himself had made, proving that a "Communist Council of the Red Army of Mexico" had been created, whose task would be to "organize a powerful revolutionary army of workers, peasants and soldiers of Mexico to be ready to act instantly at the command of the Council."

This time Marsh "seemed very much excited and intensely interested" in the document. The next step was to deliver the documents to the State Department. Marsh, Woods, and Nosovitsky went to Washington late in April 1921. They first met with J. Edgar Hoover, who went over the documents and allegedly expressed his belief that "the Secretary of State would be pleased with what Mr. Marsh submitted." Marsh then went to the State Department. "In a pleasant frame of mind" upon his return, he said he believed "that the recognition of Mexico would be delayed by the documents." According to the *New York American*, he left the documents in one of the department's offices but was unable to meet personally either Undersecretary Fletcher or Secretary Hughes.[60]

In 1925 Henry Fletcher recalled the documents but of course denied that they had any influence on the State Department's decision regarding recognition of Mexico. For his part, Linn Gale, whom the *New York American* reporter interviewed at his Washington bookstore, confirmed these facts and further stated that "it was he [Gale] who advised Nosovitsky to make public his confessions of the fake 'Red Scare' manufactured against the Mexican people."[61]

There is no conclusive evidence that the forged documents influenced officials in the State Department to delay U.S. recognition of the Mexican government. However, they are a testimony of the unscrupulousness of certain individuals in their attempts to go to any length in order to defend their interests. It should also be considered, however, that had Marsh and Woods thought their efforts would come to nought, they probably would not have invented and paid for such a conspiratorial scheme. Marsh and Woods's plot attests also to FBI involvement and the Department of Justice's willingness to use fabricated material as a political tool against the Mexican government. In addition, the documents' significance lies in that they survived the actual intrigue and subsequently entered the pool of rumors. After Nosovitsky left Mexico, the same documents were brought to the attention of the State Department as scandalous evidence of Mexican Communism.

In April 1921 a State Department intelligence agent reported from Mexico that he had seen documents written by a "messenger" who was on his way from Mexico to a "Bolshevik conference" in Europe. The "date for a general uprising" in Latin America would be decided at this conference. Since the end of February, the agent stated, the messenger had been studying the Mexican situation and had outlined plans "for the coming social revolution." Obregón's government was but a toy in the hands of his ministers,

> the majority of which are acting under instructions from Moscow. There is a real government now in Mexico the existence of which but a limited number of people know; that is the provisional communist government which can overthrow Obregón in twenty four hours. This government consists of a Council of six—four members of Obregón's cabinet are members of this council, one is an American a resident of Mexico for years and another is a representative of the Third International.[62]

Point by point, the agent's report followed Nosovitsky's forged documents: "The Red Army, organized by the Council, is a very strong organization, having in its ranks one fourth of the regular army in Mexico, workers, policemen and peasants." The agent's report concluded that even though Obregón had expelled North American Communist Gale from Mexico in May 1921, "he was only doing it to hoodwink the United States." The report also claimed that if he really wanted to overcome Bolshevism, Obregón should arrest the major labor leaders—Gasca and Morones—and jail his ministers Calles and de la Huerta. The report recommended that Felipe Carrillo Puerto and other radicals in the government should be included in the sweeping changes of the administration.[63]

The agent reported further that a Bolshevik Revolution was being prepared in Mexico and that at the head of its "Red Army" was President Obregón. The military intelligence agent reported that the Council of State, led by Communists, "is at present secretly granting valuable land and oil concessions to the Japanese government."[64] The same documents resurfaced in 1924 and would be used to demonstrate that President Calles's administration continued to employ subversive strategies to trick the United States.

Negotiating Diplomatic Recognition

Although it cannot be concluded that the forged documents influenced the State Department, it is undeniable that the specter of Bolshevism haunted its intelligence agency and Secretary of State Hughes. Speaking before a chamber of commerce, Hughes drew a parallel between Soviet Russia and Mexico under Obregón, according to the Mexican newspaper *El Universal*. He charged that the Mexican government was a disciple of Soviet advisers who taught Mexican officials "communist ruses."[65] When the representative of the International Committee of Bankers, Thomas Lamont, approached Hughes to obtain the green light to begin negotiations with the Mexican government on foreign debt payments, the banker tried to explain to the secretary of state that Mexico should not be placed in the same category as Soviet Russia. Lamont emphasized that the disagreements between Mexico and the United States were due to concrete economic problems, not ideological differences.[66]

Lamont did not believe that the Mexican government was infiltrated by agents of the Third International or by anarchists. The banker and his partners did criticize the Mexican constitution—not because they considered it radical, however, but because it was impractical when measured by the yardstick of business standards. Lamont's lobbying in the State Department and Congress opened the way for the United States to negotiate with Mexico on foreign debt payments and later, in August 1923, to recognize the legitimacy of the Mexican government.[67]

However, the ideological premises on which the State Department refused diplomatic recognition of the Mexican government had not lost their validity. Individuals who had criticized the Mexican Constitution since 1917, calling for drastic measures to force the Mexican government to desist from applying its clauses, remained in high places in the administration. Henry Fletcher was named undersecretary of state, and Matthew Hanna went from the embassy in Mexico to the State Department to be in charge of Mexican affairs. The two maintained close contacts with military intelligence. These officials, as well as the government agencies they represented, continued to reject Mexican economic nationalism as a legitimate means to improve the country's welfare.[68]

Surveillance of Mexico by the different U.S. intelligence apparatuses persisted and was a sign of the seriousness with which the State Department continued to view Mexican economic nationalism as a threat to U.S. national security. The First World War had been a tremendous stimulus to the U.S. economy, so the possibility of overproduction if Latin American markets failed to materialize was viewed with concern. Latin America absorbed manufactured products from the United States and provided the raw materials, among which oil was the most valuable. This vital flow had to be preserved. Therefore, throughout the 1920s the State Department felt a deep concern regarding the possibility that nationalism—for some officials still synonymous with Bolshevism—would end the expansion of U.S. capitalism in Latin America. When the U.S. diplomatic team arrived in Mexico following diplomatic recognition, their overriding task was to attempt to turn back the clock to the prerevolution status quo. Their work became difficult when they realized that Calles was not Obregón and that Mexico appeared to be an ally of the Soviet Union.

Chapter 2

MEXICO IN

SOVIET

CALCULATIONS

With certain frequency, the dailies *Pravda* and *Izvestiia*, as well as academic and political magazines issued by Soviet institutions, published articles on Mexico in the context of strong criticisms of capitalism and descriptions of the Soviet Union as the land of great promise for justice and liberty. The People's Commissariat for Foreign Affairs (Narodnyi Komissariat Inostrannykh del o Narkomindel) published *Mezhdunarodnaia Zhizn'* (International Life). The Comintern expressed its viewpoints and directives through *Kommunisticheskii Internatsional* (The Communist International), its official and doctrinaire organ, as well as through the more popular weekly, *Inprekorr* (International Press Correspondence), which was edited in German, English, and French (although not in Spanish). The Comintern's trade union organization, the Profintern, published *Krasnyi Internatsional' Profsoiuzov* (the Red International of Labor Unions) and *Mezhdunarodnoe Rabochee Dvizhenie* (International Workers Movement). Peasant and agrarian questions were discussed in the magazine *Agrarnye Problemy* (Agrarian Problems) and *Na Agrarnom Fronte* (In the Agrarian Front).[1]

The newspapers and magazines went beyond a mere presentation of news. Their objectives were political in nature, and facts were adapted for political and agitational ends, both in terms of content and style. The writers were not just leaders of the Bolshevik Party, but a specialized team, *mezhdunarodniki* (the internationalists), with expertise in international relations and different geopolitical areas. These ideological commentators gathered materials on the different countries, analyzed them, and sent them to the corresponding commissariats.[2] The local Communist parties and the Soviet embassies were another source of demographic and economic data, and information was gathered on communications, the ethnic composition of each country, and scientific statistics in order to keep the Soviet government up to date on developments abroad. Generally, the establishment of diplomatic relations facilitated studies on a given country, whereas the absence of such relations limited them. The Bolshevik leaders did not completely trust the information provided by foreign Communists, suspecting that it lacked a global vision, and underestimated the importance of economic relations beyond their country's own borders.[3]

The Comintern had an information department that kept it abreast of international developments. The department employed specialists who read the main newspapers and magazines of all political tendencies, abstracting the most important news articles that would later be published in a weekly bulletin. The information with greatest relevance for propaganda effects were reports concerning the weakness of rival trade union confederations and workers and peasants' affiliation to Comintern organizations. In addition to having propaganda value on an international level, such news encouraged Soviet workers to continue in their own efforts for a better future despite momentary difficulties.[4]

Before 1926, the Orientalists—experts on Asia and the Middle East—also published articles on Latin America. In reality, studies on Asia and the Middle East took priority over other regional specializations on the understanding that the Asian colonial and semicolonial countries shared the historical characteristics of underdeveloped Western countries. It was not until the Soviets recognized the United States as a world economic power in the 1920s that they also began to take a specialized view of the region under the latter's influence. From 1926 onward the Comintern had a Latin American Secretariat and a team of regional experts who elaborated materials for other Soviet institutions.[5]

Mexico as Seen by Soviet Ideologues

The articles published about Mexico in Soviet newspapers and magazines generally magnified the importance of the proletariat, but underestimated the Mexican government's efforts to reconstruct the country based on its own resources and to consolidate its national sovereignty. The Soviet articles had little to say about the national bourgeoisie and tended to belittle revolutionary nationalism. Defining Mexico as a semicolonial country dominated by foreign capital and still characterized by feudal relations of production and socialization, these reports affirmed that by itself Mexico would be unable to generate the social forces for its national liberation. They portrayed Mexico's efforts at economic development as failed struggles against imperialism. The government's fight against the Catholic Church, its efforts at distributing land among the peasants, and the struggle of anarchists and workers to avoid becoming dependent on the government were praiseworthy but inexorably subordinated to the forces of imperialism and thus doomed from the start.[6] Due to the perception of Mexico's subordinate position in the world capitalist system, no author could explain the content of the 1917 Constitution without ascribing it to the direct influence of the Bolshevik Revolution.[7]

The agrarian history of Mexico was known in the Soviet Union through the distinguished Hungarian economist Eugen Varga, director of the International Agrarian Institute and its monthly magazine *Agrarnye Problemy*. Varga compared Mexico with China, where prior to 1927 the Kuomintang and the Communists collaborated in carrying out an agrarian reform. For Varga, the experience of the two countries suggested the possibility that a social revolution could be led by the organized peasantry instead of by the proletariat—as proscribed by traditional Marxist doctrine—in countries in which the working class was the weakest link in the class structure. This possibility, however, faced a threat in the form of the asphyxiating domination by the United States. Despite its limitations, the Hungarian economist said, the Mexican agrarian reform had improved the conditions of the urban proletariat. Like other commentators on the Mexican revolution, Varga was perplexed by the government's policy of arming the peasants whenever their backing was needed and disarming them once the threat had passed. Instead of allowing the peasants to defend the agrarian revolution against the opposition of the landowners and imperialism, the government repeatedly put a break on the revolutionary process.[8]

Mexico played a minor role in Moscow's foreign policy because of its geographical distance and because of the secondary importance given to U.S. imperialism vis-à-vis British imperialism in Soviet Russia's global strategy at the beginning of the 1920s. However, when the United States began to acquire increasing relevance on a world scale, Mexico also became a strategically important venue for Soviet Russia. Now emerging as an economic and technological power, the United States became a coveted commercial partner and a possible source of capital investments to develop the concessions that, as of 1921, the Soviet government placed at the disposal of foreign capital. At the same time, as the United States increased its role as the hegemonic power in the Western Hemisphere, the Soviets began to consider the countries it dominated and oppressed as potential allies.

Whereas Argentina was viewed as a laboratory to study the confrontation between British and U.S. imperialism, Mexico—in the direct sphere of U.S. influence—provided the Soviet ideologues with fertile terrain to debate issues such as colonialism, imperialism, revolution, and class struggle. The numerous articles published about Mexico throughout the 1920s highlight Soviet government and Comintern officials' arguments on foreign policy and its interrelations with the ideological sphere of Soviet power.

The debate that developed on Mexico and the rest of Latin America was overshadowed by Lenin's theory of imperialism. Through the prism of this theory, Soviet ideologues generally ignored the particular form of each country's integration into the world capitalist system at the end of the nineteenth century. Those Leninists who became interested in Mexico—including Lenin himself—viewed it through historical laws they considered universal in nature. According to Lenin, capitalism in its final phase of development grew within a worldwide system of colonial oppression and financial strangulation that the majority of the world's peoples suffered as a result of a handful of advanced countries (the United States, Great Britain, Japan) at war with one another for a division of the spoils.[9]

In countries such as Mexico, Egypt, Turkey, and Argentina, imperialism had indeed placed insurmountable obstacles for the development of national capitalism. As a result, finance capital had become such a powerful and decisive force in economic and international relations that the circumstances of countries that enjoyed political independence were subordinated to it. Imperialist domination also signified the nonexistence of a national bourgeoisie or its dependence on foreign capital. Based on this conception, the Soviet ideologues drew the conclusion that struggles by nationalists—such as the Mexican revolutionaries or the Chinese—could not change a country's economic and political structure because during the period of capitalist imperialism semi-colonial countries "constitute[d] a link on the chain of world finance capital."[10]

Imperialist rivalry, initially between the United States and Great Britain, meant that disputes for markets would be regulated by military force. Thus, for the Bolshevik Party and the Comintern, it was inconceivable to think that the Mexican government could manipulate such rivalries for its own benefit instead of merely being its victim. It was true, of course, that imperialism had penetrated the precapitalist economic structure, creating a modest industrial class and an incipient working class in a predominantly peasant country, but by themselves such social forces were incapable of acquiring consciousness of their historical duty and of fighting "the capitalist imperialism of the United States."[11]

The ideological controversies and political confrontations that took place between Bolshevik leaders reflected different reactions to and theoretical formulations regarding unexpected and unforeseen political events and conjunctural situations. Whereas some Comintern activists emphasized the revolutionary potential of the Mexican proletariat, other ideologues sustained that in a country with a predominately peasant population and with a national bourgeoisie numerically reduced and weakened by foreign ownership of property and industry, the proletariat was born politically dead.

However, Soviet ideologues' definitions and redefinitions of Mexico had less to do with the real Mexico and more to do with adapting their theoretical premises to a world that did not follow the expected revolutionary road. The party and the Comintern ultimately had to redefine their perception of the world and change the strategies they were to use several times during the 1920s. The way of perceiving Mexico, of conducting foreign policy, and of leading the Comintern's activities changed with each twist and turn in events.

Diplomacy and Revolution in Soviet Russia

To guarantee its national security and prevent the formation of coalitions hostile to the Bolshevik government, the Soviet Union sought to strengthen its economic and political relations with Western countries. The pressing need for capital and technical know-how forced the Bolsheviks to put aside their apprehension and mistrust toward the capitalists and seek closer relations with the West. In fact, the diplomatic relations Soviet Russia established during the first part of the 1920s were not necessarily determined by ideological considerations. The Soviet leaders were willing to reach a compromise with any system provided it could guarantee the survival of Bolshevik power. For example, when negotiations were conducted in 1922 on economic cooperation and normalizing diplomatic relations with Italy, the fact that Benito Mussolini's fascists had seized state power was not important. In the same year, behind the back of the other countries with which it had negotiated to reestablish commercial relations, Soviet Russia signed the Treaty of Rapallo with its former adversary, Germany. Thus, by 1924 the Soviets managed to establish diplomatic recognition and commercial agreements with the main global powers except the United States.

Soviet Russia's diplomatic success at the beginning of the 1920s was also due to the pragmatic approach the European powers adopted with respect to the Bolshevik Revolution. Although during the first years of the revolution, Western countries had sought to weaken Soviet power, the introduction of the New Economic Policy (NEP) in 1921 and the return of a market economy, encouraged the premise that it was possible to negotiate with Soviet Russia. European countries believed at the time that their own reconstruction following World War I could not be undertaken by turning their backs on Russia, which could offer markets for their products.[12]

However, one of the peculiarities of Soviet diplomacy was the superposition of diplomatic affairs and party politics. The Comintern's objective was to lead the Communist parties and the international workers movement in the overthrow of the very same governments with which the Soviets had established diplomatic relations. As expressed in 1919 by Grigori Chicherin, the commissar for foreign affairs, the Bolsheviks' fundamental commitment was to join with the world proletariat—but not with the bourgeoisie, with whom protocols and treaties could, of course, be signed—to overthrow capitalism and radically change its reality.[13] Throughout the 1920s, the Bolsheviks tried to obscure the superposition of their foreign policy and ideological struggle, arguing that the Comintern was an organization comprised of national Communist parties and was totally independent of the Soviet state. Although the Comintern was made up of Communist parties from several dozen countries representing many different national realities, it was at the same time the international political arm of the Bolshevik Party, and in the hierarchy of Soviet institutions, the government and the Comintern were subordinated to party decisions. Decisions orienting the work of the government and the Comintern were made by the top leadership of the party.

Both the government's foreign policy as well as the Comintern's strategic line changed according to the interpretation that the Bolshevik leaders adopted concerning the stability or fragility of the capitalist system and concerning the friendliness or hostility of the outside world toward the Soviet government. When this interpretation changed, the Comintern's tactics would change several times, and each change was reflected in its relationship with the Communist parties and the organizations under their influence.

After the Bolsheviks' victory in Russia, Lenin and his collaborators believed that the revolution in the West was imminent and that the Bolsheviks had the experience and the authority to indicate the road ahead to labor leaders. During this period, the Bolsheviks supported the creation of Communist parties in the West and Asia and sought the unqualified affiliation of trade unions and mass organizations to the Comintern, considered the sole party of world revolution. Their optimism ended with the aborted Communist insurrection in Hamburg in 1923, which was crushed by the social-democratic government.

Between 1923 and 1928 the Bolshevik leaders believed that the capitalist system was in full recovery and had stabilized, and that peaceful coexistence between the two social systems was possible. This interpretation of world reality translated into a tactical line of collaboration with social-democratic and nationalist forces with the objective of gaining positions for Communists in governments and among the masses. This line's most spectacular failure occurred in China in 1927, where the Kuomintang under Chiang Kai-shek collaborated with and later massacred the Communists who participated in the nationalist ranks.

In 1928 the Comintern radically changed its political line based on the belief that capitalism was in crisis and the West was preparing to attack and destroy the Soviet Union. The deep crisis to which world capitalism had succumbed in 1929 seemed to confirm what was only a thesis in 1928. Moreover, under the influence of the failure of the policy of tactical cooperation with social-democratic, labor party, and nationalist forces, the Comintern changed its line, condemning as social fascists all such political tendencies and the unions and mass organizations that supported them. The Comintern gave orders to Communist parties to destroy their rivals.

Although it is true that during the first half of the 1920s the foreign policy of the Soviet Union focused on consolidating commercial and diplomatic relations with other governments, the Comintern's objective continued to be world revolution. However, as Stalinism—or to be more precise, the personal power of the party general secretary Yosef Visarionovich Stalin—became consolidated in the second half of the decade, the perceived needs of the Soviet state took priority over the original objectives of the Communist International to organize and lead the revolution. The close relations between the Communist Party of the Soviet Union and national parties never ceased to operate. The national Communist parties continued playing the role of organizers of the workers and peasants movements, but they also served to support the defense and expansion of the Soviet Union. In this way, the Bolsheviks were able to utilize social movements close to Communism as well as international solidarity with the Soviet Union as a subtle and effective diplomatic instrument working on their behalf.

The Convergence of Diplomacy and Internationalism

Initially, Lenin and the Bolshevik leaders were convinced that the October Revolution had awakened the working masses from their millenary slumber and spurred them to struggle against world imperialism. From Moscow, "the headquarters of world revolution," the Comintern was to provide the masses with ideological and material support to defeat their enemies. In launching its activities, the Comintern was bathed in optimism and faith in the imminent internationalization of the revolution.[14]

The Bolshevik Revolution had attracted numerous sympathizers among the working class, the socialist movements, and progressive intellectuals. However, Lenin and the Bolsheviks were not interested in a movement composed of sympathizers, but in an organization of committed and disciplined militants, a combat party ready to seize power. The political parties that were not willing to adopt the Leninist structure could not enter or belong to the new Communist International because they would weaken it with their reformism, opportunism, or "parliamentary cretinism," to use Karl Marx's phrase. For the struggles ahead, soldiers of the revolution would be needed.[15]

When Lenin sent Mikhail Markovich Gruzenberg (known by his party name Mikhail Borodin, the prototype of the ideal Communist militant) to the United States and Mexico in mid-1919, the Bolshevik leader took the first steps in implementing the revolution's diplomatic policy. Born in 1884, Borodin had been a revolutionary since he was sixteen years old. He participated in the 1905 revolution, was jailed and later exiled. In 1906 he emigrated to the United States and studied philosophy and law at Valparaiso University in Indiana, and participated in the Socialist Party of America. Borodin returned to Moscow in July 1918 and was recruited to work in the Commissariat for Foreign Affairs and at the same time in the Comintern. In this dual capacity, Lenin sent Borodin to the New World to economically support the Soviet commercial mission established in New York in 1918 and, using Mexico as a base of operations, to organize and finance Communist parties in Latin America.[16]

Initially, the Bolsheviks believed that after the revolution some of the diplomats of the old regime would follow the new government's dictates. Although some declared their loyalty to the Soviet government, for conviction or convenience, most refused to accept the new regime's legitimacy or to hand over the country's embassies and consulates abroad to representatives of the Bolshevik government. As a result, in several countries the People's Commissariat for Foreign Affairs (Narkomindel) could not recover their diplomatic missions, some of which became centers for anti-Soviet activities.

At the same time, the governments for which the diplomats of the previous regime had been accredited continued to consider them the legitimate representatives of the Russian state and ignored the Bolsheviks' exhortations to refuse their credentials. Given these circumstances, the Narkomindel named their representatives without consulting the governments that normally would extend accreditation. In the United States, for example, Boris Bakhmetev was the Russian ambassador named by the provisional government. Because President Wilson considered him the personification of Russian democracy, Washington did not recognize Ludwig K. Martens, whom the Soviet government designated in January 1919 to head the commercial mission in New York.[17]

Due to foreign military intervention in Russia and the resulting blockade, the Soviet mission in New York was left without financial means to continue functioning. One of Borodin's tasks was to obtain such funds. Moscow gave Borodin the royal family's crown jewels—worth approximately half a million dollars—which he was to introduce into the United States as contraband to be turned into cash. Detained in Haiti, Borodin gave his suitcase, with the jewels sewn into the lining, to a traveling companion and proceeded to the United States, planning to recover them at a later date.[18]

Borodin was also given the task of obtaining Mexican government diplomatic recognition and, with the money the jewels were to have provided, of promoting the Communist movement. British and U.S. intelligence services believed that Borodin had been named as Soviet government representative to Latin America in the same way that Martens had been designated for the United States. They also assumed that Borodin had instructions to convince the Mexican government to supply food and raw materials to

Russia. According to the same espionage agencies, he traveled under the guise of being the Mexican consul general in Soviet Russia, with a Mexican diplomatic passport issued in Moscow.[19]

Without funds, however, Borodin could not complete his mission in the United States. In addition, his presence attracted the attention of the Bureau of Investigation, so he had no alternative but to cross the border to carry out the other part of his mission. Because he did not know Spanish, American comrades supplied him with an interpreter. Once in Mexico City, he noticed that one of the capital's newspapers, *El Heraldo de México,* had an English-language section and that its articles were noticeably left-wing. Borodin sent his interpreter to investigate and as a result became acquainted with the editor of the section, Charles Phillips, who in turn presented the Soviet envoy to Manabendra Nath Roy.[20]

During and after the revolution, Mexico became a refuge for American socialists who opposed U.S. participation in the European war and military conscription. Charles Phillips was one of them. Roy was a different kind of refugee: an Indian nationalist, his original mission was to obtain German money and arms, which were to be smuggled into India to fight the British colonial government. To this end, Roy traveled from India to Indonesia and from Japan to China. Detected and hunted by the British, Roy had to cross the Pacific Ocean and seek hiding in the United States.[21] There he met an underground network of Indian nationalists waiting, in vain, for the twenty million German and Irish Americans who would support their anti-British crusade. Once the United States declared war on Germany in 1917, however, the government persecuted the Indians for their ties with Germany. Roy was briefly arrested in New York and to avoid further persecution escaped to Mexico, which "in a state of permanent revolution, seemed like the promised land."[22]

In Mexico, Roy became acquainted with officials close to Carranza, and through his articles in *El Pueblo* concerning British imperialism's exploitation of India and the need for social revolution, he met the leaders of the Mexican Socialist Party. Through them, he became friends with American opponents of the war, in particular Charles Phillips.

Roy was the type of person Borodin needed. After the two established ties of mutual confidence, Borodin told Roy about the loss of the jewels and his urgent need for money. Roy provided Borodin with five thousand dollars for the commercial mission in New York and helped him organize the rescue of the lost gems that he considered "property of the revolution."[23] Despite some attempts, Borodin never recovered them, and since then the loss of the crown jewels has become one of the legends in the history of the Comintern, together with tales of untold Moscow gold intended to finance the activities of the Communist parties.

According to Roy, Borodin managed to meet with top Mexican government officials and with President Carranza himself. He raised with them the possibility of creating a Latin American bureau of the Comintern as a common anti-imperialist front. Supposedly, Carranza made no concrete commitments but put government channels of communications at Borodin's disposal to allow him to maintain contact with Moscow. Charles Phillips—alias Shipman—gave another account, however: "Carranza was glad to see Roy, but the harried old man refused to meet Borodin even informally. He was not going to let himself in for anything like recognition of Soviet Russia at a time when Generals Obregón, Calles, and De la Huerta were openly threatening to revolt over the presidential succession."[24]

With or without direct contact with Carranza, Borodin interpreted the Mexican government's signs of hospitality toward foreign leftists as an ideological trend favorable to the Bolsheviks and as a willingness to recognize the Soviet government. Although Carranza had not actually recognized the Soviet government, Roy gave the impression that he had. With this impression, the Bolshevik emissary went on to the following point on his agenda: to convert the Mexican Socialist Party into a Communist Party. Borodin also believed that the Mexican government would not object to the creation of a Communist Party or to its affiliation to the Comintern as long as its public pronouncements were moderate.[25]

Clearly, it was Borodin who proposed that a national congress of the Socialist Party be called. At the end of August, more than a dozen delegates met, representing unions and workers groups, anarchists and socialists of various shades, both Mexican and foreign. According to Phillips and Roy, Borodin ran the congress from behind the scenes: "His advice helped us get over Morones. And without Borodin we could hardly have thought of affiliating the enlarged party with the Third (Communist) International."[26]

The congress did not transform the Socialist Party into a Communist Party, although it did adopt Communist goals such as socialized property, control of production and distribution of the means of production, and the construction of a society of the working class. Although the Socialist Party did not change its name to the "Communist Party," the delegates' attitude moved the party in that direction.[27] It seems that the group close to Roy and

Borodin, which wound up with the leadership of the party, made the concession to obtain the government's tolerance of their activities.

During the congress, internal divisions in the party emerged, not only in the struggle for the leadership, but also in clashes between the different currents within the organization: the anarcho-syndicalists and the reformists versus the group headed by Borodin. Possibly knowing that he represented a minority in the congress, Roy and his group hid from the others Borodin's decision to select Roy and Phillips to accompany him to Moscow to represent the Mexican proletariat at the Second Congress of the Comintern.[28]

Soviet Diplomacy Following Borodin's Return to Moscow

After leaving Mexico in December 1919, Borodin was fully convinced that he had planted there the seed of the future Latin American revolution. It was necessary, however, to strengthen the embryonic Comintern organization he had established with logistical support and ideological orientation from the Bolsheviks. With this in mind, he traveled to Amsterdam, where in October 1919 the Western Bureau of the Comintern had been established with the aim of forging regular ties between Moscow and the Communist movement in Europe and the Americas, given the problems inherent in the blockade of Soviet Russia. Its work would have to remain covert.

In February 1920, the Amsterdam bureau organized an international conference, which was supposed to have been secret. The Dutch Communists were in charge of the Amsterdam bureau and organizing the conference. Lacking experience in clandestine operations, they could not avoid police infiltration. When the police presence was detected, the conference was suspended. In fact, it was Borodin who discovered the police, who were hiding in the meeting room closet with a listening device. In addition to the Dutch police, the conference was attended by Nosovitsky—the Justice Department agent who in 1921 would forge the documents concerning the existence of a Mexican Red Army—pretending to be a Communist activist.[29] Because Mexico was an agenda point at the Amsterdam conference, Nosovitsky, and therefore the Justice Department, would have firsthand knowledge of the Russian-Mexican connection.

The Western Bureau of the Comintern in Amsterdam never became consolidated, nor could it provide the hoped for assistance for the Third International's bureau in Mexico, which in the meantime languished for lack of material resources and guidance. In April 1920, the Amsterdam bureau was dissolved and its authority and tasks transferred back to Moscow, where preparations were underway for the Second Congress of the Comintern.

Returning to the Soviet capital, Borodin reported to Lenin and the Comintern leadership on his trip to Mexico. Roy and Phillips, who reached Moscow separately, also reported to the Bolshevik leaders on the "highly interesting experiment in revolutionary strategy" being carried out in Mexico. Lenin apparently listened with interest, but felt that revolution in the New World was not imminent and so ordered Roy to work from then on toward mobilizing the oppressed and exploited masses of Asia "in a gigantic revolutionary movement" that would in due course engulf Mexico.[30]

In his conversation with Lenin, Phillips recalled that although the Bolshevik leader's knowledge about Mexico was rudimentary, he was interested in the Mexican peasant movement, the national and indigenous question, and the strength of anti-imperialist sentiments more than in Mexican socialism, which he said was bound to be elementary. For Lenin, what was most important was Mexico's strategic location in the Western Hemisphere as a neighbor to the United States.[31]

The Second Congress of the Comintern was inaugurated in July 1920 in Petrograd. Mexico was discussed during the deliberations on colonial and semicolonial countries, and was mentioned by the U.S. delegates Louis Fraina and John Reed. Using Lenin's theory on imperialism, Fraina described Mexico and the rest of Latin America as a colonial base of the United States, which should be fought by promoting revolutionary movements. Without even mentioning the political changes resulting from the Mexican Revolution, he described how Mexico and Latin America passively suffered the aggressiveness of the oppressor without mounting a resistance to U.S. political and economic hegemony.[32]

The second time Mexico appeared on the agenda of the Comintern was at the Congress of the Peoples of the East in Baku, Azerbaidzhan, in September 1920. This congress was considered to be the continuation of the Comintern's Petrograd congress, which in turn had been continued in Moscow in July. The theme of the Baku congress was the unification of the Eastern peoples with the revolutionary workers of the West under the banner of the Comintern in a crusade against British imperialism. In Baku, Reed was the most important speaker, and he backed the aspirations of Mexican revolutionaries for national sovereignty. Idealizing their achievements, Reed said, "After many years of civil war, the people formed their own government, not a proletarian government, but a democratic one, which wanted to keep the wealth of Mexico for the Mexicans and tax the foreign capitalists."[33]

Fraina and Reed presented two different perspectives on Mexico, but both perspectives were encouraging in terms of their belief in the possibility of developing a revolutionary movement capable of challenging U.S. imperialism. It appears that Fraina won more respect among the delegates and the Soviet leaders, although Reed's influence was significant. It was Reed, however, not Fraina, who was elected to the Executive Committee of the Comintern as a representative of Communists in the United States. At the time, a rumor circulated that Fraina had been a Justice Department informer. Due to his fervor and revolutionary idealism, and in order to avoid clashes between him and other American comrades, the Comintern sent him to Mexico to implement the trade union policy that the congress had just adopted.[34]

The Soldiers of the World Revolution in Mexico

In 1919, the Bolsheviks believed in the imminent victory of the Soviet system in the West, and the question of revolutionary versus reformist trade unionism did not concern them. However, following failed attempts that same year to create Soviet republics in Hungary and Germany, and after the reformist International Federation of Trade Unions—also known as the Amsterdam International—reorganized its contingents and obtained a new lease on life, Moscow feared that weak Communist forces would remain isolated. At the beginning of 1920, the chairman of the Comintern, Grigori Zinoviev, proposed that the Red International of Trade Unions (or Profintern, per its Russian acronym) be established as a confederation that would bring the workers movement together under the aegis of the Comintern. Lenin himself made declarations on the need for Communists to work in "reactionary trade unions" the same way Russian revolutionaries had done so in their country. With this in mind, the Bolshevik leaders discussed the matter with different foreign delegations before and during the Second Congress of the Comintern. Even though the immediate reaction of the trade unionists from the capitalist countries was to refuse to have anything to do with the reformists, the Comintern imposed its criterion that the Communists had to work in the reformist trade unions.[35] For the Bolsheviks, the trade unions represented an enormous concentration of the popular masses shaken by the depressed economic conditions following

World War I. This panorama would have to be taken advantage of in order to radicalize the workers movement. The Communists should work to convert the unions into "conscious organs of struggle to liquidate the capitalist regime and bring about the victory of communism."[36]

Although the Red International of Trade Unions was not founded until July 1921, the Comintern emissaries who arrived in Mexico during the first months of that year were in Moscow when its creation was being discussed. They were inundated with the heated arguments that finally led to the Profintern's creation, and as disciplined soldiers of the revolution they implemented the new trade union line. The American Louis Fraina and the veteran organizer of the Japanese workers movement, Sen Katayama, who was more than seventy years old at the time, were selected to head up the Comintern mission to Mexico, with Charles Phillips as their assistant. Mexico City was to be the headquarters of the Profintern coordinating committee for the rest of Latin America. Of the three, only Phillips was familiar with Mexico and knew Spanish.

Phillips left Moscow in November 1920 accompanied by Natalia Alexandrovna Mikhailova, an eighteen-year-old woman who worked in the Comintern as an interpreter. She was attractive, uninterested in revolution, and anxious to leave Russia. To Phillips, who had separated from his American companion several months previously, Natalia's courtship was pleasant, and he married her so she could accompany him. The couple arrived in Mexico in January 1921. Several weeks later, Katayama arrived and then Fraina, who was also married in Moscow to a Comintern employee named Esther Nesvishkaia.[37]

When the internationalists arrived in Mexico, they found that the Mexican Communist Party—founded in November 1919 as a split from the Socialist Party—existed in name only. Its original members were no longer to be found. Only José Allen, party general secretary, and a group organized in the Young Communists Federation, headed by José Valadés, remained loyal to the idea of building Communism in Mexico.[38] However, the Cominternists were ready to roll up their sleeves and get to work reconstructing the Communist ranks, encouraged by what they perceived to be the apparent climate of freedom of speech and the right to protest that existed at the time in Mexico. Taking advantage of the enthusiasm of the small handful of Mexican Communists, the Comintern activists channeled their energies into organizational and propaganda work.

The trio sent by Moscow established an office of the Latin American division of the Profintern, in charge of disseminating its principles, seeking trade union affiliation to the new Communist labor confederation, and electing their delegates to the founding congress of the Red International of Trade Unions. To further these goals, the office published a weekly, *El Trabajador*, and *Boletín Comunista*, which among other items circulated the principles guiding the Comintern, summarized in twenty-one points. According to Phillips, their work was made easier because at the same time that the Communists were publicizing the Profintern congress, the Moronistas were meeting with AFL leaders to organize the Pan-American Federation of Labor. For some union delegates, the name of the planned federation smelled too much of the Monroe Doctrine, and they were therefore hesitant to affiliate. The Communists took advantage of this discontent and invited dissident Cromistas, along with anarcho-syndicalists and independent trade unionists, to an anti-CROM convention.

This convention was held in February 1921 and out of it came the General Confederation of Labor (CGT). Although at its own congress the CGT named a delegate to represent it at the founding congress of the Profintern, it agreed to support the Communist labor confederation only provisionally and to adopt a definitive position only after the delegate's return from Moscow and upon hearing his report on the congress proceedings. However, behind the backs of the CGT congress delegates, and probably instructed by Katayama, the delegate to Moscow took with him a letter of affiliation from the CGT to the Red International of Trade Unions that had not been approved by the CGT congress.[39]

With the Comintern's money, Katayama, Fraina, and Phillips launched a publishing house, the Biblioteca Internacional, which issued books and pamphlets about and by distinguished European trade union and socialist leaders. Paid with Comintern funds, the Communists attached to the office of the future Profintern traveled the length and breadth of Mexico, seeking ties with trade unionists in the provinces. Perhaps viewing the government's tolerance toward their activities as a sign of the state's weakness and their own strength, the Communists made a splash with their presence in the streets of Mexico City on May 1, 1921, and by raising their banner over the roof of the central cathedral. Similar mass demonstrations were reported in Morelia, Michoacán.[40]

Obregón reacted to this militancy in the streets with repression and the deportation of the foreign activists. The government expelled Phillips from Mexico and deported him to Guatemala. Without Phillips, Katayama's work was hindered but not halted. The tireless Japanese revolutionary continued in English with his propaganda work in favor of red unionism. Mexican comrades translated his broadsides into Spanish and later distributed them in the most important trade unions. Katayama continued to urge workers to affiliate to the Comintern and to wash their hands of the CROM, the AFL, and their respective leaders.[41]

Katayama's exhortations from the underground—which had little direct contact with Mexican reality, but was in fact filtered through the activity of Mexican Communists—had very limited effect. In addition, in their struggle to win the trade unions, the Mexican Communists not only had to confront the CROM, but now the CGT as well. In its September 1921 congress, the CGT condemned Soviet Russia's policy of persecuting the anarchists, expelled the Communists from their ranks, and retracted their tentative plans to join the Profintern.[42]

Katayama did not give up. In a letter to Moscow, he wrote, "I am standing firm and will do everything necessary to struggle against imperialism in the Americas, of which the Mexican government is a puppet."[43] Once again assisted by Phillips—who with Natalia returned clandestinely from Guatemala to Mexico under the name Manuel Gómez—Katayama and the Communists from the youth federation insisted that it was necessary to "continue the struggle in the CGT through our Communist members in the trade unions to formulate a practical program to reform the CGT, to have the unions adopt the program and in this way to regenerate and rejuvenate the CGT."[44] But Katayama could give little practical orientation to the workers. When labor strife erupted in the Tampico oil fields, he did not hesitate to write immediately to the workers, urging them to affiliate to the Profintern. Believing in the propagandistic power of the Soviet example, he had a pamphlet concerning Soviet trade unions by Profintern leader A. Lozovsky translated and published, adapting the introduction to Mexican circumstances. His fighting spirit notwithstanding, by the end of the year Katayama was to write to Moscow that despite having admired the commitment and sacrifice of Mexican Communists such as José Valadés, "it is very difficult to organize Mexicans."[45]

The last heroic act of the Comintern emissaries in Mexico before they concluded their mission was to relaunch the Mexican Communist Party in December 1921. Katayama left Mexico in October, before this congress was held, but he participated in its preparation. When the congress met, twenty-one delegates attended, representing one thousand Communists. Fraina reported to the Comintern that the "most significant feature of the Congress was its sobriety and steadiness. Mexican congresses as a rule are flamboyant, hysterical, the sonorous phrase and the excited gesture being dominant. This was absent at the Congress. Instead, most of the time of the Congress was used in the work of the various commissions, where every phase of the Mexican problem was earnestly discussed and acted upon." Fraina did not openly participate in the congress discussions but, like Borodin in 1919, met with the Mexican party leaders on the days leading up to the congress. Although the thesis and resolutions of the congress agreed with Comintern policy on a majority of the issues under discussion, the Mexicans did not allow their arms to be twisted when it came to the point on elections in which the Bolsheviks wanted them to participate: "Let us first, it was said to me, build the party and get the workers confidence, and then we can go on to the program of participating in the elections."[46]

Fraina reported that the Mexican Communists wanted a revolution and wanted it now, although he and Katayama did not feel conditions were ripe for an immediate insurrection. In Mexico, no single social class could exercise total political power, not even the bourgeoisie, which "governs thanks to the weakness of other classes." Katayama and Fraina—the latter admitted—"somewhat misjudged the situation, imagining that the movement was larger or capable of being made bigger than could be carried through." Finally, Fraina suggested that the Comintern send an experienced Russian militant to guide the work of the reborn Mexican Communist Party. He was to leave for South America to investigate the conditions for organizing people and for disseminating propaganda in the region.[47] Phillips, alias Manuel Gómez, and Natalia went to the United States in the spring of 1922.

Thus, by the end of 1921 the first stage in relations between the Mexican Communists and the Bolsheviks had come to an end. The Mexican Communist experiment had failed, principally because the Third International's ideologues and emissaries underestimated the scope of the changes wrought by the Mexican Revolution: the restructuring of relations between the state and society, the close ties established between the state and the workers' movement, and the marginalization of the Communist and anarcho-syndicalist trade unions, which were jealous of preserving their independence. The Soviet leaders and Comintern representatives evaluated conditions in

Mexico through a teleological vision of sociopolitical stages and had the incredible illusion that Mexican generals could be easily attracted to the Communist ranks and that the Mexican proletariat would respond to their exhortations. The proletariat was less revolutionary and the state more active than the Comintern anticipated, however.

Chapter 3

SOVIET RUSSIA

IN MEXICAN

POLITICS

The way in which events of the first years of the Bolshevik Revolution were presented in Mexico indirectly reflected the country's own conjunctural political situation and its relationship with the United States. Due to fear of further social upheavals—given Carranza's reluctance to implement the reforms contained in the Constitution—and to the fear of the consequences of pressure from the United States to force Carranza out of office, most of the newspapers fell under the anti-Communist spell. A favorable portrait of the Bolshevik Revolution might provoke further convulsions. As a result, much of what the newspapers reported concerning Soviet Russia and its supposed or real influence over Mexico was often distorted or fabricated.

The news of the February and October 1917 Revolutions reached Mexico through the European Communist press, Spanish anarchist periodicals, news agencies, and foreign newspapers. In all cases, the information was incomplete and reflected the moods and ideologies of the sources in question. Because Mexico's main metropolitan newspapers had no reporters at the scene of the events, they depended on external sources for news about the Bolshevik Revolution. Thus, together with the content, they inevitably reproduced the biases, half-truths, and prejudices of their sources. For the same reason, the first articles published in Mexico on the revolution reflected the European powers' illusion that an opposition to the Bolshevik government would emerge and replace it. This illusion was frequently what inspired the speculative and sensationalist front-page articles that obfuscated Soviet reality.[1] Nor should it also be ruled out that the shrill tone of the news was probably due to the desire of each of the sources in question to attract readers and demonstrate how astute its newspaper was. In addition, the attitude that each newspaper assumed with respect to Russia depended on which position they had taken during World War I—that is, in favor of Germany or the Allies. *El Demócrata*, founded in 1905, received German financing and defended Berlin. *El Universal*, founded in 1916, and *Excélsior*, established in March 1917, were spokesmen for the Allied cause in Mexico.[2]

Germany, which benefited from the unilateral armistice signed with Russia in 1918, considered the Bolsheviks to be Russia's legitimate rulers, so *El Demócrata* followed the same line. Given its stance and progressive editorial policy, *El Demócrata* was the only newspaper to publish Lenin's historic proclamation, "To all workers, soldiers and peasants"; the Bolsheviks' commitment to provide peace, land, and bread to the Russian people; and their promise of worldwide emancipation of the oppressed from slavery and exploitation. *El Demócrata* also published Lenin's high-sounding pronouncement on the abolition of private property and privileges, as well as his promise of equality for all ethnic groups living in the Russian Empire. Despite receiving contradictory information, *El Demócrata* wanted its readers to have the impression that the Bolshevik government was growing and consolidating.[3]

In contrast, *Excélsior* and *El Universal* centered their coverage on the destructive forces of the revolution: the outbursts of popular anger against the aristocracy, the looting of property, and the street assaults on "well-dressed people," which Lenin approved of according to their articles. Both newspapers related accounts of protests by workers and government employees against Soviet power and of internal struggles within the leadership amidst hunger, epidemics, and terror. Observing the Soviet scene, albeit from afar, *Excélsior* and *El Universal* concluded in 1919 that Bolshevism was "an ominous phenomenon."[4]

As time wore on during the 1920s, the quality of the coverage on the Soviet Union improved thanks to a diversification of news sources and more direct access to the sources of information. The first reflections by European intellectuals such as H. G. Wells and Bertrand Russell following their trips to the land they had considered the workers' paradise began to be published. Alongside the critical and introspective articles on Soviet reality, enthusiastic pieces were always run: writings by idealists such as the French author Henri Barbusse or the Mexican Rafael Ramos Pedrueza, for whom the defense of the Soviet homeland was an act of faith launched against detractors entrenched in the enemy camp.[5]

The Bolsheviks Are Here

From their first reports at the end of 1918 and throughout 1919, *El Universal* and *Excélsior* depicted a Mexico threatened by Bolshevik "contamination." Before the October Revolution, these newspapers had attributed popular demands to the promises left unfulfilled by the Mexican revolutionaries, and they had blamed the economic difficulties Mexico was experiencing on inflation, the currency devaluation, or the government's erroneous monetary policies. The newspapers rained insults on the Industrial Workers of the World and its Mexican counterpart, the Casa del Obrero Mundial (House of the World Worker). After October 1917, however, the newspapers hurled the same invectives at the Bolsheviks and Bolshevism.[6]

Even though the anti-Bolshevik hysteria had its origin in the United States, the Mexican media—especially *Excélsior*—was willing to spread the scare campaign in Mexico. In reality, the 1919–1920 red scare in Mexico was a replica of the same phenomenon that developed north of the border. Most of the evidence the newspapers presented to their readers concerning the "Bolshevik threat" was fabricated by or acritically reprinted from the U.S. press. It is likely that these types of articles were published by the U.S. press or in the Mexican media as part of a disinformation campaign.

From the end of 1918 on, articles painted a picture of waves of nameless, faceless Soviet agents crossing the borders of South America, Europe, and the United States, then waiting to plant the seeds of Bolshevism among unsuspecting workers, innocent peasants, and new army recruits. These agents, according to the newspapers, brought with them "the terrible Bolshevik ideas that are being tenaciously fought everywhere in the world because they are believed to be at the root of unrest and social disturbances."[7]

Articles of this type sought to exonerate the Mexican government from responsibility for social unrest and popular opposition to the regime. With this in mind, the newspapers increased the intensity of their diatribes on Mexican Bolshevism. *El Universal* used the false fear of Bolshevism to shift responsibility for social upheavals from the Carranza government to a foreign foe. *Excélsior*, on the other hand, used "the Bolshevik nightmare" to call the public's attention to the incapacity of the government. In addition, to inspire a certain fear of the United States among the public, it published articles—supposedly reprinted from the U.S. press—on the threat Communist ideology represented to the national security of the United States and therefore to relations between the two countries.[8] It announced, for example, in May 1919 that a hub of Bolshevik propaganda had just been uncovered in the Tampico oil fields, precisely when workers at the Pierce Oil Corporation went on strike against the company and the latter refused to negotiate the union's list of demands. *Excélsior* distorted the information on the strike and presented the labor conflict as the workers exaggerated acceptance of "the ideas professed by Trotzky and Lenine [*sic*]." The daily supported the military commander's decision to close down the Casa del Obrero Mundial for being "the Bolshevik center" in Tampico. In a disapproving tone, the newspaper reported a strike in Orizaba of twenty thousand textile workers who cheered for Russia and shouted "death to the aristocracy" while marching in the streets.[9]

By 1920, *Excélsior* discovered that Bolshevism was not only affecting labor unions, but was also penetrating the army barracks and reaching the peasants. In Campeche, for example, CROM activist Jose Prevé, "a Muscovite from the Soviets," and a group of poorly equipped Indians were apparently going from ranch to ranch "trying to influence the peasants with outside and corrupt theories." Prevé, according to the ever vigilant capital daily, advised the peasants to stop working, attack the rich, and take "what rightfully belongs to them because they produce the wealth."[10]

But just as *Excélsior* described the "pernicious" influence of the "depraved" Bolsheviks, at the same time it sought to assure its readers that the workers, with a few exceptions, were immune to such sedition because they realized that their salvation could not be achieved by destroying capital. *El Universal*, for its part, said Bolshevism was bound to fail because it would come up against the positive actions of the Mexican government, which had guaranteed an improvement in the population's living conditions.[11]

Vilified or praised, *Bolshevism* had been established by 1920 as a watchword, a reference point at certain levels in Mexican political culture. Despite all the negative propaganda, it was associated less with the Bolsheviks in power in Soviet Russia than with a force bent on subverting the existing order or on eliminating obstacles in the way of universal emancipation. Mexican conservatives in and out of government—like their counterparts in the United States—considered it a threat to the Mexican social order.

On the other hand, influenced by the Communists or by the aura that surrounded the October Revolution, the trade unions and peasant organizations associated Bolshevism with uncompromising radical reforms and considered the Soviet government an ally. With its assistance, they could overcome the obstacles placed in the way of emancipation. For at least a time, the radical wing within the Mexican administrations in the 1920s thought that the Mexican government could utilize an alliance with the Soviet Union to its benefit as a lever to counteract the hegemonic power of the United States.

The Radical Intellectuals in Power

One of the most important results of the Mexican Revolution was the eruption of workers and peasants into the political arena and the subsequent broadening, when compared to the Porfiriato period, of the spectrum of political participation. The other significant change was in the social composition of the governing elite—the upperclass before the revolution, but the middle class after the revolution. An additional new element characterizing postrevolutionary administrations was the involvement of a radical intellectual elite in important political posts.

This intellectual governing elite matured politically during the armed phase of the Mexican Revolution. Some of their representatives participated in the Constituent Assembly in Querétaro in 1916. Ranging between twenty and thirty years of age during the period of the revolution, these intellectuals were willing and anxious to work for their country. Zapata's intellectual heirs took the agrarian project to the government to implement it from the heights of state power. Another intellectual current, originally Maderist and then recruited by Carranza, also believed in the virtues of state power to bring about reforms that none of the revolutionary factions had been able to implement.[12] They knew it would be difficult to carry out the 1917 Constitution, but they hoped to be able to radicalize or influence the government's policies on land distribution and to raise the lower classes from ignorance and poverty. Marte R. Gómez was probably sincere when he described himself as "radical and honorable, with no concerns other than fighting for the realization of those ideals that can be summarized as the desire to improve the collective well-being of which we speak so much and do so little."[13]

The radical intellectual elite viewed itself as the consciousness of the government it was serving. Although it never coalesced as an autonomous group, it consisted of individuals who believed in the possibility of instilling a program and ideology in the revolution that would strengthen not only the state, but also education and social welfare. These intellectuals criticized the previous administrations as instruments of political aggression and defenders of political privilege, and they believed that the government was obligated to improve the social inequalities created by the dominant economic system. In general, the radical political elite believed that the government should be at the service of the people.[14]

Despite censuring the administrations they served, however, the intellectuals rarely went over to the opposition. For example, the economist and sociologist Rafael Nieto—whom Jesús Silva Herzog called "the vacillating Marxist"—criticized the legal framework of the Mexican Revolution as incapable of resolving social inequalities in which so few had everything and the majority had nothing. Despite his criticisms of Carranza's administration, Nieto was undersecretary of the treasury and held posts in subsequent administrations until his death in 1926. The economist and historian Jesús Silva Herzog occupied numerous posts in the Finance Ministry during the 1920s because he was convinced that only by working within the system could deficiencies in the government be rectified. Before confiding to José Vasconcelos that "one thing is the revolution and another the stupidities and the 'crimes' committed in its name,"[15] the lawyer Manuel Gómez Morín put his talents at the service of the Finance Ministry when it was headed by Adolfo de la Huerta in 1921 and then collaborated with Calles in improving public finances so that Mexico could be more independent and economically sovereign. It is well known that before passing over to the opposition in 1928, when Vasconcelos was minister of education, he distributed textbooks that included contributions from established as well as modern socialist political thinkers. His goal was to broaden Mexicans' cultural horizons.

Ramón P. de Negri served in the foreign service, the secret service, and numerous administrative posts from the Carranza administration to Emilio Portes Gil's; his friend Juan de Dios Bojórquez did the same. The agricultural engineer Marte R. Gómez occupied different government posts, and with diligence and tenacity worked to speed up the land distribution process. When at the end of the decade the government backed away from applying agrarian reform policies, he decided to maintain a low profile until the official attitude changed. Strident radicals could also be found in public administration—such as deputy Rafael Ramos Pedrueza and the Communist senator Luis Monzón. Although they were thorns in the government's side, the "danger" they represented to the government's stability was deliberately exaggerated by the press.

The radical political elite adhered to socialism, but it also sought to adapt currents of European thought to Mexican national traditions so that they could be used to forge an authentically Mexican political and social program.[16] The Bolshevik Revolution made a deep impression on some of the administrative and intellectual cadres of the Mexican Revolution. However, from a distance and without a thorough understanding of Soviet developments, these intellectuals looked to the example of the Bolshevik Revolution for inspiration and for ways of employing one or another of its ideas. Antonio Díaz Soto y Gama felt the Soviet land distribution program was "the complete, absolute integral realization of the socialist ideal" as contained in Marx's *Communist Manifesto*. Vasconcelos admired the mass education program of Commissar Anatoli Lunacharsky. Although not a socialist, Manuel Gómez Morín was for a brief period—at the same time that he administered the Banco de México—a consultant to the Soviet embassy, advising the Russians on how to cement commercial relations between the two countries so that Mexico could diversify its markets. Jesús Silva Herzog's curiosity to learn about the methods to be followed in industrializing an underdeveloped country led him in 1928 to request that President Portes Gil send him to the Soviet Union as ambassador so that he could study the Bolshevik Revolution firsthand. Some visionaries among these intellectuals—de Negri, for example—hoped that Mexico would be engulfed by the wave of "world revolution," which would sweep away the old economic and political structures that the Mexican state could not or did not want to eliminate.[17]

The radical elite was anti-imperialist but at the same time quite aware of Mexico's geopolitical reality. This understanding tempered their ability to formulate and implement a radical program within the country. However, what dampened the elite's radical spirit was, above all, its unequivocal participation in constructing the Mexican state, based as it were on the principle of class conciliation and a functional relation with the United States. The contradictions that continually arose between the radical elite's ideology and the government's policies were reconciled by the interdependence between the state and its administrators. The radical elite genuinely believed in the leading role of the state as promoter and defender of the well-being of the lower classes, but it also depended on the government for its employment and livelihood. For its part, the Mexican government needed the economists, lawyers, engineers, and agronomists for their tech-nical knowledge as much as for their dedication and honesty on the job.

It was this intellectual elite that promoted the establishment of diplo-matic relations between Mexico and the Soviet Union and that later main-tained close ties with the Russian diplomats, although relations ended up being established in 1924 for the state's own considerations.

Carranza's Diplomacy toward Soviet Russia

After the October Revolution, Mexican policy toward revolutionary Rus-sia was unclear. In September 1918, U.S. Ambassador Henry Fletcher asked Cándido Aguilar, foreign relations minister, about Mexico's attitude to-ward the Bolshevik government, given that "the peaceful Russian citizens of Moscow, Petrograd, and other cities are being made victims of a cam-paign of generalized terror and subject to all sorts of executions." The min-ister did not respond.[18] Although the Foreign Relations Ministry requested reports on the situation in Russia from the Mexican embassies in neighbor-ing countries, the Mexican government did not line up with the United States to condemn the Bolshevik government. In fact, the Mexican govern-ment was slow in formulating a policy toward Soviet Russia, mainly be-cause it had more important matters to deal with, and in its foreign affairs Russia was not a priority. In any event, the government adopted a wait-and-see attitude while it was still being determined whether the Bolsheviks would remain in power and be recognized by the Western powers or the Russian opposition supported by foreign troops would topple the Soviet government.

In 1918, the Foreign Relations Ministry lost all contact with its represen-tatives in Russia. The Mexican embassy in Petrograd closed its doors after the revolution, but unlike the embassies of the allied countries, which moved to northern Russia under the protection of foreign troops, Mexico did not reopen its diplomatic mission. The consulate in Moscow remained functioning until mid-1919, despite the chaos caused by the civil war and foreign intervention. Shortly thereafter, it too was forced to close its doors.

One fine day, a group of Soviet soldiers entered the offices of the Mexican consulate and detained the commercial attaché, Basilio Blidin, taking with them diplomatic seals, archives, and blank passports. On July 1, 1919, the soldiers jailed Jorge Villardo, another embassy official, on charges of being a citizen of an "imperialist" and "reactionary" country. Five days later Vil-lardo was informed that he was to be shot unless he would give safe conduct to two Bolsheviks to Berlin, provide them with fake Mexican passports, and present them at the border as consular employees. All indications are that Villardo took to heart the soldiers' warning that if he revealed the identity of his traveling companions "in whatever country I was living, they'd kill me; that if I accepted these conditions they would let me go free, and that if not, they'd shoot me and arrest my family."[19]

Despite inconsistencies in Villardo's account or in the report by Leopoldo Ortiz, business attaché at the Mexican embassy in Berlin, it is most likely that one of the two Bolsheviks whom Villardo took to Berlin and later presented to Ortiz was Borodin. After the encounter, Ortiz reported to the Foreign Relations Ministry that Villardo, who identified himself as secretary of the Mexican consulate in Moscow, arrived at the legation with one Michael Gruzenberg, "who was presented as the Mexican vice-consul in Moscow." Borodin, using his true last name as an alias, led Ortiz to believe he was "an American from California who said he had a deep sympathy for Mexico." Ortiz had the impression that Borodin was an intelligent businessman "who was thoroughly familiar with the political and social changes in Russia." He did not suspect that before him stood a Bolshevik leader whom Lenin had sent to the New World to radicalize the continent, nor did he suspect that the young Villardo, who "deserves my confidence," covered up Borodin's true identity, probably fearing for his own life.[20]

Although perhaps some officials of the government personally knew Borodin during his brief stay in Mexico in 1919, it is most likely that Carranza had no direct contact with the Bolshevik emissary. After all, as a result of press reports, the president had to be aware that the Bolshevik Revolution had been heatedly debated at the Paris Peace Conference as a threat to peace. In addition, after the Communist International was founded in March 1919, with the explicit goal of "advancing toward the heart of Europe," the European countries rejected the Bolshevik government as a partner among equals.[21] 1919 was also a year of intensive anti-Mexican propaganda in the U.S. press. Such negative publicity spurred Carranza to counteract it by circulating his treatise, *Carranza's Doctrine and Indo-Latin Rapprochement* among the Hispanic population of the United States. Conceived as the antithesis of the Monroe Doctrine, Carranza's book indicted U.S. hemispheric foreign policy as an attempt to seek the subjugation of Latin American countries, whom Carranza exhorted to close ranks to improve their position with respect to those who "look down on us because of our material inferiority."[22]

In addition to his counterpropaganda, in July 1919 Carranza sent Cándido Aguilar, his son-in-law and former foreign relations minister, to Europe to purchase arms and to the United States to try to influence public opinion and obtain a loan for the ailing Mexican economy. Aguilar went to Italy to negotiate with the renowned Casa Ansaldo the construction of a foundry, which would allow Mexico to become self-sufficient and face the periodic embargos imposed by the United States on its arms shipments to Mexico. Supposedly, the Italians promised to keep the factory equipped with the most up-to-date technological innovations in exchange for regular shipments of Mexican oil.[23]

Before leaving for Italy, Aguilar met U.S. interim Secretary of State Frank Polk in Paris. Polk belonged to the anti-Carranza bloc within the U.S. government. During their conversation, the secretary of state took the opportunity to make a casual allusion to the supposed insistence on the part of the British and French governments that the United States intervene in Mexico in defense of their interests. Polk indicated that Washington was resisting a drastic action against Mexico, but if the three governments were to agree on a serious course of action, he would let Aguilar know. In fact, rumors were circulating at the time in diplomatic circles concerning a secret agreement between the United States, Great Britain, and France. Alberto Pani, the Mexican ambassador to France, had repeatedly expressed concern over "the climate of open hostility toward our revolution and particularly, toward President Carranza's government."[24] Not completely certain if the agreement actually existed, the Mexican government acted extremely cautiously throughout 1919. In addition, Carranza's former allies, especially Alvaro Obregón, were becoming his adversaries. Discontent with the government was rampant in various parts of the country, and its legality was being questioned.[25]

This was the context in which Roy contrived the account of the meeting between Carranza and Borodin. He probably embellished the incident in his autobiography. It was true that Carranza was seeking an independent foreign policy vis-à-vis the United States, but Roy took too many liberties in describing a meeting between the two political leaders in which they supposedly agreed to join forces to struggle against U.S. imperialism.[26] Charles Phillips's version seems to be closer to the truth—namely that Carranza declined to meet with Borodin for fear that the Americans would interpret any rapprochement with the Soviets as a provocation. In reality, there is evidence that the president rejected any suggestion to initiate official relations with the Bolsheviks.

In October 1919, two Soviet government officials approached Ramón P. de Negri—then Mexican consul general in New York and an ardent supporter of the Bolshevik Revolution—and asked him to explore the possibility of establishing a Soviet trade mission in Mexico. De Negri was enthused with the idea and sought the president's consent. Carranza rejected the idea as inconvenient.[27] De Negri did not give up and insisted: "I feel that it is of great importance for our government to study the tendencies of Soviet Russia's administration because of the sympathy it has displayed for our government, and because the U.S. government, despite its intransigence toward that regime, now seems to be repentant, willing to send special agents to Russia to study the current situation and because the governments of England and Italy are inclined to recognize the Russians."[28]

He exaggerated the U.S. government's change in heart toward the Soviets, however. In reality, his allusion to agents being sent by the United States to Russia refers to a secret visit by government advisor William C. Bullitt to Moscow in February 1919 to try to get the Soviets to pay their foreign debt to U.S. creditors, without at the same time making peace with the revolution.

But Carranza did not allow his arm to be twisted, and his attitude toward Soviet Russia continued to be marked by caution. Moreover, at the same time that de Negri was urging him to draw closer to the Soviets, he received disturbing news of the Communist International's supposed sinister designs for Mexico. From Rotterdam, the Mexican consul provided details on the establishment of the Comintern bureau in Amsterdam, which was also to be in charge of Bolshevik propaganda in Mexico "to encourage strikes, insurrections within the army, destruction and bloody revolutions."[29] This version of events in Rotterdam was the one reported in diplomatic circles and intelligence agencies concerning the meeting of the Comintern at the beginning of 1920 in which Borodin participated and which we know was infiltrated by the Dutch police and the Justice Department agent Nosovitsky.

Shortly thereafter, in May 1920, Carranza was overthrown. In light of the documents available today, Obregón's publicist Emile Dillon exaggerated when he claimed Carranza had introduced Communist doctrines into the country and had spent government money on Communist propaganda "regardless of the consequences."[30] In the 1930s Marjorie Ruth Clark's appre-

ciation of Carranza's position seems closer to the truth. Carranza had hoped
to make use of Soviet Russia against the Allies and especially against the
United States without appearing to sympathize with its ideology. "If he did
encourage Communist propaganda it was because he hoped to utilize it in
the intricate political game he was playing," she wrote.[31] The shifting sands
the government was treading upon prevented Carranza from completing
his game. His position in office was increasingly precarious due to the anti-
Communist, belligerent attitude of the Americans and to his sharply receding social policies. Little by little, Carranza was losing support within
and outside the country. Moving close to Soviet Russia would have been a
false move.

Obregón's Diplomatic Balancing Act

Alvaro Obregón's successful rise to power in 1920 was due in part to his
military exploits during the revolution and to his political skill in attracting both the peasantry, for whom the government still had not fulfilled its
promise of land distribution, and the workers, who felt the government had
not rewarded them for their dedication to the revolutionary cause. Obregón
included peasant leaders with ties to the Zapatistas in his cabinet. During
his presidency, he distributed almost a million hectares of land, more than
the combined total distributed during the presidency of Carranza and the
interim presidency of de la Huerta in 1920. Obregón compensated his labor
allies by strengthening the Labor Ministry. However, he did not seek to
redistribute wealth, but rather to balance out the conflicting interests of
different social groups. Pacifying the country and bolstering support for the
government were urgent priorities, despite both domestic and foreign pressures to put a halt to the process of distributing the nation's wealth.[32]

Obregón's popular policies were based on the desire to buffer social antag-
onisms between the landowners and peasants, as well as between management and labor. The president was convinced that the workers' well-being
depended, above all, on the country's economic recovery through an equilibrium between the productive agents—on the one hand, the availability of
credit and capital investment, and on the other, the disciplined participation of labor without limitations such as strikes. To achieve these goals, it
would be necessary for the powerful to be more revolutionary and for the
revolutionaries to be less so. For example, when the struggle for power
between the socialists and their adversaries was at its height in Yucatán in
1920, Obregón warned the former that the revolution was now over and

that their objectives had to be achieved gradually. The message to the landowners was exactly the opposite, with the president declaring that "revolutions do not end as long as they don't fulfill their goals." Obregón hoped that his collaborators would govern in favor of all social classes, rather than in favor of one at the expense of another.[33]

However, conciliating the interests of landowners and peasants, employers and workers in Mexico was anathema among the government's radical collaborators in the 1920s. Class conciliation only hid the drastic inequality and ancestral injustice that the armed revolution had not eradicated. The peasants kept up pressure to have land distributed, and strikes multiplied in the workplace, where employers opposed pro-labor legislation and trade union campaigns among the workers.[34]

For governors such as Felipe Carrillo Puerto in Yucatán and Adalberto Tejeda in Veracruz, as well as for the radical politicians in the government, the policy of class conciliation reflected the administration's cowardice. Francisco Múgica, Ramón P. de Negri, Marte R. Gómez, Jesús Silva Herzog, Rafael Nieto, Luis Monzón, Aurelio Manrique, and Antonio Díaz Soto y Gama believed that the road forward, as shown by the Bolsheviks, was to be found in the government's determination to carry the revolution through to its ultimate consequences.

The enthusiasm of the Mexican radical elite for the Bolshevik Revolution stemmed from its own ideological commitment to social justice. Its objective was not to replace the Mexican legal system with the Bolshevik model, but rather to learn from Russian success in mass education, the establishment of cooperatives, party organization, and military discipline. The kinship that the radical elite believed existed between the Mexican and Bolshevik Revolutions was based on their idea that the processes shared common objectives. Raising the banner of commitment with the popular classes, the intellectual elite in the government felt it had the right to pressure the administration to complete its promises and to apply the revolutionary laws.[35]

Obregón knew that some of his collaborators were more radical than was necessary to smooth out the differences that existed among the government, the states, and various group interests. However, the president also had a trick up his sleeve to balance political disparities and calm his opponents.[36] To temper the restless revolutionaries and neutralize the dissident radicals without at the same time antagonizing them, Obregón sent several of them to the Soviet Union with expenses paid. He therefore did not object when the CROM wanted to send one of its leaders to Russia and felt it was convenient that Luis León, loyal idealist but inexperienced collaborator, see the "workers paradise" firsthand. By financing José María Sánchez and Rafael Ramos Pedrueza's trips to the Soviet Union, the president was able to get rid of the irritating radical governor of Puebla and the boisterous federal deputy. He tried to persuade Francisco J. Múgica, another thorn in his side, to accept the post of ambassador to Russia when diplomatic relations were established with the Soviet Union in 1924. Múgica rejected the offer, preferring to stay on the run until Obregón's presidential administration came to an end.[37]

The president did not compromise with radical critics of his government and, in fact, sought to neutralize them. If they were foreigners, he simply had them expelled from Mexico, which is exactly what occurred in May 1921 when street protests reached the Chamber of Deputies and demonstration leaders actually barged in on the legislature while it was in session. Speaking to Congress in September 1921, Obregón reported that in May twenty-eight "foreign agitators of the popular classes" had violated Mexican law and had been expelled. Among them were Linn Gale, accused of antigovernment and anti-CROM propaganda; Charles Phillips, alias Frank Seaman; his wife Natalia; the anarchist Sebastian Sanvicente; and others.[38] Probably without being aware of it, Obregón had helped to dismantle the Comintern team that had arrived in Mexico at the beginning of the year to mobilize the workers against the government.

Obregón and the United States

As in his domestic policies, Obregón also walked a tightrope in foreign affairs. The president was well aware that in the United States his government was characterized as Bolshevik and that Bolshevism was used as a pretext to undermine his authority. He was quite conscious of the damage caused by a distorted picture of Mexico abroad and exerted great effort to correct this image both before and as soon as he took office in December 1920. Adopting a propaganda strategy completely different from that of Carranza, he had publicity generated about Mexico and himself based on what he thought the world wanted to hear, instead of replying to or denying every accusation and prejudice. Even before taking office, he warmly welcomed foreign businessmen. Later, through his publicist Emile Dillon, he portrayed himself to the business community as having an interpretation of the meaning and scope of the Constitution different than Carranza's. He would not favor the worker above the businessman because such a policy would throw relations between capital, labor, and human intelligence off balance. The agrarian problem, in Dillon's words, was not the lack of land, but the absence of investment and projects on abundant extensions of land. Under the Carranza government, Mexico had stagnated because Carranza had subordinated social programs to his efforts to stay in power. What Carranza had achieved was to bring Mexico and the United States to the brink of war.[39]

When Warren G. Harding entered the White House in March 1921, Obregón publicly expressed his satisfaction with the election of the new president, although he doubted the wisdom of including Albert Fall in the government. In an apparent acceptance of the Monroe Doctrine, he expressed support for the Pan-American union as the best guarantee against the greed of European and Asian powers, and recognized the United States' leadership in the Western Hemisphere.[40] His strategy was to pacify Americans' fears that Mexico was ungovernable. He also aimed to guarantee the northern neighbor's recognition of his government and at the same time ensure the flow of foreign capital to Mexico with the objective of being able to carry out a domestic and foreign policy without U.S. interference.

Obregón sent several representatives to the United States to sound out the possibilities of recognition. He was aware that there were several pressure groups, in addition to the bankers and the oil interests, with whom a rapport could be established to obtain support for his government. The AFL had lobbied in the United States on behalf of the Mexican government during the recurring crisis between the two countries, so Obregón decided to take advantage of the moment to send labor leader Luis Morones to Washington to arrange a meeting in the White House through the AFL. Although Morones did not obtain any tangible results, he left his hosts with the impression that Mexico was willing to satisfy the Americans' "requirements."[41]

Small businessmen in the United States also favored diplomatic recognition of Mexico. Their position was similar to the AFL's. Both groups believed in the virtues of good relations between Mexico and the United States in order to create favorable conditions for U.S. investments. A Mexico weakened by poverty, the repression of the popular classes, and entangled relations with the United States would have a negative effect on the workforce as well as on the U.S. economy. Unemployment in Mexico would force its workers to emigrate to the United States and in the process take jobs from Americans. It was to the advantage of both sides that the Mexican economy expand, its job market grow, and markets develop for U.S. products.[42]

Recognizing Bolshevik Russia

The Mexican government's main foreign policy objective was undoubtedly to achieve U.S. diplomatic recognition in order to reestablish capital investment flows to Mexico. But even while seeking to bolster the country's economic sovereignty, the government wanted to preserve Mexico's political sovereignty as well. Without U.S. recognition, Obregón would not feel tied down, although he would still be limited in terms of the ability to act independently of the "colossus from the north."

An example of Obregón's desire to act independently occurred in February 1921, when he was approached by a Russian Red Cross representative, D. H. Dubrovsky, with a request for Mexican assistance for the population of the Volga region, hard hit by a severe foot shortage. In other circumstances, response to such a request would have been viewed as nothing more than a humanitarian act. In the given situation marked by the intransigence of the major powers in providing the recognition vital for Mexico, collecting and shipping grain to Russia became a clandestine endeavor. Obregón wanted to help the Soviets but was forced to hide his efforts so that they would not be erroneously interpreted.

The Soviet request was known only to de la Huerta, the finance minister, and to General Angel Flores, a close collaborator of Obregón, who was put in charge of obtaining the grain. The ten thousand sacks of corn and three thousand sacks of rice crossed the Atlantic without the news being made public. Dubrovsky also obtained five thousand sacks of corn from Carrillo Puerto but was unable to hire a ship to transport the cargo.[43]

Obregón's caution backfired. U.S. and British intelligence agencies learned of the clandestine shipment and suspected that the sacks of corn and rice sent to alleviate the famine in the Volga region were diverted to feed the Red Army. While the Mexican government was still negotiating with Dubrovsky, the U.S. embassy in London cabled the State Department: "Received information last Saturday from source extremely reliable in the past [that] Obregón has signed political and commercial treaty with Lenin."[44] In the summer of 1921, while the Mexican humanitarian aid was still at sea, the Justice Department investigated the maneuver. The case was presented to the State Department as an illicit move, with Secretary of State Hughes requesting additional information from the U.S. embassy in Mexico on Dubrovsky's visit "at the personal request of President Obregón to arrange for the shipment from Mexico of two boat loads of supplies for the Red Army."[45]

Despite the limitations to maneuvering imposed by the absence of diplomatic relations with the United States and the negative publicity generated by the supposed ties between Mexico and Soviet Russia,[46] Obregón did not stop exploring the benefits a discreet relation with the Russians could bring to Mexico. He had ample evidence of Russia's heightened role as a trade partner of the European nations and that country after country was establishing diplomatic relations with a government that had previously been considered a pariah in European politics.[47]

Perhaps these were the circumstances that motivated Obregón to explore the possibilities of establishing commercial relations with Soviet Russia when the opportunity arose. In June 1922, the Mexican consul in Denmark, Lázaro Basch requested authorization by the Foreign Relations Ministry to visit Russia and promote business opportunities between the two countries. Obregón gave the green light. Basch shared the view, common at the time, that in introducing the New Economic Policy in 1921—which reestablished market relations and offered concessions to overseas companies—Soviet Russia had become a gold mine for foreign investment and trade. In addition, it was believed that the Bolsheviks had inherited enormous wealth left over from the Czarist regime. The West was unaware, however, of the degree of economic devastation caused by seven years of world war, civil war, and generalized unrest.[48]

Basch spent several days in Petrograd and Moscow. From there he wrote a letter to the Mexican representative in Berlin in which he described the warm reception offered by the Soviets, gave his favorable impression of the organization of government institutions, and referred to the auspicious conditions for establishing commercial and diplomatic relations.[49] It is very likely that Basch wrote this letter under the pressure of the prevailing censorship of correspondence directed abroad because when he returned to Denmark, he gave a totally different version of his trip.

The Mexican consul's visit raised suspicions in Denmark, which at the time did not have diplomatic relations with Moscow. To save face with the Danes, Basch wrote an anti-Soviet article and gave an interview to a semiofficial Danish magazine in which he described his visit to Russia as a failure. He said that in addition to being uncomfortable, it was cold, and there was not much to eat. Most importantly, the Soviets had rejected his proposal to promote trade with Mexico before diplomatic ties were established; trade would follow diplomatic recognition, his Soviet hosts insisted. In addition, Basch declared that Mexico disassociated itself from Bolshevism. The same article appeared later in the *Christian Science Monitor* under the headline, "Russia Refuses to Grant Mexico Commercial Treaty."[50]

Basch's initiatives pleased the Danes but irritated Obregón. The Foreign Relations Ministry prohibited Basch from making further declarations.[51] Perhaps Obregón did not want to close the door on the possibility of future relations with the Soviets.

A year later, Obregón named Juan Manuel Alvarez del Castillo as Mexican ambassador to Germany. At that point, negotiations with Soviet Russia seriously began. The circumstances were clearly favorable: negotiations with the United States on foreign debt payments had ended satisfactorily, foreign bankers had extended credit lines to Mexico, and talks on diplomatic recognition were about to conclude. It was also known that Albert Fall, one time archenemy of Bolshevism, was now reconciled to the revolution following the adoption of the New Economic Policy. Prospects were encouraging for U.S. oil companies, such as the Sinclair Oil Company, of which Fall was a partner, to strike it rich.[52]

When Obregón sent Alvarez del Castillo to Germany, his main objective was to undermine support in the Chamber of Deputies for Adolfo de la Huerta's candidacy for president. Alvarez del Castillo was de la Huerta's intimate friend and in the Chamber of Deputies had headed a group of legislators organized in the National Cooperative Party, which had launched the finance minister's candidacy. Obregón, meanwhile, had selected Plutarco Elías Calles as his successor.[53]

Alvarez del Castillo, who was twenty-nine years old in 1923, lacked experience in diplomacy, and when he left Mexico, Obregón had not conferred on him any specific task. The new Mexican ambassador had studied law and was acquainted with the different currents in world socialism. The books and authors he read had convinced him that state socialism was the best economic system for promoting equality and the collective good.[54]

Once in Berlin, Alvarez del Castillo met the Soviet ambassador, Nikolai Krestinsky. A lawyer by profession and of the same generation as his Mexican counterpart, Krestinsky had a long history in the revolutionary movement. He had been a member of Lenin's party since 1903 and had been arrested for his revolutionary activities and exiled to Siberia several times.

After the revolution, he was director of the state bank and was briefly commissar of finances before leaving for Germany. He was also Moscow's main negotiator with German industrialists interested in investing in the Soviet Union.

Alvarez del Castillo was fascinated with the Russian and listened with enormous interest to his reports on Soviet successes in land collectivization, state socialism, and agrarian socialism. The two diplomats visited each other frequently and felt at home like old colleagues. In their meetings, Krestinsky would inquire about the state of relations between Mexico and the United States, whose attitude he condemned. He indicated that Moscow was interested in suspending cotton imports from the United States and buying the product directly from Mexico. Although enthused about commercial prospects and closer contacts between the two countries, Alvarez del Castillo could not be more committal as long as he did not have authorization from Obregón.[55]

Obregón's answers to Alvarez del Castillo's enthusiastic letters were circumspect: Mexico could initiate conversations with the Soviet Union exclusively on products that could be sold in each of the countries' respective markets. Talks on diplomatic relations would follow the reestablishment of commercial relations. After the United States granted diplomatic recognition to Mexico in the summer of 1923, Krestinsky asked that Mexico negotiate in the open with the USSR. The deputy commissar for foreign affairs, Maxim Litvinov, notified Mexico that in the new and more favorable circumstances the Soviet Union would accept the negotiation of a trade agreement only after it received diplomatic recognition.[56]

De la Huerta's rebellion, which took place between December 1923 and May 1924, prevented further negotiations—partly because Alvarez del Castillo resigned his post in Berlin to join his old friend in Mexico. De la Huerta appointed him foreign minister and commissioned him to go to the United States to prevent Washington from supplying arms to Obregón. When de la Huerta was defeated, Alvarez del Castillo followed him into exile in the United States.[57]

Negotiations between Mexico and the Soviet Union were renewed after the rebellion was defeated. Talks were concluded in July 1924, a few months before Obregón left office. Mexico was not prosperous, but it was hoped that U.S. diplomatic recognition would stimulate a flow of credits and investments into the country. True, the Bucareli agreements angered many inside and outside the government. Vasconcelos, for example, was annoyed that the discussions were conducted with such secrecy. Obregón's radical collaborators objected to the agreements because they granted U.S. citizens the right to cash indemnities for any losses or damage to properties during the revolution and to the concession to the U.S. government that constitutional Article 27 would not be retroactively applied. Some felt that the spirit of Article 27 was being violated, and others questioned the legitimacy of the revolutionary regime. In response to all the objections, Obregón replied that he did not want to go down in history with his administration unrecognized by the main powers of the civilized world. To achieve recognition, some concessions would have to be made, which any government would make if interested in reaching an understanding with other countries.[58] In fact, after the United States reestablished diplomatic relations with Mexico, other countries, except Great Britain, followed suit.

The renewal of diplomatic relations with the Soviet Union in 1924 influenced public perceptions of the Mexican government. The conservative press did not hail the move but was pleased that Mexico's new ally was moving away from drastic economic measures and was applying the sensible New Economic Policy. The left within Mexico's government, as well as the labor movement and peasant organizations, including some Cromistas, welcomed Obregón's initiative to assert Mexico's autonomy and independence with respect to the United States. However, what the ties with the USSR reflected was the president's policy of "not putting all your eggs in the same basket." Obregón perceived that a radical stance would reap political dividends. In fact, with the decision to establish diplomatic relations with the Soviet Union, he offset his critics, who had accused him of having become a stooge of the Americans following the signing of the Bucareli agreements.

Part Two

THE

REVOLUTIONS

ARRIVE AT

CROSS-PURPOSES,

1924–1927

It is the instability of Mexico which is so maddening: a land so rich, so beautiful; a race, the Indians, so tender, lovable; but all smeared over with a slime of political intrigue and treachery in which my own country has played its shameful part.

—Edward Weston (1924), in Newhall,
The Day Books of Edward Weston

The policies have changed. Now the free market is allowed and the theaters, trolleys and newspapers, etc. cost money. But Lenin has preserved an oasis of socialism in Russia—the government officials and their employees—, while allowing the rest of the country to live as capitalist. From what we can see, the second phase of our revolution will be a struggle between these two principles, the socialist and capitalist ideals.

—Marietta Shaginian (1923),
in Chentalinski, *De los archivos literarios del KGB*

Our social revolution, different or similar to the Russian revolution, better or worse oriented, more or less betrayed, needs intellectuals capable of fully understanding its technical aspects and who can explain them to the masses who only understand them intuitively.

—Marte R. Gómez (1925),
Vida política contemporánea

Chapter 4

▼

THE

UNITED STATES

CHALLENGES

MEXICO

In October 1924, James Rockwell Sheffield arrived in Mexico as the new U.S. ambassador. For this wealthy and conservative Republican lawyer with little experience abroad, life in Mexico would be an unending nightmare. As he once wrote to President Coolidge, his only comfort "from the distressing official contacts" was to look out over the blooming roses in the embassy gardens.[1]

Without any diplomatic background and feeling little sympathy for the country to which he was assigned, Sheffield did more harm than good for relations between Mexico and the United States. This novice in the foreign service shared the commonly held view of the time that diplomacy should be at the service of U.S. economic interests and that in the final analysis all questions of international politics involved business interests.[2] Sheffield's distorted perceptions and subjective evaluations of a physical and social environment he did not understand, in addition to his ideologically tinged interpretations of the information he received, were the raw material with which he concocted his recommendations to the State Department. His misunderstandings and misconceptions of the Mexican political milieu created tensions and increased the latent conflicts between the two countries. Even worse, Sheffield was willing to believe any rumor that circulated in the diplomatic milieu or any gossip tossed around in journalistic circles. Thus, under the influence of his own prejudices—reinforced by the insistence of big business that the State Department not relax pressure on the Mexican government to annul constitutional Article 27—Sheffield did not negotiate, but acted as though he carried the proverbial "big stick" in his dealings with Mexican officials. When he was removed from his post in 1927, relations between the two countries were at their lowest point in a decade.

To begin with, Sheffield had the misfortune to reach Mexico City shortly after diplomatic recognition was granted to the Soviet Union. Ever since the press reported the establishment of diplomatic relations with the USSR, the U.S. embassy indicated its malaise because "the activity of communist agitators in this country is about to be intensified." The rumors about such activities were believable "if one may judge by the apparently increasing intensity of purely industrial disputes."[3] Consul Arthur Schoenfeld reported that according to experienced observers in Mexican affairs, "there is no natural tendency in Mexican national psychology toward active agitation affecting industrial labor"; hence, the disturbances "can only be explained by the presence of foreign agitators who are deliberately stirring up industrial strife." Even though Aarón Sáenz, the foreign affairs minister, tried to explain to the U.S. diplomat that the industrial disputes were due to management's resistance to improving the working conditions of its employees, Sheffield was not convinced.[4]

Before his arrival, Sheffield probably read the correspondence between the embassy and Washington, and should have been informed about the U.S. position toward its southern neighbor and the experiences of former ambassador Henry Fletcher, who resigned in 1920.[5] Before he even arrived, he was disposed against Mexico, though, and his first contacts only confirmed his prejudices. By sheer coincidence, he arrived in the Mexican capital in the same month, October 1924, that the Soviet ambassador, Stanislov Pestkovsky, reached Mexico's shores. He could not have helped but notice the warm reception Pestkovsky received when he and his family disembarked at the port of Veracruz. The day chosen for Pestkovsky to present his credentials to the Mexican government was symbolically the anniversary of the Bolshevik Revolution, November 7. Mocking diplomatic protocol, Pestkovsky removed his tuxedo as soon as he finished his official obligations that day and met with workers and intellectuals to celebrate the anniversary of the Russian Revolution.

The U.S. embassy knew about Pestkovsky's every move. An official was assigned to follow Pestkovsky and report to the ambassador what was said at the November 7 meeting; as a result, the State Department heard firsthand that the speakers spoke of "the Communist plan to acquire control in Mexico." Washington was also informed of Pestkovsky's comments concerning the advantages of the Marxist theory of revolution, which allows for a "precise" analysis of the political and social situation. In addition, the Soviet ambassador was said to have told the assembled workers—and in the process the U.S. embassy's emissary—that a Communist party "disciplined and centralized like a good army" was what allowed the Bolsheviks to win in Russia.[6] For the Americans, such an unorthodox diplomacy was an anathema.

The U.S. embassy's consternation over Pestkovsky's undiplomatic exploit reflected the State Department's persistent view of the Soviet Union as an international wrongdoer. This position, first adopted by Secretary of State Lansing and then codified as the official State Department position, continued with Lansing's successor, Bainbridge Colby. In 1920, Colby proclaimed that Washington could not recognize or have friendly relations with a government determined "to conspire against our institutions." In 1923 Secretary of State Hughes declared that "those in control in Moscow have not given up their original purpose of destroying existing governments wherever they can do so around the world." Following the death of Warren G. Harding in 1923, President Calvin Coolidge pursued the same policy of denying the Soviet government's legitimacy until Moscow showed a willingness to "take up the burdens of civilization with the rest of us." Even in 1928 Secretary of State Frank Kellogg expressed Washington's concern with Soviet interference in other countries, referring to its "extensive and carefully planned operations for the purpose of ultimately bringing about the overthrow of the existing order in such nations."[7] After diplomatic relations were established between Mexico and the Soviet Union, the semiofficial and distinguished magazine *Foreign Affairs* editorialized that "Russian influence in Mexico will be exercised in a sense unfavorable to the United States and it will not be agreeable if we are to have a base of communist propaganda established to the south of us. Still, we should probably mind this less than one of Japanese influence."[8]

Sheffield was not aloof from the discussions taking place between his colleagues and in the press concerning Communism in Mexico, and he felt uneasy in a country that recognized the legality of the Soviet government. His displeasure was so great that he refused to attend Calles's presidential inauguration in November 1924. He argued that "the presence of a Soviet representative in the diplomatic corps might create an embarrassing situation" for the United States, which did not recognize Moscow. Without actually saying so, Sheffield also wanted to insult the Mexican government. He wanted to make it clear that although the transition from Obregón to Calles was the most peaceful transfer of power in Mexico in fourteen years, it should not be taken as a cause for celebration, but accepted as a matter of course. Secretary of State Hughes had to admonish Sheffield and urge him to participate in Calles's swearing in ceremony; his presence would not signify U.S. recognition of Soviet Russia.[9]

Sheffield's tribulations in Mexico were just beginning. Since the Bucareli agreements in 1923, the social reforms codified in the 1917 Constitution had become a dead letter. The Americans hoped that Calles would maintain the status quo, while the press and the U.S. Embassy expressed pleasure at seeing the Mexican government fight the "red enemy" in its own country. The embassy was optimistic because although "Calles seems to be trying to help the proletariat, he evidently does not intend for the Communists to have a free and unrestrained hand." In addition, the U.S. business community had the impression that Calles would not tolerate "Bolshevik interference" with private property.[10]

However, in April 1925 the embassy reconsidered its appreciation of Calles. According to Sheffield, the Mexican president had not halted application of agrarian laws: his attitude toward the trade unions was too friendly, and in helping resolve the country's problems, he had failed to fall back on Americans and "the educated Mexicans of the Díaz regime." Both the ambassador and a military intelligence agent were alarmed over the increasing political importance of Morones, who, it was rumored, had presidential aspirations, and the CROM, which he led, was supposedly more influenced by the Soviets than by the AFL.[11]

Even though there appeared to be no connection between the establishment of diplomatic relations with the Soviet Union, which took place in 1924, and the announced renewal of Calles's reform program one year later, Sheffield was quick to make and tenaciously sustain such a connection. He was always convinced that the Mexican and Bolshevik Revolutions were one and the same.

In the United States it was noted that members of the Mexican cabinet were divided on the pace and extent to which the government's revolutionary program should be implemented. U.S. officials were conscious that their antagonism to the reforms motivated some Mexican authorities to advocate caution in applying land distribution policies. Alberto Pani in the Finance Ministry preferred a climate of political stability with which to attract foreign capital. The agrarian engineer Marte R. Gómez, on the other hand, put a greater value on a radical agrarian reform policy than on any good that could result for Mexico from foreign capital. These two conceptions of the economic recovery program—one based on the idea that foreign capital was needed to undertake national construction, and the other based on national self-sufficiency—were to dominate Mexican political thinking throughout the 1920s. Between these two alternatives, a third position was postulated by Morones and the CROM. U.S. observers viewed this position as opportunist—not based on any political principles and motivated only by the hunger for power on the part of the CROM leaders. Morones was opposed to radical agrarian reform in words only because his adversaries in the government were after him and were gaining support among the peasantry, among whom the CROM was not very popular.[12]

When the U.S. government decided to become publicly involved in Mexican affairs, it did so precisely by taking advantage of internal divisions occurring below the surface of events. In May 1925, six months after his arrival, Sheffield returned to the United States to confer with Secretary of State Kellogg. The ambassador was convinced that Mexico needed a stern warning. Following their discussions, Kellogg made public a U.S. admonition to the Mexican governmental elite that it should stop implementing constitutional reforms.

Indicting Mexico before the World

After Calles took office as president, Secretary of State Kellogg thought conditions in Mexico had improved. He attributed the changes to Ambassador Sheffield's managing to "protect," as he worded it, U.S. and other foreign properties, thanks to which relations between the two countries were more friendly. However, he believed that the illegal confiscation of property for which no compensation was paid put Mexican authorities on the spot: "The Government of Mexico is now on trial before the world," the secretary of state proclaimed on June 12, 1925.[13]

Kellogg's declaration hit like thunderbolt. The Mexican government rejected his declaration, considering it arrogant, a threat to national sovereignty, and an encouragement to opposition forces to rise up against the government. The CROM sent an "energetic protest by the Mexican working people" against Kellogg's pronouncement. The entire national press backed Calles.[14]

The secretary of state dismissed the Mexican protests with the sweep of a hand:

It is hoped by the Department that after the preliminary excitement has subsided and the rallying of all present dissenting elements around President Calles in view of the fancied threat by foreign interference has abated, the point of the Secretary's statement will sink in and that the more conservative and better elements of this Government will seek to back up President Calles in the execution of the program so auspiciously inaugurated and from which there has lately been such unfortunate deviation.[15]

Kellogg was sure that his pronouncement would have the desired effect because a rumor circulated that preparations for another revolution were under way in Mexico. In addition, he was aware that there were divisions concerning the pace and scope of the reforms, that the "revolutionary family" was divided between Obregón's supporters and Calles's, and that the country was fragmented into regional military and political strongholds, known as *cacicazgos*, which no government could hope to control. In June 1925, Kellogg decided to take advantage of the internal divisions in Mexico and conditioned U.S. military assistance, in case it were necessary, on a Mexican commitment to protect U.S. lives and property.[16]

The *New York Times* publicly inquired why a new crisis had erupted between the two countries. Colonel James Reeves of military intelligence could not provide an explanation for the sudden change in relations between the United States and Mexico, which "has beyond doubt mystified the American people." The colonel correctly supposed that Kellogg's message could be viewed as "U.S. interference in purely Mexican affairs and as an attempt to dictate to and coerce the present Mexican administration toward selfish ends of American interests."[17]

Captain Bogart, from the general staff of military intelligence, found Kellogg's declaration to be an indication that "the U.S. government is ready to go to any extreme in order that American and other foreign rights and interests in Mexico be adequately protected and the international engagements and obligations of the Mexican government be met." In addition, he continued, Kellogg wanted to distance himself from "an established government of Mexico whose policies might differ but little from those of Soviet Russia."[18]

Could there be other reasons to explain Kellogg's menacing declaration other than those invoked by the ambassador and military observers? Two additional explanations underlying those already given might be advanced.

In March 1925 the Soviet commissar for foreign affairs, Georgi Chicherin, made a speech in which he referred to Mexican diplomatic recognition of the USSR. He made an ill-fated declaration about the Soviet Union's popularity in Mexico and the advantages of having relations with Mexico as a base from which the Soviet Union could expand its political contacts in the New World.[19] Chicherin's declaration was a bombshell dropped at the least opportune moment in relations between Mexico and the United States.

At the same time, beginning in autumn 1924 the documents forged by Nosovitsky once again began to circulate. Possibly, they provided additional ammunition for Kellogg's salvo. Published in a single pamphlet, the same documents that Nosovitsky had fabricated in 1921 appeared at the end of 1924, this time with Calles appearing as the commander of the "Red Army of Mexico" in place of Obregón. The pamphlet, entitled *Red Rule Hangs over Mexico*, was published by Eagle Industrial Associates. This association of private detectives focused on keeping U.S. businessmen abreast of political developments in Mexico and on providing companies with services "in handling Mexican matters" with its experience in elaborating propaganda and counterpropaganda.

According to Nosovitsky, the association had come across the documents and used them for their own objectives, possibly without even knowing that they had been forged. After Nosovitsky discovered that it was the Eagle Associates office that had published the pamphlet, he realized "that an active campaign against the present Mexican government is being attempted."[20] In the same office, one of Nosovitsky's assistants found a letter addressed to Plutarco Elías Calles and dated February 8, 1924. The letter was signed by Manabendra Nath Roy, who in 1925 was being sought by British intelligence for his Comintern activity in favor of Indian independence, and it clearly put the Mexican president on the spot. "Esteemed Comrade Calles," it began, thus seeking to demonstrate that although on the surface Calles was a nationalist, deep down he was an authentic revolutionary. In the letter, Roy reproached Calles for his faintheartedness and warned that he had nothing to fear: the course of history could not be halted because "you have a wrong conception about the class struggle when you say that the Mexican proletariat could come nearer the social revolution by waging its battles on a national revolutionary platform." Calles's fear that the United States and the other capitalist countries would attack Mexico if the Mexican proletariat affiliated to the Communist International was unwarranted because "the class struggle had reached a degree of development which welded the power of the proletariat against the bourgeoisie."[21]

Investigating further, Nosovitsky discovered that the letter to Calles was a fake and suspected that it had been written on the initiative of the Eagle Associates. Upon closer examination, Nosovitsky felt that the letter was the work of Adam Pontewicz, a member of the U.S. Communist Party and an informant for the detective agency.

The letter, as well as the pamphlet *Red Rule Hangs over Mexico*, would not have merited so much attention if diplomatic circles had not taken such an interest in the documents. The British embassy in Mexico sent both documents to the foreign office in London. If the pamphlet reached the British embassy, there is no reason to doubt that it also fell into Sheffield's hands in the U.S. diplomatic mission. Sheffield, who was hypersensitive to anything he believed to be Bolshevik tinged, could well have added this document to the pile of complaints against Mexico that he was to lay before Kellogg in Washington in May 1925.

As was common in the United States, Kellogg's diatribe against Mexico provoked opposing reactions. An editorial in the *Macon Telegraph*, for example, hyperbolically called the declaration "the worst diplomatic blunder in American history." The liberal magazine *The Nation* rejected it as one more U.S. insult against a friendly government. AFL president William Green said he was "seriously concerned that there should even be the implication that our government would lend aid and support to a movement against the constitutional government of Mexico."[22] Conservative opinion, on the other hand, sided with Kellogg's firm attitude toward Mexico.

Yet Another Plot against Mexico

Not satisfied with Kellogg's insult, in 1925 pro-interventionist politicians in Washington hatched another chimerical plot to overthrow the Mexican government. This time they tried to approach Adolfo de la Huerta, exiled in the United States since 1924. Henry Lane Wilson, former ambassador to Mexico, once again lobbied for the U.S. government to put an end to "erroneous Mexican radicalism." In a private letter he wrote—with an impressive dose of cynicism—that if Calles yielded to Kellogg's demands, the peasant activists and trade unionists would overthrow his administration. If Calles defied the U.S. government, de la Huerta, in connivance with our government, should make sure he fell. If we had to have problems in Mexico, we should put Mexicans on the front line.[23]

The plan to use de la Huerta in the United States and his followers in Mexico can be corroborated in the Sonoran leader's *Memorias*. De la Huerta tried to justify and explain his conduct during the 1923 military uprising, and although not everything he says is trustworthy, the details he provides of the U.S. plan can be considered correct in general terms. According to the former president and ex-minister's account, a group of U.S. businessmen approached him to head up a revolution in Mexico. They would provide money, ships, and airplanes to assure a quick victory. To get on de la Huerta's good side, they declared that they had been wrong in 1923 and 1924 in supporting Obregón instead of him. In return for installing him in office, the businessmen demanded a commitment for concessions to build highways, ports, and dams. The profits derived from the lucrative enterprises would pay the expenses involved in the uprising. The deal did not go through, according to de la Huerta, because he realized that the State Department was involved in the affair. It seems the plan failed not only because of de la Huerta's alleged scruples, but also because the accomplices could not reach an agreement over the division of the spoils even before they had a chance to usurp political power.[24]

In February 1926 another plan to overthrow the Mexican government was presented to the State Department by Howard T. Oliver, president of the executive committee of the New York–based organization, the Mexico Pilgrims. Oliver presented the plan to Undersecretary Joseph Grew in hopes that the State Department would back the organization's effort to form a strong antigovernment force by combining U.S. businessmen and "the revolutionary groups" in Mexico.

Even though Grew advocated the use of a heavy hand toward Latin America, he believed that the United States had an obligation "to keep the peace and to ensure constitutional government in those countries." He felt that the Mexican government might have manifested "a strain of oriental shortsightedness" in thinking that it could remain in power without the support of the United States, but he also believed in the inviolability of constitutional formalities. His response to Oliver was emphatic: "Not only would this Government not listen to consider for a moment the question of fomenting revolutions in a country with which we maintained friendly relations, but if any facts concerning such movements came to our attention, we should in good faith bring those facts to the attention of the government concerned."[25]

However, Secretary of State Kellogg's diplomacy at the time was a combination of timidity and bravado, with more of the latter in his policies toward Mexico. Increasingly, within the State Department Kellogg delegated decision-making powers to his former law partner Robert Olds. As Olds's influence grew, Undersecretary Grew's waned, to the point where he was left in the dark on the measures the State Department planned to carry out in Mexico.[26]

Facing a Renewed Wave of Reforms

In the summer of 1925, the Mexican government expelled U.S. citizen Bertram Wolfe for his participation in the Mexican Communist Party and trade unions. His expulsion left a favorable impression on the U.S. embassy but did not deceive the diplomats.[27] Sheffield saw no reason to soften the hard-line approach in his dealings with the Mexican government. By then, he had an evaluation of each and every one of the members of Calles's cabinet and had reached the conclusions that they were not only bad but inefficient and were marked by greed and Indian as opposed to Latin nationalism, hating everything that was not of their race. Sheffield lamented that so little white blood circulated in the veins of Mexico's leaders.[28]

In December 1925 the Calles government drafted laws, scheduled to take effect in January 1927, that reaffirmed the leading role of the state in directing the national economy. The laws regulating oil exploitation and foreigners' rights to own land in border zones and coastal areas were considered confiscatory and exacerbated Sheffield's hostility toward Mexico. The new draft law on land ownership prohibited foreign nationals from owning properties within fifty kilometers of the coastline. In addition, foreign companies could have only minority participation in agricultural enterprises and were forbidden to seek protection from their own government in any business dispute with Mexico. The oil law required companies to obtain concessions from the government, valid for fifty years, thus replacing their property rights on land on which they had been drilling and extracting oil for many years previously. Before sending the proposed legislation to Congress, Calles renewed payments on the foreign debt—interrupted when the 1923 military rebellion broke out—to soften the impact such laws would have in the United States.

Close to 70 percent (50 percent according to the Mexican government) of the oil companies refused to obey the measure.[29] Both decrees ran counter to the Bucareli agreements, which had exempted oil companies from the provisions of Article 27 if they could demonstrate that they had been exploiting the oil fields prior to May 1917. Calles's bill showed that the current president was not required to comply with agreements adopted by his predecessor.[30]

Once positions were defined, the United States responded by attacking Mexico with a deluge of diplomatic notes and a propaganda war. In January 1926 the military attaché at the U.S. embassy blurted out that Mexico "has festered the modern shibboleths of socialism and the most archaic type of communism existing in the world, and collectivism and syndicalism are jumbled with more complete chaos than is to be found even in Russia."[31] In reality, the Mexican government's attempts to put the 1917 Constitution back on course brought the two countries to the brink of war.

Diplomatic Skirmishes and Propaganda War

Because the State Department expressed its opposition to the new laws only through diplomatic notes, some oil companies and banks took the defense of their interests into their own hands. In private talks with Mexican officials, representatives of these companies and banks claimed to express the State Department's point of view in letting it be known that a major international war might erupt if Mexico did not desist from applying the announced legislation. During a visit to the Mexican embassy in Washington, for example, a representative of oil magnate Harry Sinclair insinuated to Ambassador Manuel Téllez that "authorities higher up" had prevented him from reaching an agreement with the Mexican government. Elmer Jones, who represented the International Committee of Bankers in Mexico, wanted the president of Banco Nacional to believe that if Mexico did not retreat from its stance, "the United States would come into Mexico City with armed forces and set up a government that would respect American lives and property and would continue to support such a government until it could maintain itself on its own accord." Ambassador Sheffield continued to insist that the State Department adopt a more aggressive policy to protect U.S. companies.[32]

The diplomatic skirmishes between Mexico and the United States went hand in hand with a propaganda war waged by both countries' presses. In Mexico City, John Page, correspondent of the *Public Ledger* and the *New York Evening Post*, ran back and forth to the embassy to keep Sheffield informed of the gossip he had obtained concerning the wave of opposition that had arisen against the pressures exerted by the United States. In the course of his work, Page learned that labor leader Morones was about to go to the United States to organize a propaganda campaign against Sheffield. On another occasion, he told the ambassador that Robert Haberman, the U.S. socialist employed by the Mexican government, had called Sheffield that "damned fool" who should keep out of Mexican affairs because "we can make more noise in the United States" than he could in Mexico. In another discussion with Sheffield, Page intimated that Dr. Ernest Gruening, who had gathered materials for his history of the Mexican Revolution, was about to return to the United States "to arouse opposition in the United States Senate to the State Department's Mexican policy" and would lobby for recalling the ambassador. This professional rumormonger reported to the ambassador that Minister Sáenz "told Mexican newspaper friends of mine yesterday that you had outlived your usefulness in Mexico, and that he was getting tired of seeing you around. The United States government itself is on trial before the public opinion of the world for its improper use of superior power in an attempt to coerce the governments of Mexico and other weaker American republics."[33]

The atmosphere in Mexico was becoming tense. The Mexican government did not sit back with its arms folded in the face of incessant insults, both open and veiled. Through its own propaganda channels, it rejected the U.S. threats and declared that they not only affected Mexico, but menaced all of humanity as well. Mexico's resistance was a struggle on behalf of all the peoples of Latin America.[34] Professor Frank Tannenbaum of the University of California, who had been in Mexico gathering data for his agrarian history of Mexico, stopped in at the embassy, apparently after consultation with some Mexican government officials. The objective of his visit was to make it clear that if the United States overthrew Calles, his successor could be Morones or someone even more hostile to Washington. Tannenbaum insinuated that it would be cheaper for the United States to pay indemnization to its citizens whose property had been confiscated than to wage war on Mexico.[35]

Dismayed, the State Department was forced to admit that the Mexican propaganda had accomplished its purpose and had influenced U.S. public opinion. Undersecretary of State Grew noted in his diary on February 1, 1926, "We are cordially hated there and it is not easy to foresee what the final outcome will be."[36] The State Department was on the horns of a dilemma: if it continued to refute the Mexican government, it would have to give more information to the press concerning the "injurious tendencies of actual and proposed legislation," thus influencing public opinion and creating an antagonistic attitude toward Mexico. It was likely that pressure would mount for Washington to break diplomatic relations, or worse, to intervene militarily in Mexico. Grew proposed a wait and see attitude: "There is no use in being anything but courteous and patient unless or until the legislation is applied in such a way as adversely affects vested American interests in a retroactive manner. We are carefully watching how events unfold, to avoid placing President Calles in a position where he must act ruthlessly in order to save face."[37]

The press ignored Grew's appeal to avoid exacerbating the American public's emotions and raising anti-Mexican sentiments with sensationalist news reports. The propaganda incited by the press continued and was reproduced in the Mexican newspapers. In April 1926, for example, *Excélsior* published a story from the *New York Times* supposedly based on "documents" that uncovered the existence of "secret meetings" held in Moscow in January and February in which plans were hatched to "provoke revolutions and other disturbances in various parts of the world," among which was a plan to provoke an armed conflict between Mexico and the United States.[38] Evidently, these news reports and fabricated accounts reflected an interest in such an armed conflict. Ambassador Sheffield was one of those who headed up the pressure group that believed that only through force could U.S. rights in Mexico be safeguarded.[39]

Preparing for a Diplomatic Showdown

Toward the end of 1926 and the beginning of 1927, Sheffield's prayers seemed to be answered. The U.S. government accused Mexico of being the hub of Bolshevism in the Western Hemisphere and, therefore, a threat to the security of the United States. The immediate pretext for this accusation was Calles's public support for Nicaraguan Liberal Party presidential candidate Juan Sacasa and the secret shipment of arms to that Central American country.[40] The United States viewed with alarm Mexico's dispute of U.S. hegemonic pretensions in Central America and feared that the Mexican challenge could weigh in negatively in the other Latin American countries. These factors radicalized Washington's position and precipitated the conflict between Mexico and the United States. Mexican politician leaders and the U.S. press interpreted the conflict as a prelude to war.[41]

To justify an aggression, the U.S. government had to present conclusive proof to the public that Mexico was under Bolshevik influence. The opportunity arose in mid-1926, when the Soviet government removed Stanislav

Pestkovsky and sent Alexandra Kollontai as his replacement to the embassy in Mexico. At that time, the public associated Kollontai's name with the Bolshevik Revolution, in which she had played a major role, rather than with the theory on the role of women in the new society, which was her major concern in 1926.

To reach Mexico from Norway, Kollontai planned to travel via the United States. However, the State Department denied her a visa, charging that her mission was not what it was claimed to be—namely, to strengthen friendly and commercial relations between the Soviet Union and Mexico—but rather subversion. In addition, she was denied a visa so that the American public would not be misled into believing that the Soviet Union had good intentions.[42] The conservative press and politicians hailed the State Department's attitude as "wisdom in excluding . . . an accredited agent of the Soviet government who is proceeding to take up her duties in a country which is known to be a center of Communist activities directed against the United States and the republics of Central America."[43]

Alexandra Kollontai crossed the Atlantic directly en route to Veracruz, from where she traveled by train to the capital. In the port of Veracruz, Governor Heriberto Jara showered the Soviet ambassador with attention. When the train arrived at the Buenavista railroad station in Mexico City, U.S. Consul Wood was present among the crowd in order to assess the welcoming ceremony the Communists had organized for the new ambassador. He reported that some seven hundred persons were present, waving red flags, and that "the crowd sang snatches of a song, presumably The International, but since I am not acquainted with the music or words, I cannot exactly say what it was." Wood noted the ambassador's proverbial beauty and elegance and ended his report by indicating how pleased he was that the CROM—which he wrongly considered to be a left-wing organization—was not present.[44] Apparently, the event lacked the accustomed revolutionary enthusiasm. Kollontai's swearing in ceremony was also inconspicuous. However, even though her stay in Mexico was brief and marked by a low public profile, her seven-month presence was enough to spark rumors and result in fabricated news reports that she instigated revolutionary disturbances north of the border and south all the way to the Panama Canal.

Kollontai's arrival in Mexico was like a gift from above for Robert Olds, the assistant secretary of state, because it gave him the hoped for pretext to incite public opinion in the United States against its southern neighbor. On November 16, 1926, he invited representatives of four news agencies to a press conference at which he painted a sensational and detailed picture of Communist activities in Mexico and Central America. He urged the journalists to give the news its due importance in the media, but only the Associated Press heeded his advice.[45]

Olds's attempt to make Mexico appear as the Bolshevik malefactor did not prosper. As a result, in December 1926 the Division of Mexican Affairs at the State Department drafted a memorandum seeking to prove that the institutions, laws, and members of the Mexican cabinet were permeated with radicalism. In January 1927 the memorandum prompted President Coolidge to inform the press that U.S. lives and property would have to be protected in Mexico: "We do not care how this is done, but only know that it must be done."[46]

On January 12, 1927, Secretary of State Kellogg presented to the Senate Foreign Relations Committee a report entitled *Bolshevik Aims and Policies in Mexico and Central America*, together with a dossier of supporting documents. He wanted to spread the view that Mexico was the beachhead of the Soviet Union's master plan to launch the world revolution:

> The Bolshevist leaders have had very definite ideas with respect to the role which Mexico and Latin America are to play in their program of world revolution. They have set up as one of their fundamental tasks the destruction of what they term American imperialism as a necessary prerequisite to the successful development of the international revolutionary movement in the New World. Thus, Latin America and Mexico are conceived as a base for activity against the United States.[47]

To back up his charges and make a convincing case, Kellogg turned to the Division of Eastern European Affairs and its chief, Robert F. Kelley. This specialized division of the State Department had been created in 1924 and since then had been supplying information to the Division of Mexican Affairs whenever it was deemed appropriate. Kelley—who graduated from Harvard University, where he studied Russian—had gained experience in espionage activities during the First World War. His knowledge was put to use after the war by the State Department and the Bureau of Investigation when they needed to compile information on suspected radicals and subversives.[48]

In 1926, Kellogg asked Kelley to provide the information needed to accuse Mexico on the Senate floor of sponsoring the Communist movement in the Western Hemisphere. Kelley had enough material to make a case against Mexico. In the previous year he had already alerted Kellogg when the Anti-Imperialist League was formed on the Comintern's initiative. According to information provided to Kelley from his men in the field, based in the U.S. consulate and intelligence station in Riga, Latvia, Mexico was selected to be the league's headquarters. The league's main objective was to "organize a revolutionary movement in the territorial possessions of the United States."[49] In addition, Kelley further explained to the secretary of state that "one of the chief aims of Bolshevik revolutionary policy in this hemisphere is to unify the anti-American movements and tendencies in the various countries of Latin America into a single movement embracing the whole American continent, in order to form what the Bolsheviks term a united front against American imperialism."[50]

A year later, in 1926, the documents Kelley supplied to Kellogg, which the latter presented to the Senate as evidence of Mexico's sinister designs, consisted of 107 pages and included clippings from Soviet newspapers that referred to Mexico and documents from the State Department itself concerning Communism in Mexico. The dossier also contained extracts from Comintern publications, declarations by leaders of the Soviet Communist Party, material from the organs of the U.S. and Mexican Communist parties, clippings from official newspapers, and statements made by AFL and CROM leaders and Mexican presidents. This rich selection covered the period from 1920 to the end of 1926. Kelley added a cover letter to the dossier that provided the key to interpreting the activities referred to in the documents and an outline of the institutional framework to explain how the Soviet system functioned.[51] After the documents were presented to the Senate, the news leaked to the newspapers, which did their part to use it as venomous propaganda against Mexico. President Coolidge added his two cents as well.

Everything that had transpired between Mexico and the United States throughout 1925 and 1926 was enough to convince the Mexican government that its northern neighbor was preparing to break relations or even to launch a military action. All indications are that it took the different U.S. threats literally: reports from businessmen that the State Department prevented them from submitting to Mexican law; the propaganda in the press; and Kellogg and Olds's direct and indirect intimidating warnings that Mexico not interfere in Central America. Anticipating a military intervention, Calles transferred five thousand soldiers from Sonora to Tampico and instructed his closest collaborators—Portes Gil, General Arnulfo Gómez, and

General Lázaro Cárdenas, commander-and-chief of military operations in Tampico—that in case of an invasion, they were to burn U.S. oil fields. Calles also sent messages to Mexican embassies abroad, asking that they use their funds to counteract the American propaganda against the Mexican government.[52]

Through its agents and consuls, the State Department observed the troop movements in Mexico. Once again with a distorted perception of events in Mexico, in February 1927 the State Department sent a circular letter to all U.S. consuls to be alert to shipments of Russian arms and munitions to Mexico. Such an absurd circular provoked equally comic responses. From Guadalajara, Consul Dudley Dwyre reported that three Americans told him that they had seen a horse-drawn cart loaded with arms and munitions leaving the railway station. Supposedly, the boxes were labeled with the word "Russian."[53] Several days later, Sheffield did not hesitate to lend credence to the malicious rumor that Alexandra Kollontai had organized the emigration of fifteen hundred Mexican workers to industrial centers in the United States, "where they would maintain close contact with other foreign workers and endeavor to instill into them the principles of communism, in the hope of fomenting hatred against the cause of capitalism."[54]

George Seldes—a seasoned journalist from the *Chicago Tribune* and during the revolution a correspondent in Russia, from which he was expelled in 1922—also fell prey to the hysteria ignited around Mexico at the beginning of 1927. The *Chicago Tribune* had sent Seldes to Mexico in 1926 to cover the anticipated outbreak of hostilities between Mexico and the United States. Seldes reported these events two years after they occurred, writing that the charming and cultured Kollontai "directed a communist plot in a dozen countries." The fantastic rumors made the modest embassy Kollontai was in charge of into a monumental building with numerous departments, "each devoted to a Central or South American country or group of islands, or to a special function such as press propaganda or to supporting leagues or clubs or movements anti–United States in aim and spirit." According to Seldes, the embassy sent agitators throughout Mexico and especially to the oil fields, textile factories, and railway unions: "Russian agents, disguised as peddlers, go through the countryside ostensibly selling cheap goods, but really preaching red doctrines. Sometimes when a peasant says, 'I cannot buy, I am too poor,' these Moscow agents reply, 'Arise and take. Take the land. Take the factories. Prepare for the dictatorship of the proletariat.'"[55]

The oil companies and agroindustry took advantage of this climate to continue pressuring the State Department to take vigorous action in Mexico. Even though some companies had moved their businesses out of Mexico months previously and set up shop in Venezuela—with the result that Mexico ceased to be a vital venue for investment—in their opinion the nationalist legislation that they had been unable to overturn continued to set a dangerous precedent for the rest of Latin America.[56]

Policy under Fire

While Mexico was preparing for war, in the United States criticism grew of the U.S. government's foreign policy in Latin America. Senator from Idaho and president of the Senate Foreign Relations Committee, William Borah ridiculed the government for refusing Kollontai a visa and mocked the State Department's narrow criteria as contrary to the country's traditions:

> Here is a woman who has attained a distinction in the diplomatic service, represents a government which has been recognized by all of the great powers of the earth. She is on her way as ambassadress to a friendly country. And she is not permitted to visit the United States on her way. It seems to be thought that our institutions would not stand the strain. Are our institutions so frail? Or have we sacrificed and forever discarded every tradition which once gave us a unique distinction among all nations?[57]

The Senate itself rejected the documents that Kellogg had presented as proof that Mexican policy was directed from Moscow. Instead, it passed a resolution stating that the controversy between Mexico and the United States "relating to the alleged confiscation or impairment of the property of American citizens in Mexico" should be resolved through arbitration.[58]

From Mexico, the president of the CROM pointed out to the secretary of state that the labor confederation was inspired by Mexican, not Russian, ideas: "First, it is not true as you know, and we have irrefutable proofs that you do know it, that the theories and activities of Bolshevists from Russia and from the United States influence the Mexican government or the Mexican laboring masses, notwithstanding the efforts propagandists of these ideas have been making for some years, but which have practically ceased because they have failed here."[59]

As a result of its strained policies toward Mexico, the State Department was attacked from all sides: antiwar organizations, the AFL, the Quakers, the liberal press in the United States, and most of the Latin American media. In 1927 journalists Scott Nearing and Joseph Freeman published their book *Dollar Diplomacy*, in which they lambasted "American imperialism" in Mexico. Cordell Hull, Democratic senator from Tennessee and future secretary of state, wrote in April 1927, "The lack of vision, practical knowledge and morality in our foreign policies has been disastrous in the extreme." The United States had sown suspicion, contempt, and bad will.[60]

The U.S. business community was divided over the intimidating policies directed against Mexico. It is known, for example, that Henry Ford objected to U.S. intervention in Mexico because, by the end of 1926, after less than a year doing business there he had captured the expanding automobile market in Mexico City. Intimidation and war were simply bad for business. Herbert Hoover of the Commerce Department and bankers Thomas Lamont and Dwight Morrow opposed a break in relations, to say nothing of war with Mexico. Other business leaders who promoted the "open door" policy with Mexico felt that embargoes, diplomatic threats, and military intervention were prejudicial to the development of trade and investment. Last but not least, the different types of boycotts wound up favoring European competitors.[61]

Under widespread pressure, Secretary of State Kellogg reconsidered the State Department's policy toward Mexico and subsequently refused to sanction the department's role in advising business interests and intervening on their behalf in dealings with the Mexican government. Kellogg advised company representatives that in the future they would have to negotiate their demands directly with the Mexican government. Even the Office of Naval Intelligence changed its stance and complained to the State Department about Sheffield's belligerent conduct. In response, Kellogg cabled the ambassador, reprimanding him to stop threatening Mexico with U.S. intervention.[62]

On April 25, 1927, Coolidge made a speech to the press in New York that Mexican authorities perceived as the least threatening declaration in the recent period: Washington would protect the property of Americans abroad as it did at home, but would not assail Mexican legislation as it had previously in similar circumstances.[63] By mid-1927 the State Department decided to seek a solution that would satisfy all sides involved in the oil conflict. To begin with, Kellogg urged Coolidge to replace Sheffield with Dwight Morrow, the vice president of that financial giant the J. P. Morgan Company.[64]

The decision to name Dwight Morrow was most opportune. His style of diplomacy would be in keeping with the savoir faire that businessmen with many years of experience in Mexico had recommended to ambassadors. James Smithers, who had represented the J. G. White Engineering Corporation since the Porfiriato period, constantly urged U.S. ambassadors in Mexico to conform to the different standards of conduct characteristic of Mexican society.[65] In addition to adopting a conciliatory attitude toward the problems that for so long had complicated relations between Mexico and the United States, Morrow would move away from the ugly question of Bolshevism. The new ambassador would use softer language and assume a cordial approach toward Calles to achieve through diplomatic courtesy what his predecessors could not accomplish through coercive means.

However, the "new course" of U.S. diplomacy toward Mexico was not to the liking of the rest of the embassy diplomatic corps or of military intelligence. In October 1927 Consul General Alexander Weddell wrote the State Department that he doubted it was possible to reach an understanding with Mexico. The United States should not trust a country that—like no other "with the possible exception of Russia"—would hire an artist to paint a mural on the walls of one of the most important ministries that contained "visible expressions of contempt of and hostility to a neighboring country" with which it claimed to have friendly relations. Weddell was referring to the permission granted to Diego Rivera to paint, without any restrictions, the murals at the Education Ministry, which the artist covered with dollar signs, used the Statue of Liberty "as a mere table decoration," and depicted honorable citizens such as John D. Rockefeller, Henry Ford, and J. P. Morgan as symbols of U.S. imperialism. A government that allowed such an affront did not deserve the trust of the United States.[66] For Weddell and military intelligence, Mexico continued to be the breeding ground for Latin American Communism.

Chapter 5

▼

THE SOVIETS
MISUNDERSTAND
THEIR MEXICAN
FRIEND

Stanislav Pestkovsky belonged to the group of Old Bolsheviks. Stalin knew
him from when they shared an office at the People's Commissariat of Na-
tionalities, created by Lenin in 1918. Because this commissariat did not
originate from a previous ministry, it lacked personnel and, initially, lacked
clear goals. What the office did do was prepare party propaganda. Pestkovsky would have preferred to have worked in the People's Commissariat for
Foreign Affairs, but was rejected and assigned instead to head up elabora-
tion of political propaganda.[1]

Pestkovsky was born in Poland in 1882; his family belonged to the no-
bility. While a student, he joined the Russian Social Democratic Party (out
of which the Bolshevik Party later emerged) and participated in the 1905
revolution. Until 1913, when he fled to England, Pestkovsky had been exiled and condemned to forced labor in Irkutsk. When the 1917 revolution
erupted, Pestkovsky returned to Russia and Lenin named him commissar
of the Petrograd telephone and telegraph exchange.[2]

In 1919, Pestkovsky joined one of the first groups in opposition to the
Bolshevik government. The democratic centralist tendency, as it was
known, criticized the excessive centralization of political power in the
hands of the party, restrictions on initiatives by local soviets, and rigid top-
down control in industry, the party, and local government. This group accused the government of moving closer to a dictatorship of the party instead of aspiring to a dictatorship of the proletariat.[3] Pestkovsky never
openly supported Trotsky's theory of permanent revolution, but in 1922 he

was one of many Bolsheviks who had concluded that the road to world revolution was going to be long and difficult. In preparing for this long road a group of officials in the apparatus of the soviets, party, and Comintern founded in 1922 the International Organization for Aid to Revolutionary Fighters (Mezhdunarodnaia organizatsiia pomoshchi bortsam revol'utsii [MOPR], or International Red Aid, as it was called).[4] Sending Pestkovsky to Mexico could have been Stalin's way of getting rid of a critic because he had applied the same official ostracism to Alexandra Kollontai and other oppositionists who criticized the growing Stalinist dictatorship in the party and Soviet government.

Stanislav Pestkovsky's Revolutionary Elan

Pestkovsky's life was entwined with that of the party, and he considered International Red Aid (MOPR) a branch of the party. Expanding the MOPR network in Mexico and Latin America, with the goal of providing material and spiritual relief to the "captives of capitalism in prison," Pestkovsky believed he was aiding the expansion of the party and advancing the revolution.[5] With an unbreakable faith, the Bolshevik leader arrived in Mexico in mid-1924 to put his life's ideals into practice.

The internationalist Pestkovsky imbued his diplomatic tasks with a revolutionary spirit. Perhaps he shared the opinion, common among Comintern officials, that the Mexican government was a puppet of U.S. imperialism. The proletariat, therefore, required his professional attention; as a result, when not attending official cocktail parties, Pestkovsky dedicated his time and the embassy's resources to assisting the Mexican Communist Party (MCP) while at the same time getting his feet wet in the reality of the country. He helped to keep the MCP's press afloat, studied the history of the Mexican workers' and peasants' movements, and acted as advisor to trade union leaders with the aim of winning them away from the CROM and affiliating them to the Communist Party and the Comintern.

Despite the failure of the attempt to attract reformist and anarchist unions to the Profintern in 1921,[6] the Soviet government thought it would be an easy task in 1924 to carry out the Comintern's line in Mexico. After all, a few months before the Mexican government gave the green light to establish diplomatic relations with the Soviet Union, its ambassador in Berlin, Pascual Ortiz Rubio, met with Nikolai Krestinsky, the Russian envoy to Germany. At the meeting, according to Krestinsky's interpretation of the conversation, Ortiz Rubio transmitted the feelings of the Mexicans:

"Our government and all of us are your disciples and we're doing what you've already accomplished"; also, Calles "is almost a Bolshevik." Although Obregón was a pragmatist and not a theoretician, Ortiz Rubio led Krestinsky to believe that the president belonged to the left-wing within the petty bourgeois government in power.[7]

It was surely this type of information that contributed to the perception by Chicherin, the commissar for foreign affairs, that relations with Mexico would provide the USSR with the legal cover to be able to expand their underground contacts in Latin America and the United States. As soon as he was informed about Mexico's favorable view of renewing relations, Chicherin approached Comintern president Grigori Zinoviev to suggest the best person for the post of ambassador because "he can be of great use in carrying out our American tasks. Attention should be placed (on the nominee) from the point of view of Comintern tasks."[8]

The Comintern asked Zinoviev to use the opportunity afforded by the Fifth Congress of the Comintern, which at that moment was meeting in Moscow, to discuss with the U.S. delegates "the best way of taking advantage of future personnel in the embassy in Mexico." Faced with Mexican insistence, Chicherin pressed Stalin to name an ambassador and proposed Pestkovsky. Stalin was in agreement without mentioning his own interest in seeing Pestkovsky removed from the scene of his political maneuvering.

Soldier of the revolution that he was, Pestkovsky went to Mexico to carry out the Comintern's orders in loyal and disciplined fashion. When these orders did not coincide with the government's wishes, the ambassador, guided by his revolutionary conscience, on more than one occasion shunted diplomatic scruples to the sidelines.

Pestkovsky's Daily Routine in Mexico

On November 7, 1924 (the anniversary of the triumph of the October Revolution), Pestkovsky presented to President Obregón his diplomatic credentials as Soviet ambassador to Mexico. In his speech, the ambassador extolled the similarity of ideals for which both countries were fighting. He spoke of the sympathies of the Soviet workers and peasants for the efforts of the Mexican masses to shake off the heavy burden of imperialist oppression. This struggle was the best guarantee that relations would be close between the two countries. Finally, he said that the Soviet Union appreciated Mexican diplomatic recognition because it knew that tremendous obstacles had to be overcome to be able to take the move.

When it was Obregón's turn to reply, he too stressed the objectives shared by Mexico and the Soviet Union, such as improving the lot of the poor and long oppressed masses, but he avoided making any connection between diplomatic recognition of the USSR and Mexico's relations with the United States. Yes, Mexico and the Soviet Union were tied by common objectives,[9] and recognition of the USSR by Mexico was the act of a sovereign country, an act of solidarity with another nation that also sought to free itself from subjugation by the forces at loggerheads with the country's welfare.

After the ceremony at the National Palace, Pestkovsky changed clothes and in the afternoon met with the Communists, the workers, and other sympathizers of the Russian Revolution. The meeting was held at the San Ildefonso Preparatory School, at the time the center of a passionate controversy on the aesthetic value of the murals painted by Diego Rivera, David Alfaro Siqueiros, and José Clemente Orozco, who declared their works part of the war against "bourgeois individualism" in art. The press and intellectuals opposed to revolutionary muralism thundered that the paintings were not art, but rather political propaganda that denigrated Mexico and represented the "dregs of society."[10]

In front of the murals and before an enthusiastic audience, Pestkovsky traced the history of the Bolshevik Revolution and emphasized the role played by the Communist Party in its victorious outcome. The Russian ambassador spoke in English, with Bertram Wolfe translating the speech into Spanish. Wolfe then quoted a letter from Emiliano Zapata to his collaborator Genaro Amézcua, in which the peasant leader from Morelos compared the Mexican and Bolshevik Revolutions in high-sounding words: "We would gain a great deal, human justice would gain a great deal, if all people of our America and all the nations in old Europe understood that the cause of the Mexican Revolution, like the cause of unredeemed Russia, is and represents the cause of humanity, the supreme interest of all the oppressed." Someone recited a poem dedicated to Lenin and sang the ballad "The Communist Valentine."[11]

In a letter to assistant commissar of foreign affairs, Maxim Litvinov, Pestkovsky wrote of that memorable meeting and the warm reception he had received in Mexico. On that occasion, he reported, fifteen hundred persons were present, and the affair lasted four hours. Leaders of the Agrarian League units from Michoacán and Veracruz who could not attend sent greetings and invited Pestkovsky to their communities. Even the railway workers union, independent of both the CROM and the Communist Party, sent a delegation. Pestkovsky believed that he had also been well received by the diplomatic corps.[12]

The Soviet diplomatic mission was small: the ambassador; his wife and daughter; the secretary, Leon Haykiss; and the typist, Isaac Zeitlin, who did not know any language but Russian and could barely use a typewriter. Later to arrive were Viktor Volinsky as press secretary and Grigori Lapikian as labor attaché, although the U.S. embassy suspected that Lapikian was, in reality, involved in espionage.[13] The journalist Carleton Beals described Pestkovsky as "a big, booming man with gnarled tobacco teeth showing through a dark beard . . . a brusque, tactless, but jovial man, very obstinate, aggressive and quick-tempered," and referred to the ambassador's wife as "a simple, kindly person, more a homebody than a typical diplomat's wife."[14]

The truth be said, the Soviet embassy had little to do. Pestkovsky's first responsibility was to assist Russian immigrants in regularizing their stay in Mexico. Because trade between the two countries was practically nonexistent, the ambassador had time to spend studying Mexican history and trying to understand the revolution. After less than a month in Mexico, he sent his first observations to Moscow. Far from what Ortiz Rubio had led Krestinsky to believe regarding President Obregón's radicalism when he visited him in Berlin, Pestkovsky observed that Obregón made economic concessions to the Americans to preserve the country's political independence. The Russian revolutionary believed this independence to be a utopian dream. In addition, the government that claimed to represent the workers broke strikes organized against foreign companies, but allowed them against Mexican firms. Of all the popular movements, Pestkovsky noted, the agrarian struggle was the most noteworthy. However, peasant struggles were weakened by rural power brokers, the caudillos who led the movement, and the anarcho-bandits.[15] Pestkovsky was sensitive to any analogy with Russian reality and saw similarities between Mexican agrarianism and the *makhnovschina*. This antilandlord and antigovernment peasant movement was led by Nestor Makhno in the Ukraine in the first years of the revolution, but was repressed by the Bolsheviks with particular zeal because it was also directed against their rule.[16]

The ambassador cultivated good contacts among Mexican officials, the diplomatic corps, and intellectuals. However, his closest relations were with Mexican and foreign Communists. Communist propaganda and revolutionary organization were closer to his heart than the life of protocol and etiquette. Thus, his work had two sides: one visible, the other hidden.

Openly, the ambassador organized meetings to mark the death of Lenin, the victory of the Bolshevik Revolution, and May Day. His parties at the embassy became the talk of the city because he invited both the Communists as well as the diplomatic corps, whom he asked to wear informal clothing. Sometimes, Diego Rivera would drop in straight from his scaffolding, still covered with paint. Pestkovsky showed Soviet films and served tea. He routinely invited all government ministers and the president, who with the same frequency declined the invitations. Sometimes Calles would claim he had too much work, other times that he had previous engagements or that the invitation from the embassy had arrived too late.[17] Although Calles evidently did not want to be seen as becoming too close to the Soviets, other Mexican officials did not have the same qualms. Emilio Portes Gil, Jesús Silva Herzog, and Manuel Gómez Morín regularly visited the embassy or at least came on some occasions. Ramón P. de Negri became an intimate friend of the ambassador.[18]

In periodically organizing sessions to exhibit the latest Soviet films, the ambassador obviously had more than mere entertainment for his guests in mind. The Bolsheviks were also promoting their revolution through the arts and entertainment. Films, more than other forms of artistic creation, were designed to arouse admiration for the heroic events of the October Revolution, in their emphasis of the participation of the masses and in their commitment to the revolution. The films were also a means of political education and promoting the interests of the Soviet state. Among the movies shown in Mexico were Sergei Eisenstein's *Strike* (1925), in which workers heroically resisted oppression and were defeated; *The Battleship Potemkin* (1926), based on the story of a mutiny on the Czarist ship in 1905 and the street demonstrations in Odessa; and *Mother* (1926), based on Gorky's novel in which a mother decides to follow in her son's footsteps and join the revolutionary struggle. All these movies sought to legitimize the revolution and the government that emerged from it.[19]

On a more discreet level, Pestkovsky collaborated with the Mexican Communist Party, providing ideas and money for its official newspaper, *El Machete,* and for the combative organ of the Anti-Imperialist League, *El Libertador.* The funds at his disposal must not have been very plentiful. In July 1925 he wrote the Commissariat of Foreign Affairs that he not only lacked political information, and therefore a line to follow, but also resources to continue working. He also tried to explain to his superiors that Mexico was an exceptional country, with a large field for action—more important for the Soviet Union than Norway or Greece because "we have an entire continent to emancipate from foreign imperialism."

Pestkovsky urgently needed money for diplomatic expenses and a secret fund—the former to be able to invite Mexicans to dinner and make political friends, the latter to be able to continue publishing *El Libertador*, through which the Soviets could extend their influence throughout Latin America. He also wanted to publish an embassy magazine in Spanish to report on the social achievements of the Soviet Union. In total, he needed more than three hundred dollars a month for press expenses.[20]

However, Pestkovsky's good intentions and concrete efforts raised eyebrows in Moscow. He was not sufficiently discreet. On one occasion, he not only made a denigrating comment concerning Mexican officials in an encoded report, but maintained relations with worker and peasant organizations and the Communists that were too openly visible. In February 1925, Litvinov admonished Pestkovsky to be more attuned to diplomatic protocol and to maintain a low profile.[21]

Most likely Pestkovsky ignored this warning and did what he thought best. In his diary, he noted: "Already beforehand I had received information from the communist circles that the Japanese ambassador proposed to different 'left-wing personalities' (among them D. N.) their 'help' in the fight against the United States."[22] He decided to see the Japanese diplomat and propose that they coordinate their activities. Although he did not have a concrete proposal to make to his Japanese counterpart, he did want to scout out the terrain. Naive or distrustful, the Japanese ambassador asked Pestkovsky if the Russians' objective was to "expel" foreign capital from Latin America. The reply was that nothing was being proposed that was not strictly legal; the objective was to prevent the political and economic subordination of the Latin American countries to the United States and Britain. Pestkovsky himself admitted that the meeting was arranged by means of trial and error because he had no official information on the state of Russian-Japanese relations or instructions on the suitability of "coordinating" activities with the Japanese ambassador in Mexico. But Tokyo's representative, in addition to not concretely committing himself to anything, took his distance from his Soviet colleague. As he confessed several days later, he did not want to attract the attention of U.S. intelligence services to the possibility of a Russian-Japanese conspiracy against them at the precise moment when a friendship treaty was being signed between Japan and Mexico.[23]

On another occasion, although he received no invitation to attend the 1925 May Day parade, Pestkovsky went to the bull fight stadium where twenty thousand people were gathered to mark International Workers' Day. He was the only diplomat present. Calles and other ministers were, however, in attendance. The speakers were labor leaders Ricardo Treviño and Luis N. Morones, in that order. In addition to distinguishing between good capital and investment that violated the Mexican Constitution and legislation, Morones said, "We will close our borders to those who seek to provoke divisions within the workers movement and against the Mexican Workers Confederation."[24] Pestkovsky knew the words were directed against him.

By that time, Pestkovsky had already won the animosity of the CROM and a cold shoulder from Calles. Morones and his team knew of the subsidies Pestkovsky was providing to the Mexican Communist Party to sustain their press, which vehemently denounced not only "yanqui imperialism," but also the CROM's subordination to the Mexican government and the AFL. However, what was unacceptable was the growing influence of the Communists, financially supported by the Soviet embassy, in the railway workers union, which had slipped out of the CROM's control.[25]

At the beginning of May 1925 the newspapers in Mexico and the United States published a speech that Chicherin had delivered in March at a meeting of the party executive committee in Tiflis, Georgia. Assessing the state of the Soviet Union's foreign relations in the context of Washington's refusal to recognize the new nation, Chicherin made the following observation: "We have succeeded in re-establishing diplomatic relations with a neighbor of the United States, Mexico, and this gives us a political base in the New World."[26] He added that the Soviet Union enjoyed tremendous prestige in Mexico and that on a daily basis Comrade Pestkovsky encountered expressions of warmth and sympathy for the Soviet Union. The commissar concluded his broadside with the self-congratulatory comment that "Mexico gives us a very convenient base for further extension of our ties in America."[27]

The news of the speech hit like a bombshell. That same evening, after the day's newspapers had reported Chicherin's speech, a "revolutionary dance" performance was held, sponsored by the League of Revolutionary Artists and Writers. Pestkovsky was in attendance and ran into de Negri, who transmitted Calles's and Morones's enormous displeasure with Chicherin's speech. Calles was also annoyed with the ambassador's participation in domestic Communist activities.[28]

The news of Chicherin's speech could not have arrived at a less opportune moment. The German ambassador was right on the mark when he commented to Pestkovsky that the speech was viewed as Soviet interference in Mexican internal affairs and that the emphatic public presidential response had less to do with the speech itself and more to do with the strained relations with the United States. To be sure, the news coincided with a change in the State Department's attitude toward Mexico after Calles intensified land distribution and with the recall of Ambassador Sheffield to Washington for talks with Kellogg.[29] The last thing Calles needed was for the Soviets to be adding fuel to the American fire.

To Minister Sáenz, Pestkovsky tried to explain away Chicherin's speech as an inocuous reference to the development of Soviet diplomatic relations on the American continent. He understood the Mexican reaction and sympathized with the government's plight in view of its difficulties with Washington. However, in case any future incident arose, he asked that any anti-Soviet declaration be previously discussed with the ambassador and, secondly, that it be written in the least aggressive tone possible.[30] The matter went no further. Several weeks later, in June, Kellogg slammed the Mexican government. At that point, Calles became embroiled in a conflict with the United States that made the skirmish with the Soviet Union lose importance.

Russian Rubles for Mexican Railway Workers

The Communists were furious with Calles for his reaction to Chicherin's speech, a response they interpreted as a display of hostility to the Soviet Union. In the pages of *El Machete* and *El Libertador* they accused the president of subservience to the United States. The feeling of the Communists at the time was, "If Calles has declared his 'independence' from Russia, why doesn't he declare independence from the United States?" as recalled years later by Bertram Wolfe.[31]

The CROM leaders, on the other hand, began to pressure Calles to go beyond making declarations and to expel Pestkovsky and the other foreign Communists from Mexico. Upset over the growing influence of the Communists among the seventy-five thousand members of the Confederation of Railway Societies, an influence it was never able to obtain, the CROM created in 1925 a rival organization to the confederation, the National Federation of Railway Workers, but was able to attract only a handful of members.[32]

It is true that the MCP saw tremendous opportunities to gain influence among the railway workers by supporting their tenacious resistance against the CROM and defending their already won trade union rights. In its third congress held in April 1925, the party discussed possible gains and losses in its mass work. The U.S. delegate to the congress, Charles Phillips, alias Manuel Gómez, summarized the situation as follows: the peasants were well organized, but knew nothing of Bolshevism; the industrial workers did not have an effective organization but were receptive to the party's message, although the party lacked cadre to teach its politics to the working class. The party's efforts should be centered in the independent unions and especially in the Railway Confederation, where more than one comrade already worked. Because there was no better school than the struggle itself, one of the slogans with which the MCP concluded its congress deliberations was "all out for the rail strike."[33]

The CROM leaders were well aware that the Communists were holding classes for the railway workers—not only on history, sociology, economy, and political thought of "the class struggle through the ages," but also on organizational questions so that unions could remain financially and politically independent of the government and labor confederation. Bertram Wolfe, who taught the classes for railway workers, also gave practical advice: for example, how to bring the engines to a standstill by putting soap in the boilers. Wolfe was a thorn in the CROM's side, and because he was a foreigner, it was easy to get rid of him. One morning in June 1925, two policemen intercepted the American Communist on his way to work, and in July he was deported to the United States.[34]

Inasmuch as the rail workers were trying to resist CROM interference in their unions, they also opposed Calles's plans to reorganize and rehabilitate the national rail system, the Ferrocarriles Nacionales de México, a company with majority state ownership. Heavily damaged during the revolution and the subsequent rebellions, the company was in debt and embroiled in labor conflicts. A detailed study indicated that although in 1909 the company's profits stood at 41 percent of its revenue, by 1926 they had fallen to 6 percent. In 1910, the average worker's salary stood at 56.13 pesos monthly, but in 1927 was 124.78 pesos, a 225 percent increase. The government wanted to sell the company to a private owner in order to free itself from the weight of a 260-million-peso debt, but the deal fell through because the potential buyer conditioned the purchase on a reduction in both the workforce and workers' salaries. For political reasons, the government could not agree to such a proposal, so it passed the company over to the Communications Ministry, and as a result, the workers became employees of the federal government and, by law, forbidden to strike. The new administration adjusted salaries and the size of the workforce. In December 1926, the mechanics declared a strike, and the company fired them.[35]

CROM president and minister of industry, commerce, and labor Luis Morones declared the strike illegal and replaced the workers with strikebreakers. In February 1927, workers from other unions in the Confederation of Railway Societies went out on strikes in solidarity with the mechanics. The strikers faced the army and the scabs, with resulting injuries and deaths. From that point on, the company would negotiate only with the CROM.

The Soviet embassy supported the railway workers in their resistance to the company reorganization and their decision to strike. Full details on Soviet embassy support are not known, but the Communists did not make a secret of the financial aid they received from the Soviet Transportation Workers Union via the embassy. The fifty thousand rubles (approximately twenty-five thousand dollars) did not arrive until March 1927, when Pestkovsky had already left, and Alexandra Kollontai was ambassador.[36] Thanks to the Soviet donation, the union was able to move to larger headquarters, where it could provide housing to the families of strikers who could no longer pay their rent. In addition, the funds were also used to organize a soup kitchen and publish an information bulletin. When the money ran out, the bulletin ceased publication, and the union had to give up its headquarters. The strikers were weakened by financial tribulations suffered from that point on. The unions lost members as the railway workers went back to work, convinced that they could not struggle against both the company and the government. The strike went down in defeat.[37]

The aid provided by the Soviet embassy to the railworkers touched off an uproar long before the funds actually arrived. At its convention in March 1926, the CROM decided to send a protest note to Pestkovsky and demand that he put an end to the "moral and economic support" for the Communists, "enemies of the CROM and our government." The Soviets had no right to impose their beliefs and control the activities of the Mexican labor movement.[38]

According to U.S. intelligence, President Calles met with Pestkovsky and warned him that if he did not cease his involvement in trade union affairs, his diplomatic credentials would be revoked. Supposedly, Pestkovsky asked for a two-day grace period to be able to consult with Moscow. When he again met with Calles, he announced that Commissar Chicherin had decided that should Mexico sever relations with the Soviet Union, the Russian ambassador in Paris, Christian Rakovsky, had instructions to release the secret correspondence traded between the Soviet government and Obregón before diplomatic recognition had been publicly announced; the contents would be none too flattering to Mexico and would thus affect relations with the United States. According to the same report, the idea alarmed Calles, who assured Pestkovsky that Mexican objections to Communist support for the railworkers were motivated by the need to cultivate good relations with the AFL.[39]

Several months later, in October to be exact, Pestkovsky left Mexico, apparently on his own accord. He had probably been recalled by Moscow for fear that he would be expelled by the Mexican government. Prior to his departure, he organized a farewell party to which, as in previous occasions, Calles was invited. Once again, the president declined the invitation.[40] The CROM expressed its satisfaction with Pestkovsky's departure and hoped that Calles would break off diplomatic relations with the USSR. Despite its insistence, however, the president maintained the association with the Soviet Union.[41]

Pestkovsky had no alternative but to leave Mexico—partly responsible for the clash in policies between the two governments because he had privileged his interests as a revolutionary above and beyond his mission as a diplomat. But the Soviet emissary could not have acted otherwise. In his conception, the Mexican state was an ally of imperialism, although involuntarily. The proletariat, although organizationally weak, was the only class that could successfully struggle against imperialism, and Pestkovsky's mission was to help it along in its historic task.

Pestkovsky's recall and departure did not become a diplomatic incident. At the time, the Soviet government was embroiled in an international conflict with Great Britain. In May 1926, when British workers declared a general strike, the Soviet unions offered financial aid, which the British Trade Union Congress rejected. The more intransigent Conservatives in the British cabinet attacked the Soviet Union for exporting revolution and in 1927 convinced parliament to break off diplomatic relations with the USSR.[42]

Despite the seriousness of the Anglo-Soviet confrontation, the Bolsheviks continued to organize aid for the Mexican workers, even after Pestkovsky's departure. Soviet foreign policy toward Mexico was based on principles that were different from its policies with respect to Great Britain. Mexico was neither a trade partner nor a world power, but had an active workers movement. Any victory achieved by the workers, no matter how small, brought humanity closer to its final goal of overthrowing the world capitalist system. According to the Soviets, a strike was a manifestation of the proletariat's revolutionary energy and evidence of the incapacity of capitalism to resolve class conflicts. Recalling Pestkovsky from the embassy in Mexico was an insignificant price to pay compared to the tremendous dividends gained by eroding capitalism, albeit in the system's periphery.

Alexandra Kollontai: Captive of Disillusion and the Red Scare

Alexandra Kollontai was born in 1872 into an aristocratic family in St. Petersburg. Already married in 1898, she turned her back on wealth and privilege and went to Switzerland to study Marxism. Returning to St. Petersburg in 1899, she joined Lenin's party, in which she specialized in giving lectures and writing articles on the problems of the day from a Marxist point of view. She passionately believed in the need for women's emancipation, but opposed middle-class feminists who, from her standpoint, wanted to expand women's rights without concerning themselves with liberating women from poverty. In contrast, Kollontai believed that the emancipation of women workers would not take place without the revolutionary struggle, but pointed out that women had specific needs due to the bonds of traditions tying them to society. Even formulated in this fashion, her ideas were rejected by the male leaders of the party, who argued that women should join the general revolutionary struggle.

In 1908 Kollontai was forced to flee Russia to avoid arrest and lived in exile during the following nine years. When the Bolsheviks seized power, Lenin named her commissar for social welfare. Kollontai drafted several bills on government support for maternity care and, in coordination with other commissariats, authored laws that established women's political and legal equality. In addition, she led a campaign to draw women out of the home and into activities and political posts. Because of her and other female party activists' considerable insistence, in 1919 the government established a department for work done by women workers and peasants.

In 1922, Kollontai left both her post and Russia after playing a leading role in the defense of trade union freedom, workers' control in the factory, and party democracy. The party characterized Kollontai's social theory as feminist and therefore different from the objectives sought by socialist construction. From then on, she spent her time in the diplomatic service, writing stories and one or another article on women's questions. Although deep down she continued to believe in the revolution as the only emancipatory force, for the rest of her life she decided to place a priority on serving the party and the government, even when the government's policy was peaceful coexistence with Western countries and when its leaders were more concerned with fulfilling production quotas and bolstering their personal power than the population's well-being. Kollontai would have preferred to leave government service, perhaps to live in France and write her memoirs, but the party did not let her do so. A diplomatic career was the only alternative open to her if she did not want to join the ranks of Russian emigres.[43] When news of her appointment as ambassador became public, no one knew the drama and personal dilemmas that engulfed her, and no one would have suspected that she lacked the revolutionary spirit that characterized Pestkovsky.

After Great Britain broke relations with the USSR in 1927, the Soviet government reached the conclusion that peaceful coexistence with the capitalist world had reached a dead end and that the West was preparing for war against the Bolshevik state. Kollontai was aware of the turnabout in Soviet foreign policy, but in Mexico her behavior did not indicate any such change. On the contrary, the ambassador tried to salvage both the appearance of normality and the damaged image of Soviet diplomacy left by her predecessor as a result of his activities. She must have been aware of articles concerning Mexico that appeared throughout 1926 and 1927 in the Soviet and international Communist press. Such articles emphasized the aggressive U.S. policies toward Mexico and Mexico's support for beleaguered Nicaragua. The commentators portrayed Mexico as a hapless victim of imperialism, whose only alternative was to succumb to the West or participate in the proletarian revolution.[44] Kollontai could not but have felt sympathy for the country of her new appointment.

Yet Kollontai was clear about the role she had to play in Mexico. Several weeks before sailing for Mexico, she told the press that "today's diplomat should scrupulously abstain from carrying out any type of propaganda or from interfering in the internal affairs of the country to which one is accredited."[45] No novice in the field of diplomacy, she knew how to scout the terrain so as not to make any false moves. She was conscious of Mexico's strategic importance for Soviet foreign policy, but was also aware of the increasingly intense U.S. pressure on Mexico. The underhanded de facto expulsion of Pestkovsky and the refusal of the State Department to allow her to pass through the United States were clear indications that in Mexico she would be walking on egg shells and should thus strictly adhere to diplomatic protocol.[46]

The morning before Kollontai left by train from Berlin to Rotterdam, Ramón P. de Negri, Mexican consul at the time, went to see her to request a postponement of her trip. He argued that the conflictive relations between Mexico and the United States could lead to war. In such a scenario, he hoped that the Soviet Union would assume a "more active role than (it had played) thus far" in its policy toward Mexico. Kollontai further reported that in passing through Berlin on the way back to Moscow, Pestkovsky met with de Negri and let it be understood that in case of a U.S. aggression, the Soviet Union would not stand by as a passive observer.[47] Kollontai herself, however, had no intention of launching a campaign of agitation, organization, and propaganda.

Even before touching down on Mexican soil in December 1926 and during her first weeks in the country, the ambassador had to behave in such a way that her conduct would cut across the accompanying extravagant or hostile slander and newspaper gossip regarding her revolutionary past, her physical attributes, and even her wardrobe.[48] Because of the uproar her appointment had sparked in the United States, the Mexican conservative press criticized Calles for having allowed an even more renowned revolutionary than Pestkovsky to represent the Soviet Union. In addition to having been denied a U.S. visa, Kollontai was not allowed by Cuban authorities to disembark to meet a women's delegation that had gathered at the port to meet her when the boat on which she was traveling docked in Havana.[49]

In Mexico, on the other hand, Kollontai received a warm welcome, although *Excélsior* tried to minimize it. When the ship in which she was traveling reached the port of Veracruz, the state governor Heriberto Jara showered her with honors. A delegation of Communists awaited her at the Buenavista train station in Mexico City, even though they didn't know what time the train would arrive.[50]

During the presentation of her diplomatic credentials to the Mexican government on December 22, Kollontai praised the political and social progress Mexico had registered, and highlighted the similarities and close-

ness of the two countries. She stressed the importance of the working
class's role in politics and the social and economic difficulties Mexico confronted due to imperialist hostility. She wanted to remove all doubts that
her main work in Mexico would not be anything other than the promotion
of trade between the two countries.[51]

Kollontai unsuccessfully tried to win the friendship of CROM leaders. As
part of a program in which trade union leaders studied the labor legislation
and policies of other countries, the CROM had sent Eulalio Martínez to the
Soviet Union. When the Mexican trade union envoy returned, he brought
back little in the way of practical experience and many tales of how he was
spied on, how his correspondence was opened, and how he was not allowed
to travel freely around the country. The CROM intensified its public vil-
ification of restrictive Soviet labor practices, contrasting them with the
generous advantages of Mexican trade union policies. When the funds from
the Russian transport workers arrived in Mexico in March 1927, the CROM
launched a campaign against Kollontai and demanded her expulsion from
the country. When the Foreign Relations Ministry did not respond to the
CROM's demand, Morones, in his ministerial capacity, prohibited the ex-
hibition of Soviet films in commercial cinemas.[52]

Like Pestkovsky, Kollontai organized evening social gatherings at the embassy, at which Soviet movies were shown and tea *à la fourchette* was
served, with Russian folk music in the background. Her parties, however,
were characterized by sobriety and decorum. She always invited each and
every cabinet minister; some went because they wanted to or out of curiosity, others as a work-related commitment. The president never attended.[53]

Despite Kollontai's best efforts, her stay in Mexico sparked more controversies than bore fruit for the two countries. When the Soviet donation for
the railway workers arrived, most likely the ambassador channeled it to its
intended recipients. Immediately the press tarred her with the "subversive"
label, although her reputation as a fervent Bolshevik contrasted with her
condition as an exile from the Soviet Union. Furthermore, Washington's
policy of continuing to accuse Mexico of being the nest of Bolshevism in
the New World also undermined the seriousness and effectiveness with
which Kollontai strove to carry out her mission. Kellogg's severe criticism
in January 1927 that Mexico sought to spread Bolshevism beyond its borders, and Sheffield's accusation that the ambassador was sending Mexican
workers to the United States to infect Americans with the Communist
virus placed her in a delicate situation with Calles.

However, despite having been denied a visa to enter the United States and experiencing U.S. hostility against her when she was stationed in Mexico, Kollontai did not interpret these moves as directed against the Soviet Union. She felt the United States was using her as a scapegoat to settle scores with Mexico. In a report to Litvinov, she sought to minimize the importance of the documents Kellogg had presented to the U.S. Senate as proof that Mexico was a continental troublemaker directed by Moscow—not because she was unaware of how precarious Mexico's situation was, but because she considered the Mexican-U.S. conflict as part of the worsening international panorama, a confrontation between progressive and conservative forces.[54] Kollontai was, if anything, surprised by Calles's tolerance toward the Soviet Union at the time when the Russian funds for the railway workers arrived. She also did not see signs that the Anglo-Soviet dispute would affect the Mexican government's posture toward Moscow.[55]

From a personal point of view, Kollontai's life in Mexico had its pleasant moments, but was also made bitter by the publication of a pirate edition of her short story *Bol'shaia liubov* (A Great Love) under the sensationalist title *Red Love*. Originally published in 1923, the story was part of a collection entitled *Zhenshchina na perelome* (Women at the Turning Point) and was based on the author's own experience; it told of a woman who sought self-realization through her work, over and against her husband's opinion. In the story, as in the rest of the collection, the writer used a sentimental and romantic plot to popularize her theory on female emancipation and women's liberation from bourgeois morality. The book, which was originally published in Moscow, lacked in translation the didactic quality that the writer sought to achieve.[56] Kollontai tried to halt the edition or at least to read the proofs before the book rolled off the presses, but she did not read or speak Spanish. Beals helped her improve the most vulgar alterations of the original text, but in any event the book wound up being a cheap and sensational romance.[57] Kollontai's contact with the reduced universe of Mexican feminism was, in contrast, the most pleasant aspect of her life in the country. Communist women visited her frequently, and according to the testimony of activist and singer of revolutionary ballads, Concha Michel, "after a conversation with her, we'd feel we had been oriented."[58]

All in all, however, Kollontai failed in her efforts to demonstrate that revolution and diplomacy, the Comintern and the Soviet government, functioned independently of one another because it was not so. Nor was she able to promote trade between Mexico and the Soviet Union. In 1926, the

TABLE I Exports from the USSR for 1926–1927

Country	Tons	Thousands of rubles
E.U.	235,000	81,652
Argentina	1,450	1,157
Mexico	51	105

Source: *Vneshniaia Torgovlia SSR, 1918–1940* (Moscow: Vneshorgizdat, 1960), pp. 1044–73.

TABLE 2 Imports from the USSR for 1926–1927

Country	Tons	Thousands of rubles
E.U.	213,506	508,361
Argentina	39,035	89,672
Mexico	2,633	2,729

Source: *Vneshniaia Torgovlia SSR, 1918–1940* (Moscow: Vneshorgizdat, 1960), pp. 1044–73.

two governments canceled the commercial treaty signed in 1909, but could not reach agreement on a new accord. The Soviet government complained that the text drafted by Mexican ambassador Basilio Vadillo was unacceptable because it did not take into account the differences between an economy based on capitalism and one based on state ownership of property. In turn, Vadillo rejected the text proposed by the Soviets because it included a politically inappropriate clause—that Mexico would receive favored nation status.[59] Thus, by 1927 the Mexican products purchased by the Soviets and a large part of Soviet goods sold to Mexico passed, as before, through U.S. intermediaries, without generating many benefits for the respective producers.[60]

Kollontai felt that she had exhausted her possibilities for improving bilateral relations between Mexico and the Soviet Union. Frustrated and suffering from Mexico City's altitude sickness, she asked the Soviet government to relieve her of her post. She sailed for Europe in June 1927, leaving the ambassador slot vacant and relations between Mexico and the Soviet Union on hold.

Chapter 6

▼

MEXICO AT THE

CROSSROADS

During the 1920s, the Mexican press delved extensively into the Bolshevik Revolution and, through investigative reports and commentaries, informed its readers on everything related to the ups and downs of the New Economic Policy (NEP) and to the political fortunes of Leon Trotsky. Their fate would symbolize the success or failure of the revolution. The unfolding of the Russian Revolution served as a mirror that spurred reflection on the Mexican revolutionary process. Both radical intellectuals in the government and liberal and conservative newspapers sketched parallels between the two revolutions. Although at first the Mexican Revolution was juxtaposed to the Russian Revolution, increasingly with time it was defined in opposition to the Bolshevik experiment.

When in mid-1924 the newspapers announced that diplomatic relations had been established between Mexico and the Soviet Union, the reference points defining an image of the world political situation were U.S. antagonism toward Mexico and the USSR, a NEP at its zenith, and Leon Trotsky at the height of political power. Two years later, the NEP was under attack, and Trotsky had lost power. In Mexico, both phenomena were interpreted as a setback for the Bolshevik Revolution.

The NEP: Yardstick of the Revolution

When Lenin announced in March 1921 that War Communism was being abandoned and introduced the New Economic Policy, the Mexican press hailed the change. The media viewed the transition from an extreme to a more moderate Communist policy as a recognition that a country devastated by war and revolution could not be rebuilt without capital investment. The introduction of the NEP was interpreted in Mexico as an admission that Communism had been defeated and that Lenin had won the battle to allow foreigners to invest and reconstruct the country. Russia could not exploit its raw materials, *Excélsior* said, quoting Lenin, "unless foreigners provide machinery, train Russian workers and show them the best methods of production."[1]

Once applied, the NEP was a huge success because Soviet Russia, isolated and boycotted by the foreign capitalist governments, had few options to confront the hunger and discontent among the peasants that emerged as a consequence of the drastic measures associated with War Communism, imposed in 1918. The NEP also arose as a result of the need to adapt the new reality to the complex residual social and cultural hangovers from prerevolutionary Russia, which were locked in bitter struggle with the goal of constructing a Communist society. The NEP was to provide society with the necessary breathing space to achieve such an objective and, in the meantime, enable it to withstand the consequences of the revolutionary convulsions.[2] Lenin viewed the NEP (1921–1929) as a setback on the road to socialism, but not a repudiation of socialism. The ideal of establishing direct exchange of merchandise between the countryside and the city was an immediate failure, but among the Bolshevik leaders, Lenin, Trotsky, and Nikolai Bukharin hoped that such an objective would be achieved through a gradual process. Some, Lenin among them, doubted that socialism could be built by collaborating with the NEP capitalists.[3]

Lenin baptized the NEP with the label "state capitalism." The state retained political power and control over key enterprises, allowing small capitalists and a group of foreign capitalists to do business and operate concessions. However, the Bolsheviks hoped to restrict the activity of private enterprise, and some believed that for the greatest efficiency and the best results, the socialized sector of the economy should in the long run overtake the private sector.[4]

Some Bolsheviks were opposed to the NEP, considering the policy a betrayal of the revolution and socialism. Kollontai, for example, feared a return to bourgeois values, whose amorality would prevent women's emancipation.[5] Others blamed the NEP for the slow pace of industrial recovery. In 1922, production in light industry was only a quarter of its prerevolutionary levels, and heavy industry was paralyzed. In turn, the manufactured goods produced by the factories could not find markets among the peasants, for whom their prices were too high. As a result, the expected alliance between the working class and the peasantry never took place. In reality, the price differential between agricultural produce and industrial products tended to widen. Thus, as the peasants could not buy manufactured goods, they were not motivated to sell the fruits of their own labor. These price differentials, or the "scissors effect" as Trotsky called it, put economic relations between the countryside and the city in danger and therefore also put a question mark over the political alliance between the two social classes. To correct this imbalance, the economy should be planned in favor of the socialist sector—state-run companies and cooperatives—until by their very weight they would absorb or gradually eliminate the private sector and supersede the NEP's limitations.[6]

Outside observers of the NEP with an interest in defeating Soviet power confused the transitory character of the NEP with Communism's weakness. The Mexican newspapers commented that these economic reforms confirmed the correct, measured pace of the Mexican Revolution and its evolutionary road toward the reconstruction of the state and society on new foundations. Paradoxically, after Russian society began to recover from the disintegration it had suffered during the revolution and the civil war, Mexican commentators identified Lenin with moderation in leading the revolutionary process in Soviet Russia.[7]

If Lenin signified moderation to the conservative media in Mexico, the NEP's adversaries represented ultraradicalism. After the death of the Bolshevik leader in 1924, these adversaries were considered to have betrayed his ideals. Thus, according to Mexican newspapers, the leader of the Comintern, Zinoviev, was one of the extremists among the Bolsheviks because he wanted to dismantle the NEP. *Excélsior* quoted him, when speaking to delegates at the Fifth Congress of the Third International, as saying that "capitalism was the worst of all tyrannies." According to the newspaper's account, Zinoviev manifested his disdain for the bourgeois countries, which, although they had recognized Soviet Russia, continued to be its enemies, so the struggle against them would continue. Although the revolution had not triumphed in Western Europe, Communism was growing by leaps and bounds in the land of the Soviets.[8]

Throughout 1924 and 1925, the Mexican press reported economic successes and relative political peace in Soviet Russia, which correlated with the supposed dissolution of the Comintern. In fact, one of the constant interpretations offered by the official and semiofficial Mexican media concerning the evolution of the Bolshevik Revolution was to relate Soviet economic growth to a weakening Comintern, and vice versa: stepped up activities of the Third International signified an economic downturn and loss of control by the state over the gigantic country.[9]

However, the optimism expressed by European countries concerning Soviet economic recovery and peaceful coexistence with the capitalist world did not last long. Throughout 1926 the Mexican newspapers also reported that the Supreme Economic Council had warned Soviet enterprises and the workforce that industry lacked machinery, and that production costs were rising because of careless management in the factories, deficient labor discipline, and workplace organization among the workers. From then on, the government would undertake a campaign against laziness, indifference, and administrative negligence.[10]

During the same period, the press reported that the Comintern had intensified its activities in Europe and Asia. Soviet involvement in the 1926 British general strike and the subsequent break in diplomatic relations between the two countries were headline news in Mexico. In addition, reports appeared on the Soviets' abortive attempt to radicalize China and the industrial zones of Germany. At the same time, observers of the Soviet scene were perplexed by the repressive wave that swept over the Soviet Union itself following the assassination of the Russian ambassador to Poland by a monarchist student who sought revenge for the 1918 Bolshevik execution of the Czar and his family.[11]

It is true that the Soviet leadership never had resolved its ambiguous attitude toward the NEP. The adoption of market instruments and the recognition of the necessary role of traders and small businessmen were the results of a compromise with the peasantry, but the NEP's adversaries believed it was incompatible with industrialization. The debate within the government over the NEP led to contradictory policies. After the price crisis of 1923, the state restricted the activities of businessmen and traders, reducing their state bank credits as well as their company sales. At the same time, the state raised the private sector's taxes and applied controls over the prices of their products and merchandise. The NEP's opponents increasingly came to view businessmen and traders as their class enemies, and the rivalry between private and state companies was perceived by many of them as a manifestation of the class struggle.[12] As of 1929, the NEP was dismantled and replaced with forced collectivization and industrialization centrally organized from the heights of Soviet power. The attack on the mixed economy and the gradual change over to a strictly state-controlled economy were reflected in the deterioration of the Soviet Union's foreign relations. In Mexico, this deterioration coincided with Kollontai's tenure in the embassy and with Soviet financial assistance to the striking railway workers. According to the largest selling newspapers of the day, Mexico had become unwittingly involved in the sinister designs of the Comintern. Given the bombardment of U.S. economic and political pressure, it was necessary to clearly delineate the Soviet's radical policy from the gradual Mexican process.

Leon Trotsky: The Measure of Revolutionary Character

The power struggle in the Soviet Union was also viewed in Mexico as a fight between the government and the Comintern—a struggle between good and evil. The two entities were considered separate, each trying to subordinate the other. When Lenin became ill in 1922, a war to the finish took place in Russia to determine who would succeed the Bolshevik leader. After his death in 1924, the press took it for granted that the power struggle within the Bolshevik Party was between Trotsky, the general of the Red Army, and Grigori Zinoviev, the "ultraradical" leader of the Comintern. The media seldom mentioned Stalin until 1926.

It was believed at the time that Trotsky was Lenin's political heir. His sudden disappearance from the scene during 1924, without any explanation from the Soviets, was considered significant by the communications media, even in Mexico. *Excélsior* and *El Universal* commented profusely on Trotsky's dramatic fall from the heights of power. Once they even explained the events through absurd news reports that Trotsky had allied himself with the monarchists or that he had ambitions to become a dictator.[13] After these so very absurd reports were denied, the newspapers presented him as a symbol of democracy and his opponents as autocrats. One event in particular attracted the attention of the media: when in 1925 Trotsky was removed from the leadership of the Commissariat of War, he did not protest publicly or resort to insubordination, as any Mexican general would have done in similar circumstances.[14]

El Demócrata had a different take on the dramatic events unfolding in the Soviet Union. Vito Alessio Robles's newspaper had practically given American Communist Bertram Wolfe carte blanche to write about his impressions and interpretations of the USSR following his trip there in 1924 as the Mexican Communist Party (MCP) delegate to the Fifth Congress of the Comintern. During several months in 1924 and 1925, *El Demócrata* published Wolfe's twenty-some articles without prior censorship.

From both faith and discipline, the Communists tended to embellish Soviet history so as not to give its detractors any additional ammunition. Thus, Wolfe's articles—intelligent, well written, and informative—also aimed to discredit the reports in other newspapers concerning the situation in the USSR and especially Trotsky's unexplainable disappearance. Another soldier of the revolution, Wolfe wanted to give Trotsky the prominent place in history he felt the Bolshevik leader deserved. In one of his articles, he wrote: "This Trotsky, dead so many times, arrested so many times, expelled so many times, Trotsky the sick man, Trotsky the 'bonapartist' who wants to become emperor of Russia, Trotsky the moribund . . . is marching, shoulder to shoulder with me, and my furtive glances show me a tall, strong and robust man in semi-military uniform."[15] Wolfe wrote of Trotsky's popularity, but did not mention that a campaign was being waged against the Bolshevik leader, which explains why he could not have seen Trotsky play a prominent role in the congress.[16]

While in the Soviet Union Wolfe witnessed the campaign in favor of state cooperatives and against NEP-inspired private business, which were considered speculative. To graphically describe his impressions, he shared with his readers the delicious taste of milk from a cooperative and contrasted it with an unappetizing, yellowish liquid from a private store he had to visit on a Sunday because the state cooperative was closed. Although not everything in the cooperatives was milk and honey, their evolution thus far had promised to make life easier and better for the workers. However, as long as the cooperatives' production and trade were not yet developed in all branches of light industry, the NEP would temporarily have to fill the gap.[17]

It was commonplace at the time for the press to interpret Trotsky's fall from power as the result of an ideological and institutional confrontation between moderation and extremism, between the Soviet government and the Comintern. According to this interpretation, extremism and the Comintern won the fight.

The Mexican ambassador in the USSR also sent a long commentary on the question to his superiors. Vadillo entitled his document "The Bolshevik Threat," and in it he tried to explain that the danger did not emanate from the government, which was characterized by the pragmatism of a "bourgeois administration," but from Bolshevik ideas. These ideas were generated by the Comintern's propaganda machine, which preached the "general theory of revolution."[18]

It can safely be argued that the ideas disseminated by the press and systematized by the Foreign Relations Ministry concerning the Soviet Union—its dilemmas, internal contradictions, and role in the world—influenced the way in which Mexican political leaders and commentators interpreted, by analogy or negative comparison, social developments in Mexico and the country's incessant conflicts with the United States. These same ideas influenced politicians and observers' opinions on Mexico's alliance with the USSR.

Calles "the Bolshevik"

In December 1924, a few days after having taken office, President Calles announced that the revolutionary process had entered its constructive phase. With this message, he wanted to give the impression that although he had his own political agenda, it was nonetheless a loyal continuation of the trail blazed by his predecessor.[19] Mexico's material reconstruction was unthinkable without the participation of foreign investment and capital. Like Obregón, Calles linked economic development, national sovereignty, and redemption of the proletariat and the peasantry to the needs of the capitalists. However, he also emphasized that the capitalists' interests could not take precedent over the population's well-being because material privation would spark social unrest and political upheavals. Reforms were the only alternative to revolution. He confronted the same dilemma as Obregón: how to conciliate labor's demands for improved working conditions and the peasants' need for cultivable land with the necessity to provide guarantees to the capitalists, who opposed exactly these reforms.[20] But, also like Obregón, Calles knew that his government's stability would depend on backing from the labor movement under the leadership of Luis Morones, but that at the same time he could not scorn support from Communists, independent unions, and the agrarian movements. Good relations with the United States were also, of course, a priority.[21]

For the ideas he espoused, Calles, much more than Obregón, earned the reputation of being a "Bolshevik." Before his inaugural ceremony even took place, Calles visited the United States, where, according to Carleton Beals, in a speech to American workers he pledged that "before I will betray the proletariat, I will wrap myself in the red flag and hurl myself into the abyss."[22] This anecdote may be apocryphal, but it does reflect Calles's reputation as a pro-labor, radical political leader, a reputation that accompanied him during his presidential administration. Even the young José Valadés, a member of the Mexican Communist Party, had to admit Calles's skill in convincing workers that the state could furnish them "as much as and more than the unions and socialism can offer." What the Communists promised as future conquests, Calles provided to the workers and peasants in the here and now. According to Valadés, Calles "took off our epaulets and put them on his own shoulders."[23] And whereas Pestkovsky believed that in Calles he had found a fellow traveler in the historic struggle for the emancipation of the Western Hemisphere from imperialism, the conservative newspapers, both in Mexico and the United States, viewed the new president as the prototype of a radical leader who would obstruct harmonious relations with a neighboring country.[24]

Calles sympathized with the Soviet experiment, but given the reaction such sympathy sparked among his adversaries, he sought to disassociate the Bolshevik and Mexican Revolutions. In an interview in April 1924, he answered a question concerning whether he thought that Bolshevism and the Mexican Revolution were identical. He placed the revolutions in their historical time frame as a universal tendency of societies' development, but felt that such processes had to be controlled so that their impetuous inclinations would not become a destructive force. Regarding Soviet Russia, he said it was too soon to make a definitive judgment on the country's evolution, but felt that the unfolding changes, such as the results of the NEP, appeared to be successful. Although the ideals of the two revolutions were similar, Mexico was guided by its Constitution: "We are interested in the Soviets as a system of government only in its philosophical and humanitarian aspects," Calles explained.[25]

Although at the beginning of the 1920s, being called a Bolshevik or socialist could have been either flattering or innocuous, once Calles was chosen as a presidential candidate, and especially after he took office, these epithets were harmful to his role as a statesman. On various occasions, he tried to rectify the image many held of him: "Endeavors are being made to cause me to appear as the representative of Bolshevism, as a representative of the destruction and ruin which makes Communism hated. All this is untrue. My only aspiration is that the principles of the Revolution designed for the benefit of the working people be placed into practice, for these people have suffered for many years."[26] More than Soviet Communism, it was the political tendencies represented by the German social democracy of Friedrich Ebert and the British Labour Party of Ramsay MacDonald that served as Calles's guide to modernize Mexico. It was on his initiative that the Banco Nacional de México was founded in 1925, and a year later the Banco Nacional de Crédito Rural (National Rural Credit Bank); the Comisión Nacional de Irrigación (National Irrigation Commission); and the Comisión Nacional de Caminos (National Highway Commission). A series of primary, secondary, and technical schools were similarly established. Modernizing the economic infrastructure and the transport system was aimed at reducing the political and social obstacles that prevented the mobility of businessmen, capital, and workers. The Calles administration distributed 3.19 million hectares of land to three hundred thousand families, compared to the 1.7 million hectares parceled out to 161,000 families under Obregón.[27] In addition, Calles made the CROM into an ally of the government, naming Luis Morones as his labor minister.

Such measures did not make Calles appear less committed to guaranteeing the legitimate rights of private investors. The same way he affirmed that "any revolutionary movement that threatens the authority of capital cannot but fail," he demanded that investors take Mexico's development seriously. He encouraged businessmen to think in terms of their profits, but urged them to be conscious of the impact of their decisions on all social classes. Capitalists had a social role to perform in benefiting society as a whole, which in turn benefited business as such. Calles reiterated many times that the reactionary capitalists "refuse to see that in reality, we are fighting for them and their interests."[28]

However, both American belligerence—especially after members of the Mexican Congress proposed bills to regulate foreign businesses in the country—and Chicherin's broadside made Calles's pronouncements seem hollow. Reflecting the American position, *Excélsior* interpreted Chicherin's comment that Mexico was considered a base to expand Soviet relations in the Western Hemisphere as an attempt by Soviet Russia to use Mexico as a trampoline for Bolshevik propaganda in the United States and Latin America. The United States was correct in refusing to recognize the legality of the Soviet government, and Mexico should not have done so.[29]

This time, Calles was forced to respond to the media's frontal attacks by publicly repudiating Soviet policy. The country should not be seen as an instrument of the Soviet Union's foreign policy, although Mexico did recognize the legality of the Soviet government as an expression of international justice and respect for the sovereignty of all nations, he said. He added that the Mexican Revolution was inspired by the suffering of the Mexican people and should not be slighted with characterizations at odds with the country's mentality and circumstances.[30]

Calles's unambiguous declaration created a favorable impression in political circles in both Washington and Mexico. The U.S. embassy sent a secret report to the State Department on Calles's warning to Pestkovsky, said to have been delivered in the president's office. Supposedly, Calles presented evidence that several Communists active in different unions were on the Soviet embassy payroll. According to the *Washington Evening Post*, "If the action which has been taken against the Russian Minister means that Mexico is abandoning Bolshevism, it could be said that the neighboring country has gone a long way toward normalcy and toward better and firmer relations with the United States."[31] When in October 1926 Pestkovsky left Mexico, the State Department expressed its satisfaction and hoped that Calles would go much further, even to the point of breaking relations with the USSR.

Calles not only refused to break off relations, but did not object to Pestkovsky being replaced by Alexandra Kollontai, who, in addition to being a woman with subversive ideas concerning the social order established by men, had the reputation of being politically more radical than the outgoing ambassador. As long as the Americans continued pressuring Mexico to refrain from applying the constitutional reforms, the Mexican government knew that breaking relations with the USSR would convince the United States that its influence was yielding the desired results.

The appearance of Mexico bowing to the United States would limit the country's maneuvering room in the international arena and would also affect its sovereignty, which had been the original reason for establishing relations with Soviet Russia in the first place. In addition, such a move could antagonize the administration's allies among the leftist elite in the government and the radical factions within the labor movement, who viewed Calles as their president.

The president, however, directed yet another message to the elite, which had opposed both Mexican-Soviet relations as well as the government's reform policies: far from being harmed, the middle class would benefit from Mexico's new economic policies. Taking advantage of the opportunity afforded by the ceremony in which Kollontai presented her diplomatic credentials—during which she compared the two revolutions and emphasized their common objectives—Calles abstained from any sort of comparison.

He reiterated that the Mexican Revolution was not related in any way to the Bolshevik Revolution because it had been an uprising of the Mexican people against the old tyranny and the selfish and voracious capitalism suffocating the proletarian masses. Mexico had established relations with Soviet Russia without, at the same time, judging her institutions. The bourgeoisie—which was for this very reason labeling the government as radical—did not want to admit that it might "comfortably, and without any effort in the long run, [accept] and with the passing of years, even [bless] certain acts that at the beginning it had judged as unnecessarily extreme."[32] In short, the bourgeoisie would benefit from the government's policies and should recognize this. At this stage, Calles still thought his administration could maintain good relations with the Soviet Union and the labor movement without antagonizing his allies among the ruling class.

By the end of 1926, the Calles government needed all the assistance it could get. The injection of energy and resources into the economy during the first two years of this administration was followed by a sharp economic decline. From mid-1926 on the economic crisis wreaked havoc on the ambitious projects of the administration's first years. The government's income dropped due to a reduction in oil and silver exports, which were only partially compensated for by overseas sales of agricultural produce. The United States continued to pressure Mexico through an aggressive propaganda campaign aimed at preventing the application of the oil and agrarian legislation. To carry out such reforms would cost money that Mexico had obviously stopped earning. In addition, Mexico was in the middle of an ideological and political storm sparked by Kollontai's arrival and Calles's military support to Nicaragua.[33]

In his New Year's message in January 1927, Calles—with a veiled reference to the United States—told the nation that in seeking economic and political independence, prosperity, and development, in adopting its own methods for exploiting the country's natural resources, and in defending its national rights, Mexico had come up against distrust and strong, antagonistic opposition to its government. But to maintain the country's morale, he did not mention that the government was preparing the army for a possible U.S. intervention.[34]

Calles also spoke of the successes scored throughout 1926 despite the difficulties: the government had achieved financial stability; an extensive educational program had been carried out, with several agricultural colleges built; irrigation works were completed; the army and several govern-

ment divisions had been reorganized. Conscious that Secretary of State
Kellogg and the State Department disparaged these very same programs,
characterizing them as a platform for Latin American Bolshevism, the president added:

> these projects for the redemption and the economic and social better-
> ment of the masses of Mexico, without detriment to the just rights and
> prosperity of the privileged classes, either through bad faith or the
> malice of selfish interests or lack of a proper understanding of the
> situation, have continued to be interpreted as manifestations of a de-
> structive tendency in the government. By a rancorous press campaign
> it has been sought to present Mexico as emulating or sustaining exotic
> systems of government and as conducting both at home and abroad a
> propaganda in favor of political and social systems which are abso-
> lutely foreign to our methods and our tendencies.[35]

Calles was categorical in defending the country's own road: the Soviet
methods of government would not adapt well to Mexican conditions and
did not correspond to Mexico's constitutional reorganization or the executive branch's policies.[36]

Balance Sheet of the Revolution

Mexico's economic situation worsened during 1927, however. The government's monetary reserves ran out as a result of financing earmarked for
public works projects and foreign debt payments. Even a loan contracted in
1926 could not balance the current account. Despite having adopted an
income tax, revenue from fiscal duties on imports and exports dropped and
exploitation of natural resources dramatically fell. In his State of the Nation address delivered in September 1927, Calles presented the statistics at
hand: in 1922, 30 percent of federal government income came from the oil
industry, whereas in 1924 this figure had dropped to 19 percent and in 1926
to only 11 percent. A year later, in 1927, it did not reach even 8 percent. By
that same year, petroleum exports had fallen 76 percent compared to the
exports of 1921. Agricultural exports, which had risen in the first part of the
1920s, began to decline in 1926. When exports fell, without the necessary
restructuring in agriculture to promote sustained economic growth, the
government lacked the necessary funds to purchase corn, beans, and meat
in foreign markets. The negative effects of the collapse of the export sector
included a rise in unemployment and a fall in domestic demand. The gross

domestic product fell 5.9 percent in 1927, 0.9 percent in 1928, and 5.4 percent in 1929—that is, an annual 2.6 percent decline between 1926 and 1929. This process culminated in the start of the world depression.[37] The truth be told, the restrictions imposed on the government's reform program stemmed from the structural factors inherent in the domestic economy, which postrevolutionary governments had inherited from their predecessors: the conjunctural ups and downs, U.S. opposition, and the resistance to reform offered by Mexican industrialists and landowners. One should also not forget the government's blind eye to attempts by certain Mexican elite interests to elude the reforms.

When compared to domestic investment of the Porfiriato period, the contraction in such investment in the 1920s added to the obstacles that impeded sustained economic development as a result of the reduced domestic market and the fragility of Mexican industry, which did not enjoy government protection. One of the consequences of the revolution, which seriously affected the economy in the subsequent years, was the Mexican business community's lack of confidence in the country's political stability. Industrialists stopped investing in economic branches such as textiles, steel, and cigarettes, convinced that the value of their assets was only 50 percent of what it had been before the revolution. Instead of investing capital in Mexico, they kept their funds in foreign banks.[38]

After the revolution, the government had few instruments or institutions with which to influence economic development. Although the Banco Nacional de México, the Banco Agrícola, the Comisión Nacional de Caminos, and the Comisión Nacional de Irrigación were the institutions that provided the state with the instruments for its intervention into economic life, they could not meet their objectives due to lack of financial resources.[39]

Difficulties with the balance of payments began in mid-1926 as a result of the economic recession in the United States, the decrease in mineral exports—particularly petroleum—and in gold payments made to settle the debt with the International Committee of Bankers. Traditionally, the most important tax in terms of government revenue was the tax on international trade operations and activities that exploited natural resources for export. Income from this tax represented between 30 and 40 percent of all fiscal revenue, depending on the year. Thus, although the government expected to have a fiscal surplus of thirteen million pesos in 1926, it wound up with a sixteen-million peso deficit; in 1927, it anticipated a twenty-one million peso surplus, but ended the year fifteen million pesos in the red.[40] Unforeseen expenditures involved in putting down the Cristero rebellion against the anticlerical state were considerable. As a result, the level of international reserves dropped from 39.8 million dollars in May 1926 to 15 million dollars in January 1927. By mid-1928, the government was once again forced to suspend payments on servicing the foreign debt.[41]

The drop in government income was mainly the result of a reduction in oil exports. A study undertaken by oil companies revealed that the firms reduced their business activities in Mexico and moved operations to Venezuela not only to protest the laws through which the Mexican government sought to acquire greater control over them, but also to protect their investment because a gradual salinity at the wells, according to the oil executives, placed recovery of their investments in danger and raised drilling costs, all in the context of a market characterized by falling prices. Whereas in 1922 the United States imported 129,142 barrels of crude from Mexico and 755 from Venezuela, in 1927 its imports from Mexico stood at 26,019 barrels and from Venezuela at 21,987 barrels. The following year, and from that point on, Venezuela supplied the United States with several times as much oil as Mexico.[42]

In a politically charged atmosphere, opinions were divided on the causes behind the economic decline and the administration's inability to fulfill the promises of the revolution. If, on the one hand, Calles was accused of radicalism, some of his closest collaborators criticized him, on the other, for not going far enough. The radicals within the government believed that not only Calles, but they themselves had failed despite their efforts. Ramón P. de Negri, who in 1919 had dreamed of shortly establishing relations with Soviet Russia in hopes of energizing the Mexican Revolution, by 1925 had realized that Mexico was progressing slowly, that there was little hope that Mexicans could move forward on their own, and that the only alternative was to wait for "the world revolution" to arrive to assist the process.[43] In 1927, after Calles sent him into diplomatic exile for being too radical, de Negri privately charged that the government, out of fear of the "bogeyman from the north," had diverted the revolution instead of moving toward collectivism and anticapitalism. The government, "which lacks revolutionary sincerity," was more concerned with securing the benefits of capitalism, such as credit and capital, and with directing the agrarian reform toward forms of private property than with pursuing "true social and economic justice."[44]

In 1925, Marte R. Gómez—the agrarian engineer who with the support of then governor Portes Gil launched land distribution in Tamaulipas against all odds—believed that Calles was insufficiently firm. The "political cowardice" of the group in the central government leading the agrarian reform program had combined with the ambitions of the labor leaders, in whose interest it was to "calm yanqui capitalism and the country's bourgeoisie." In observing that agrarian reform proponents in the government were powerless, Gómez complained that Morones was not radical enough on agrarian questions because the labor leader turned minister had made comments to the U.S. press that land distribution policies threatened to ruin the country.[45]

For Marte R. Gómez, land distribution was both a technical problem as well as an ethical necessity. In 1927, he was alarmed that land distribution, the heart of the revolution, was moving too slowly. At the second convention of the League of Agrarian Communities in Tamaulipas, in response to a worker who had spoken of his own recent trip to the Soviet Union, Gómez said that land collectivization in Mexico did not take place because private property in the countryside had been sanctioned by the Constitutionalists. They had betrayed the revolution. In reality, the 1917 Constitution had hindered any subsequent sovietization in Mexico.[46]

The utopian vision of an anticapitalist Mexico held by the radical elite contrasted more than ever with the dominant point of view within the government, which saw the need to project Mexico as an irrevocably capitalist country. In November 1927 Calles reiterated in an interview with the *New York Times* that "any revolutionary movement here in Mexico that threatens the authority of capital is bound to fail."[47] The president wanted to emphasize that capitalists who were respectful of Mexican laws and dignity could expect to find "untold treasures" in Mexico that awaited exploitation.

The conservative press in the capital insisted that Mexico could not allow any doubts on the country's capitalist character. Mexico depended on the United States for investments and markets, and unfortunately was in its sphere of influence. Therefore, any similarity, real or imagined, between the economic policies of Mexico and Soviet Russia only worked against Mexico's interests. The government was partly to blame because it lent itself to such comparative descriptions.

Both *Excélsior* as well as *El Universal* attributed the uncertainty surrounding the future of social programs within the framework of the capitalist system to the government's vacillating attitude—its inability to decide between capitalism and socialism. If the United States unfavorably compared Mexico to Soviet Russia, it was due to bad faith on the part of the American plutocracy and to the apparent similarities between the two countries. Mexico preserved the forms of capitalism, but supplemented them with measures that favored the working class. The problem resided in the "excessive use of Bolshevik-style rhetoric."[48] As in the Soviet Union, capitalism in Mexico was under attack by the revolutionaries, and just like in the Soviet Union in 1921 the course of the revolution had to be corrected. Criticisms leveled against capital and the enterprising initiatives of investors had to come to an end. Mexico in 1927 was where Soviet Russia had been in 1921, when Lenin ordered a step backward due to the destructive effects of the policies of War Communism on the economy, society, and morality. Mexico's advantages over Russia were that the changes had not been systematic and the Mexican leadership was not inspired by an ideal, but by individual greed.[49]

Of course, no one could seriously consider a comparison between Mexico's policies in the first half of the 1920s with War Communism in Soviet Russia from 1918 to 1921. The comparison was a ploy involving theatrical rhetoric. But the press's objective was persuasion, not precision. Its goal was to convince public opinion that Mexico was trapped between two opposite poles—the United States and the Soviet Union, each of which considered itself to be the savior of humanity—and it was caught in this position because it did not have the ability to influence the conflict between the two giants.[50] The journalists' implication was that Mexico had no other alternative but to make concessions to U.S. economic and political pressures, implement clear-cut programs, and declare the country's unshakable friendship with the United States.

However, the Mexican government was not about to adopt a policy of submission, at least not openly. The state owed its existence to the perception that it was based on and was implementing the revolutionary ideals, and that it could not follow a course of loyalty toward the United States. Despite opposition to and severe criticisms of its handling of state policies, the government could camouflage, but not abandon the revolutionary program because the lower classes continued to demand its fulfillment. The government could not declare itself entirely in favor of the capitalist class. It used the language of class conciliation and waved the banner of social justice, trying to conceal the conflicts it could not or did not want to resolve. By denying its specific class character—by manifesting an ideological elasticity and declaring its resolve to meet the needs of all—the government was constantly being legitimized. In reality, this became the revolution's policy during the 1920s: to conceal, deny, cover up, and eliminate the contradictions.[51]

From the outside, the United States challenged Mexican laws, rejecting both the essence of the state's legitimacy and Mexico's sovereignty. Mexico's international position was defined by its desire to carry out policies that were independent of the powerful, dominant, and absorbing northern neighbor. Relations with the Soviet Union helped confirm its sovereignty. This context explains why Mexico maintained relations with the USSR, even when they turned out to be so problematic.

It was apparent, however, that since April 1927 Calles was anxious for relations with the United States to improve. When President Coolidge told the press that Washington had an obligation to protect U.S. interests wherever they may be without mentioning, as had been done previously, the Mexican legislation that affected such interests, Calles responded to the U.S. president's declaration in a quite conciliatory tone despite threats of war at the beginning of the same year. He minimized the differences between the two countries and attributed them "only to a lack of understanding or divergent opinions in appreciating legal, theoretical or technical matters that in reality do not affect the facts on the ground and do not affect legitimate interests."[52] The Mexican newspapers also commented on the change in the U.S. attitude toward Mexico, but in a much less conciliatory tone. The press condemned U.S. embassy officials for not being very diplomatic when pressure from the United States was "suffocating" and "strangulating" Mexico.[53]

The sudden change in Calles's attitude toward the United States was the result of the deteriorated economy and his concern that the conflicts with Washington not embolden the government's adversaries. To guarantee political stability and maintain the hope that foreign assistance in the form of capital investment would spur economic improvement, the Mexican government was willing to reach an agreement with the United States in 1927, even at the cost of sacrificing some of its principles. When relations with the United States improved in the second half of 1927 and respect replaced belligerency, ties with the Russians became expendable.

God has made us neighbors, let justice
make us friends. The first step toward justice is to stop making false and unfair statements about Mexico.

—William E. Borah, *New
York Times*, March 21, 1927

Five in four,
five in four,
five in four,
and not in five!

—Slogan of "the Five-Year
Plan in Four," chanted by
Soviet schoolchildren

They do not know us, they do not understand us, nor do they respect us. The labels
that their orthodox and fanatic ideology has
invented present our government as petty-
bourgeois, a government, which according
to them, is allied with imperialism and is
an enemy of the working class. We are
treated with suspicion and with the same
lukewarm courtesy that they reserve for
countries considered their enemies.

—Jesús Silva Herzog (1929),
Archivo Diplomático 14-25-2

Part Three

THE

REVOLUTIONS

COLLIDE,

1928–1930

Chapter 7

THE UNITED STATES

AS GOOD NEIGHBOR

Between 1917 and 1927, U.S. foreign policy toward Mexico (and Central America) constantly violated national sovereignty under the pretext of defending international law. Although the United States claimed to be protecting the rights of each nation, in reality it was defending interests affected by economic nationalism. This policy failed in Mexico because it did not guarantee a satisfactory and permanent settlement for claims by U.S. citizens and companies that had lost land and demanded compensation for damages caused by the revolution. In fact, south of the border it deepened the animosity toward the United States. By the end of the 1920s, another Republican administration had realized that dollar diplomacy and the big stick were counterproductive methods in promoting U.S. interests abroad. In recognition that its policy had been mistaken as far as Mexico was concerned, Washington replaced its ambassador as an initial token of its good will.

Censuring Foreign Policy

In April 1927, the respected journalist Walter Lippmann wrote that U.S. economic interests in Latin America had reached the point where it was necessary to "formulate a policy as momentous as the Monroe Doctrine itself." This policy, which the United States was already in the process of defining, had to resolve the conflict that has arisen from the clash between U.S. interests in Latin America's natural resources and the rising tide of nationalism, which had already become a worldwide phenomenon.

The original objective of the Monroe Doctrine was to prevent European political intervention and expansion in the Western Hemisphere in order to protect U.S. national security. In 1904, President Theodore Roosevelt added a corollary to the doctrine as a result of the prevailing political instability in Latin America. At this point, the United States claimed for itself the right to "exercise an international police power."[1] But in its dispute with Mexico, it faced a reality different from that which had inspired the Monroe Doctrine. The Mexican Revolution was not a simple brawl between factions led from abroad, but a deep and ongoing national upheaval against the rural landlords, the clergy, and foreign concessionaires who had acquired the country's most valuable natural resources. The United States abused the Monroe Doctrine when it placed Mexico's nationalist revolution on the same level as Bolshevism. To set the historical record straight, Lippmann explained that "this revolution, which is loosely called Bolshevik and is often ascribed by careless writers to the Russian Communists, was fought out and consummated while the Czar was still on the throne of Russia. The new Mexican Constitution, which embodies the results of the revolution, went into effect on May 1, 1917, over six months before Lenin seized the government of Russia."[2] In reality, what the Mexican Revolution challenged, Lippmann argued, was the supremacy and statesmanship of the Western empires. Under attack were the extraterritorial privileges, as expressed by the courts and the special concessions that granted foreigners a higher status than the country's own population.

Not even the illustrious Lippmann managed to break from the racial discourse of the time; however, he was right on target when he pointed out some of the most important characteristics of the erroneous policies followed by the United States in Latin America. He charged that Secretary of State Kellogg and President Coolidge had committed a major error in ignoring the historical changes that had taken place and in maintaining that come what may, a property deed was untouchable. In addition, those in command in Washington considered international law, which defended property rights, to be above a nation's sovereign decisions. This position, subscribed to by the White House, left no room for a compromise solution where U.S. interests were affected. The *Kellogg Doctrine*, as Lippmann termed this intransigent approach, did not allow Mexico to confirm the oil companies' use of land because the U.S. administration rejected the Mexican constitutional principle that the natural resources belonged to the nation. Because the U.S. government rejected this principle, it demanded not only that the material damages suffered by American property owners be rectified through indemnization, but that the principle itself be annulled.

Lippmann believed in the need to protect foreign capital in other countries, but without challenging the right of nations to adopt the social system of their choice. He did not at all doubt that the interests of U.S. capital and the country in which it was invested were complementary: "Business is a much more flexible thing than the conservative theorist is ready to believe. It cannot be irreparably injured without injury to the nation which attacks it. If Mexico really tried to injure the oil business, the worst damage would recoil upon Mexico itself."[3]

Another critic of U.S. foreign policy who shared Lippmann's point of view was New York State's Democratic governor, Franklin D. Roosevelt. Roosevelt lamented the unfortunate loss in American moral leadership in the world, charging that what was really being sought was leadership of money. The up-and-coming politician argued that since the First World War, the United States had been taking advantage of the weakness of the European countries destroyed in the conflict. It lent them money, but at the same time raised its own import duties, thus making it difficult for them to pay their debts: "We have wanted to have our cake and eat it too."[4]

The United States was defending financial interests instead of developing good diplomatic relations with all Latin America. "It is not that assistance of some sort was not necessary. It was the method that was wrong," Roosevelt argued. For example, when in 1915 a revolution broke out in the Dominican Republic and the country was left without a president, cabinet, or legislature, the United States invaded the island with marines and stayed until 1927. When the chief magistrate of Haiti was assassinated, also in 1915, "we cleaned house, restored order, built public works and put governmental operation on a sound and honest basis." The world should thank us, Roosevelt said ironically, but instead "never before in our history have we had fewer friends in the Western Hemisphere than we have today."[5] Change was due. The United States would have to renounce the practice of arbitrarily intervening in the internal affairs of its neighbors. Roosevelt believed that the alternative to an interventionist policy was an association of all countries in the region, which would extend a helping hand in resolving any problems. Anticipating what would one day be the Organization of American States after the Second World War, Roosevelt looked back on "nine gray years, barren of constructive results on our part."[6] It was to be five years later, when the Democrats won the elections, that Roosevelt, now president, could practice what he had preached years previously.

The Republicans occupied the White House from 1921 to 1933. Although their attitude toward U.S. foreign policy in the 1920s was largely complacent, they also believed a change was needed. The Republican position on what constituted a sound foreign policy was expressed in the journal *Foreign Affairs* as fulfilling the Jeffersonian principle of "peace, commerce, and honest friendship with all nations, entangling alliances with none."[7] However, U.S. foreign policy could not have been more entangling. Ogden Mills, a Republican analyst, attributed the unsatisfactory state of U.S. international affairs to the inability and unwillingness of past administrations to negotiate their differences with other countries. Unlike Lippmann, Mills defended Theodore Roosevelt's corollary to the Monroe Doctrine because it recognized that national sovereignty brings with it the obligation to protect rights that others had acquired within the country's territory. In other words, national sovereignty was limited by international law. Therefore, in conditions of revolutionary upheaval, the United States could not leave its citizens without protection.

Yet Ogden Mills could see that the U.S. foreign policy of protecting its nationals collided with the interests of expanding U.S. business ventures in Latin America. Their very presence would spark concern because of aggressive U.S. foreign policy[8]: "Now that the financial reconstruction of Europe is well under way, American capital is turning more and more to the countries south of us for the purpose of aiding the development of their great resources and commercial opportunities. For all these reasons, it is important that our foreign policy towards Latin America should be clear cut and give no grounds for misapprehension as regards either the desires or intentions of this country." However, Mills's view of limited or conditioned sovereignty—which derived precisely from the application of the Monroe Doctrine to Latin American nations whose domestic policies could be a threat to North American national security—would mean that U.S. security would be placed over and above business interests and Latin American nations' apprehension regarding U.S. foreign policy, for he also stated unequivocally: "We do not shirk our responsibilities as a world power, but we still maintain our right to define what those responsibilities are and to decide under what circumstances we shall use our power and our resources."[9]

Thus, doggedly adhered to as the Monroe Doctrine was by some Republicans, the superciliousness of a world power was difficult to reconcile with the equally recognized need to negotiate with countries with which the United States sought to maintain and expand business relations. Practical experience had shown that the haughtiness inherent to the old policy had to be abandoned. With some backsliding and dissent, between 1927 and 1928 the Republicans began to act on their doubts and on the new economic challenges ahead of them.

During his visit to South America in 1928, Republican presidential candidate Herbert Hoover addressed distrustful audiences and conveyed the message that true democracy was incompatible with intervention. He declared that "it ought not to be the policy of the United States to intervene *by force* to secure or maintain contacts between our citizens and foreign states or their citizens. Confidence in that attitude is the only basis upon which the economic cooperation of our citizens can be welcomed abroad."[10] He baptized this new approach to Latin America the Good Neighbor Policy.

However, Latin Americans' fears of U.S. intervention did not dissipate with Hoover's friendly declarations. After Hoover's tour, Latin American political leaders and the press demanded deeds in addition to words as demonstrations of good faith and insisted that the promise of nonintervention be legally codified. This proposal was rejected by Charles Evans Hughes, former secretary of state, and Hoover's pledge did not become formally adopted until the FDR presidency in 1933.[11]

Meanwhile, and before the rhetoric was to become the new U.S. foreign policy toward Latin America in practice, Dwight Morrow's appointment as the new ambassador meant that Mexico had become a testing ground for negotiating a different type of commitment with the nationalist world. Morrow, known for his soft tone, was clear that his mission was to defend U.S. interests, but his idea on exactly what those interests were and how to protect them differed from his predecessors'.

Morrow's Ham-and-Eggs Diplomacy

When Morrow was appointed ambassador, one of his first tasks was to change Mexico's public image in the United States developed from many years of incompetent and prejudicial news coverage. To such an end, he could count on the support of journalists such as Walter Lippmann, Carleton Beals, and Ernest Gruening. Morrow himself provided U.S. newspapers with information on Mexico that he wished to see published in the United States and was skillful in offering news about himself and his ideas to the

Mexican media that he wanted Calles and the public to read. By establishing an effective control over the main mass media, he could, for example,
counteract the effect of a particularly virulent investigative report that the
Hearst newspaper chain published in December 1927.[12]

Precisely at the moment in which Morrow was trying to improve the
image of the United States in Mexico and settle long-standing disputes,
William Randolph Hearst published a sensational story that was splashed
across the front pages. The article provided lurid details on a supposed
Soviet-Mexican connection to finance Nicaraguan opposition to the United
States. It also included news of a "secret treaty," supposedly signed by Calles
and Juan Sacasa, Mexico's choice for president of Nicaragua. In addition,
according to the article, Mexico opposed the U.S. plan to build a canal
through Nicaragua; had donated one hundred thousand dollars to the Soviet
Union and fifty thousand dollars to striking British workers; had sent money
to Chinese radicals; and had bribed some American clergymen and the press
to publish articles favorable to Mexico. The most scandalous item in the
story published by the Hearst press was the charge that Mexico had bribed
four U.S. congressmen—William Borah of Idaho, George Norris of Nebraska,
Robert LaFollette Jr. of Wisconsin, and Thomas Heflin of Alabama—as a
means of garnering support in Washington.

The scandal backfired on its perpetrators. It was joked at the time that
Hearst had paid twenty-five thousand dollars "for these fly-by-night defa-
mations that no one in Mexico would have bought for a few hundred
pesos." A special Senate investigating committee discovered that Hearst
and his collaborators had paid a well-known document forger, Miguel
Ávila, more than twenty thousand dollars for the evidence without check-
ing into its authenticity before publishing it. It was rumored that Ávila was
employed by former ambassador Sheffield to fabricate the documents. The
Senate investigation concluded that Hearst had acted in bad faith and in
violation of the most elementary professional ethics. Senator Norris closed
the case, denouncing the Hearst newspaper empire as "the sewage system
of American journalism."[13] This time, the State Department assured the
Mexican ambassador in Washington that U.S. policy toward Mexico would
not be influenced by the publication of forged documents.[14]

In addition to influencing public opinion, Morrow changed the style and
appearance of U.S. diplomacy in Mexico. He kept the embassy's original
staff, but supervised consular officials so that they would not send decep-
tive reports on Mexico to Washington. He let Consul Arthur Shoenfeld

administer the embassy so that he himself could attend to political questions. He was surrounded by his own personnel, experts in legal affairs who helped him tackle the unresolved disputes between Mexico and the United States concerning oil, labor, and land ownership. He also took it upon himself to help the Mexican government to resolve the conflict between church and state and, above all, to restore financial stability. The ambassador selected Colonel Alexander J. McNab for the post of embassy military attaché due to his command of the Spanish language and sympathy for Mexico.[15]

Morrow rejected the idea of using force as a means to pressure another country. By the same token, he did not share Secretary of State Kellogg's premise that under international law, property rights took precedence over national sovereignty, but believed instead that "we can best defend the right of our own country when we understand the rights of other countries."[16] From his point of view, Mexican interests were compatible with broader U.S. interests. The best U.S. policy would be one that created the conditions for a content, prosperous neighbor south of the border, a country at peace with itself. Mexico's economic independence was not at odds with the protection of the legitimate rights of U.S. citizens in the country or with "a scrupulous respect for the sovereignty of Mexico."[17] The ambassador was convinced that the bilateral conflicts were the result of Mexico's economic situation and therefore saw no reason at all to deal with them as international disputes. He agreed that U.S. investments outside the United States would be under the legal jurisdiction of the country where they were located. As a result, resolving differences between Mexico and the United States could proceed only within the framework of Mexican political and social reality, and within Mexico's own legal system.[18]

Although solidly anti-Communist, Morrow did not make judgments or adopt political decisions as if he were participating in an ideological crusade. He understood full well the difference between the Mexican national and the Soviet political system. Ironically enough, anti-Communism had ceased to be a Trojan Horse for the U.S. government. By 1928 the fear that the Soviet Union would become the center of world revolution was receding in favor of considering the USSR as a country with which deals and agreements could be brokered. In the conflict between "socialism in a single country" and "world revolution," between the faction headed by Stalin and followers of Trotsky, Washington preferred the Man of Steel, believing that Stalin, not Trotsky, represented moderation. When doubts arose in political circles over who was in charge of Soviet foreign policy—the Com-

missariat of Foreign Affairs or the Comintern—Secretary of State Henry L.
Stimson felt that the Soviet government was in charge and that world
Communism was no longer a danger to peaceful international coexis-
tence.[19]

Moreover, by 1927 the United States was second in importance only to
Germany in the number of concessions it held in the USSR. General Electric and Standard Oil of New York were prominent partners of the Soviet
trade monopoly. In 1929, Henry Ford signed a contract with the Soviet-
American import-export company Amtorg—in operation since 1924—to
assist the Russians in constructing a factory to manufacture automobiles,
trucks, and other heavy vehicles. Although some business leaders did not
support diplomatic recognition, others, such as New York bankers, backed
"unofficial relations" as a means of promoting trade with their Soviet partners. When the depression heavily hit the U.S. economy, and at the same
time the First Five-Year Plan began to yield its initial fruits in the USSR,
Americans saw tremendous potential for new business opportunities amid
the world economic disaster. In 1933, the United States recognized the
Soviet government.[20]

Morrow shared the same pragmatic approach to business as his banker
friends, and it was not difficult for him to eliminate the airs of racial prejudice and cultural superiority in dealings with Mexicans—attitudes so prevalent among his predecessors. His style was so cordial and friendly that it
was known as "ham-and-eggs diplomacy" because instead of sending im-
personal diplomatic notes to the Foreign Relations Ministry, Morrow
would meet with Calles over breakfast. The ambassador tried to adapt to
the country's political culture and even began to drop in on Mexican public
officials as he pleased. A month after Morrow had arrived in the country,
Kellogg praised him for having allowed Mexico to act "on her own initiative, without any appearance of pressure from the United States."[21] This
appearance of not exerting any pressure on the Mexicans was precisely one
of Morrow's achievements: to avoid the appearance that he was really exerting pressure on the Mexicans.

The ambassador's first success centered on the negotiations concerning
the oil law. His legal advisor, J. Reuben Clark Jr., began talks with Mexican
officials by letting it be understood that his concept of sovereignty over
natural resources was no different from stipulations in the U.S. legal system.[22] This recognition of legal equality between Mexico and the United
States put negotiations between the two countries on a different footing.

Even the State Department congratulated Morrow for the progressive improvement in bilateral relations: "The rapid swing in the right direction since your arrival in Mexico has created an entirely new atmosphere, both in the Department and outside. We cannot avoid a feeling of real optimism for the first time in years."[23]

In March 1928 Morrow announced that the Mexican government recognized oil companies' rights to property acquired before the adoption of the 1917 Constitution. When the regulatory degree to the oil law was approved in March 1928, the State Department again praised Morrow for bringing to "a practical conclusion discussions which began ten years ago." If disputes should arise in the future surrounding the Constitution and legislation regulating the functioning of foreign companies, they "can be settled through the due operation of the Mexican administrative departments and the Mexican courts."[24] Morrow hoped that his example would inspire businessmen to confide in Mexican institutions and respect the country's sovereignty. He warned those Americans who felt their interests had been violated that they could no longer demand that the embassy back their protests, but would first have to take their cases through Mexican legal channels.[25]

Although some of the oil companies accepted the new law, the New York corporate executives maintained their opposition, still banking on the possibility of eliminating Article 27 from the Mexican Constitution. They contended that if they accepted the new regulations in Mexico, it could have a detrimental effect on their interests in Colombia and Venezuela. By January 1929 the companies that did not liquidate their business operations in Mexico accepted the new law, which in turn ratified their concessions.

Finally, both Mexico and the United States could claim partial victories. On the one hand, the United States defended the principle that retroactive application of the 1917 legislation violated international law and vigorously maintained its position on the inviolability of vested property rights. In response to Mexican insistence on that point, however, Washington accepted a change in the legal category of property ownership—namely, concessions—as well as Mexico's demand that vested rights on the subsoil be valid only if wells had been drilled and oil extracted. On the other side of the equation, Mexico defended its sovereign right to control its resources, renounced retroactive application of the law, and no longer placed time limits on concessioned rights. This agreement lasted until the oil industry was expropriated by President Lázaro Cárdenas in 1938.[26]

After the oil controversy, the U.S. ambassador became involved in the church-state dispute, during which religious services had been suspended. Morrow believed that settling the conflict was vital to Mexico's internal stability because "the poor almost have nothing else except the Church's solace."[27] Negotiations were arduous, but in June 1929 the clergy agreed to resume religious services. After three years of silence, once again the church bells tolled throughout Mexico.[28]

For Morrow it was easier to resolve the oil dispute than to reorganize Mexico's finances so that the country could pay its foreign debt without becoming bankrupt in the process. At the beginning of 1928 the International Committee of Bankers in Mexico concluded an extensive study on the country's fiscal and economic conditions. The report attributed the government's financial insolvency to the costly expenditures involved in defeating the military uprising of 1923–1924, a reduction in income from oil exports, and the costs of applying the agrarian reform. Land distribution undermined investor confidence, reduced productivity, and sparked uneasiness among business interests. In addition, it cost the federal government treasury dearly and frustrated any attempt to balance the budget. Another reason for Mexico's disastrous financial situation was that government had been applying social programs, such as highway construction and irrigation projects, which required heavy capital investments in credit institutions to finance.[29]

With the report on Mexican finances in hand, Morrow urged the government to reduce expenditures, thus implying that land distribution should be halted because the agrarian law required the government to pay compensation to landowners of expropriated estates. The country's precarious financial situation did not allow Mexico to meet its international obligations. Unless it improved its image abroad, Mexico could not obtain credits for development or attract capital to stimulate growth and trade. Morrow's plan was rejected by the government as well as his own bank partners.[30]

Working on a smaller scale than his original plan, Morrow was successful in influencing Calles to move back from expropriating some American landowners. However, the president abstained from agreeing to a compromise on the agrarian reform as a whole, as the U.S. ambassador had recommended. True, some of Calles's collaborators also viewed land distribution as an obstacle to development and even as a failure. Others felt continuation of the agrarian reform depended not only on the government's capacity to pay indemnization to the expropriated owners, but also on the new beneficiaries' ability to make the land productive. However, on the eve of the 1928 presidential elections, the government could ill afford to antagonize the peasantry, which was the social base of political support for the presidential candidate Alvaro Obregón. The candidate himself characterized Morrow's suggestion as inopportune.[31]

Although it was evident that the revolution had lost its radical thrust and that the workers were taking to the streets of the capital less frequently than at the beginning of the decade, the rest of the diplomatic staff at the embassy did not share Morrow's goodwill approach. On the contrary, just as before, they were outraged at the government's indulgence toward striking workers and Communist-organized rallies. Consul Alexander Weddell, for example, continued to keep the State Department informed about leftist activities and to send out issues of *El Libertador* whenever the rickety finances of the Anti-Imperialist League allowed the newspaper to be published. Insisting that there was no difference between the government and the Communists, on one occasion Weddell sent the State Department a copy of the book *Mexico-Soviet* when it was published at the end of 1927. Written by the Colombian author Julio Cuadros Caldas, the book lauded the reforms of the Mexican government and compared them with the achievements scored in the Soviet Union. Weddell faithfully cited Cuadras Caldas's viewpoint to illustrate "the political ideas animating the group in control in Mexico."[32]

The embassy refrained from carrying out the same type of anti-Communist campaign it had engaged in when Sheffield was in Mexico, probably because Morrow would not have allowed it. For example, when Abraham Rudy—a veteran of the Spanish American War and censor during World War I—visited Mexico at the end of 1927, his professional eye spotted a poster in the street inviting the public to hear a speech by Communist congressional deputy Hernán Laborde. Rudy attended and calculated that about one thousand persons were present, all wearing the insignia of Nicaraguan guerrilla leader César Augusto Sandino, who was being pursued by U.S. marines at the time. When the rally finished, an indignant Rudy rushed to the embassy to report on "these underground political movements in Mexico." To Rudy's surprise, the embassy staff told him that they knew what was going on, "but stated also that it was the policy of our government not to bother about such things."[33] Indeed, these were minor problems compared to the larger issues at hand and above all to the crisis that erupted following the assassination of president elect Alvaro Obregón in July 1928.

May 13, 1921, the day peasant congressional deputy Antonio Díaz Soto
y Gama delivered a fiery speech, and workers, led by anarchists and Communists, interrupted a session of the Chambers of Deputies. *INAH Photo
Archives, Casasola Archive no. 41855.*

President Obregón with U.S. and Mexican delegates before beginning
the Bucareli talks. *INAH Photo Archives, Casasola Archive no. 42787.*

Chaos and traffic in 1923 as a result of the work stoppage by bus and taxi drivers to protect low salaries and the rise in taxes. *INAH Photo Archives, Casasola Archive no. 43993.*

On November 7, 1924, anniversary of the victory of the October Revolution, Stanislav Pestkovsky presented his diplomatic credentials to President Obregón. In his speech, the Soviet diplomat extolled the similarity in the ideals of Mexico and the USSR. *INAH Photo Archives, Casasola Archive no. 41882.*

Thanks to working-class militancy in the streets, Pestkovsky felt he was among his own kind in Mexico. Photo shows striking trolleycar workers in 1925. *INAH Photo Archives, Casasola Archive no. 43992.*

Pestkovsky in the company of several friends and collaborators, among them Bertram and Ella Wolfe (to the right of Pestkovsky and below Wolfe, respectively), the American Communist couple who participated in the reorganization of the Mexican Communist Party between 1923 and 1925. *Hoover Institution Archives, Bertram D. Wolfe Collection.*

The headquarters of the Mexican Communist Party and its newspaper, *El Machete*, on Mesones Street. *Photo attributed to Tina Modotti.*

Rafael Carrillo was general secretary of the Mexican Community Party between 1924 and 1929. *Hoover Institution Archives, Bertram D. Wolfe Collection.*

Dressed in suit, the Russian painter and poet Vladimir Mayakovsky, who visited Mexico in July 1925. Among the Mexicans, Diego Rivera was his closest contact, and while in Mexico, he came to know Rivera's mural paintings best. *Hoover Institution Archives, Bertram D. Wolfe Collection.*

"Diego turned out to be a formidable man, with an enormous pot belly and wide face, always smiling"—from Mayakovsky's reminiscences of his trip to Mexico. *Hoover Institution Archives, Bertram D. Wolfe Collection.*

Left: Alexandra Kollontai tried to win Mexicans' friendship. As ambassador, she repeatedly invited President Calles for tea. With the same frequency, Calles declined the invitations. *National Archives, Enrique Díaz Fund.*

Below left: Kollontai's physical beauty was the special interest of her political adversaries. *Hoover Institution Archives, Bertram D. Wolfe Collection.*

Below right: Tina Modotti with Edward Weston in 1924, several years before Modotti joined the Mexican Communist Party. *Hoover Institution Archives, Bertram D. Wolfe Collection.*

A group of members of the International Red Aid. Tina Modotti was one of the organization's leaders. *INAH Photo Archives, Casasola Archive no. 46358.*

Mourners for Julio Antonio Mella, Cuban Communist and Tina Modotti's companion. Mella was assassinated in downtown Mexico City on January 10, 1929. The funeral procession attracted thousands. *INAH Photo Archives, Casasola Archive no. 46385.*

Women organizing to march in the 1929 May Day demonstration. *INAH Photo Archives, Casasola Archive no. 47264.*

Morrow and the Crisis in Government

Business leaders welcomed Obregón's reelection in 1928 because he had expressed approval for the recently enacted oil law. Obregón had also promised to renew foreign debt payments, resolve the church-state conflict, and "slowly, but effectively put a stop to all radical legislation and labor agitators."[34] However, on July 17 of that year he was assassinated.

One of Calles's first concerns regarding possible U.S. reactions was that the crisis provoked by Obregón's assassination not destroy the achievements reached in bilateral relations, jeopardize Mexico's political stability, or make it impossible for the government to meet its economic commitments. Morrow, on the other hand, feared that Mexico would overreact to the killing and was concerned that the assassins' guilt be well established so that the proof "satisfy not only the government, but the civilized world."[35] The ambassador believed he had invested considerable time and effort in improving Mexico's reputation, which an imprudent move against the suspected assassins could destroy. His fears were calmed when the suspected killers, José de León Toral and the nun Madre Conchita, both religious fanatics, were tried in accordance with all legal norms to establish their responsibility for the crime.

With Obregón's death, the problem of the presidential succession again surfaced. Calles and both military and civilian politicians were aware that the Obregonistas without Obregón and the peasant forces that had backed him would have to be compensated if peace were to be maintained. To bridge the political crisis, Calles named Emilio Portes Gil as interim president. For his cabinet, Portes Gil selected several men he could trust: Marte R. Gómez as agriculture minister and Ramón P. de Negri as industry, commerce, and labor minister, replacing Morones, who had become a thorn in Portes Gil's side. The two radical politicians—Luis L. León and Aurelio Manrique—were included in the cabinet for having been close collaborators of the fallen caudillo.[36]

The selection of prominent followers of Obregón reflected the need to avoid ruffling the Obregonistas' feathers. However, military intelligence at the U.S. embassy interpreted this entire turn of events as a return of the old radicals to power. Intelligence agent Harold Thompson reminded his superiors that León had been to Soviet Russia in 1921 to study that country, and Manrique, an unkempt "rabid socialist and fanatical agrarian," resembled "a theatrical Bolshevique [sic]."[37]

On the other hand, Morrow saw in Portes Gil's designation Calles's need not to lose his successor's loyalty. The ambassador met with the new president and concluded that because Calles refused to remain in office, given the difficult circumstances, Portes Gil was the best choice. When the ambassador attended his swearing in ceremony, during which the Tamaulipas politician assured the United States that the doors of Mexico would remain open to U.S. investment, he liked the new president's speech, but was not so certain about the other officials in the incoming cabinet. He had no doubts about de Negri's honesty but had his concerns about the minister's subordinates, who it was rumored had been trafficking rights for the oil companies with promises of confirmation.[38]

The U.S. ambassador closely observed Calles's wheeling and dealing in the creation of the Partido Nacional Revolucionario (PNR), which aimed to institutionalize the revolution through programs rather than individuals. Morrow hoped that a national reconciliation was underway and believed that the party could be a shelter for pluralism—for radical as well as conservative positions. He wanted to believe that the new party would allow all social classes to participate in the government, including those who had risen up against it, arms in hand.[39] Thus, when other officials at the embassy again insisted that Mexico was not very different from Russia, Morrow remained firmly convinced that "Russian traits of Asiatic barbarism" were alien to the Mexicans, who aspired to a British- or American-type democracy.[40]

However, a few weeks after Portes Gil took office in 1929, the U.S. press and the embassy began to cry wolf. Almost overnight, Portes Gil had armed the peasants and renewed land distribution. The *Washington Post* echoed the criticisms against the president, which multiplied as he accused the bourgeoisie of provoking restlessness in the country and threatened to expropriate the rural landowners for creating unrest in the countryside. An editorial writer for the *Washington Post* reported, "The language employed by President Portes Gil is so strikingly similar to that employed by the communist rulers of Russia that the world is warranted in assuming that there has been no change in the Calles-Morrones [*sic*] policy of seizing and turning over the property of foreigners to the peons and workers."[41]

Portes Gil ignored Morrow's suggestions to moderate the pace of land distribution and adjust its rhythm to the government's ability to pay cash compensation to expropriated landowners. He disagreed with this condition and modified the budget outlays for indemnizations, which the finance minister in Calles's administration had included on Morrow's suggestion. In 1929, more than 1,000,000 hectares of land were distributed to 140,000 peasant families, compared to 640,000 hectares divided up in 1928—more land than had been distributed in any one year since the revolution. In addition, Portes Gil announced that he would ignore any Supreme Court decision that favored the landowners in any case of peasants needing land. To explain his policy of arming the peasants, he argued that it was to allow them to safeguard their plot of land, which was their only hope in life. He explained further that in defending their own interests, the peasants were also defending the government that protected them.[42]

Morrow was aware that the Mexican government was not unanimous regarding the agrarian question. Calles, the *jefe máximo* (the supreme leader) of the revolution, insisted that the pace of land distribution depended on the government's ability to pay indemnizations. The president of the Supreme Court, Fernando de la Fuente, did not hide his frustration when Portes Gil ordered him to issue land deeds to the *ejido* (land that the state leased to landless peasants) farmers. The jurist feared that this order would discourage foreign capital inflows. On the other hand, Agricultural Minister Marte R. Gómez disagreed that social reforms should be subordinated to loan prospects.[43]

Fruitlessly, Morrow himself sought a way to moderate the pace of the agrarian reform without at the same time being accused of interfering in Mexico's internal affairs. He was distressed that the Supreme Court rejected injunctions sought by Americans whose properties were affected by the renewed surge in agrarian reform measures. When the Americans exhausted all available legal avenues, they again turned to the U.S. embassy, appealing for it to intervene on their behalf and in the process creating the same diplomatic frictions that existed prior to Morrow's arrival in Mexico. In addition—as argued by the study commissioned by the International Committee of Bankers to which Morrow had access—the agrarian reform was the Achilles' heel of the Mexican government's financial performance because it was the cause of the budgetary imbalance and of the country's inability to pay its foreign debt. Convinced he was correct, Morrow sent his aides to meet with Mexican officials and tried to speak directly with the president, as well as with both the agriculture minister and the industry, commerce, and labor minister. However, the armed rebellion that suddenly erupted in March 1929 was to shift his attention from daily political questions to military affairs.[44]

The rebellion, led by Obregonista general José Gonzalo Escobar, broke
out on March 3, 1929 (a day before Herbert Hoover's inauguration). Within
the government, the uprising silenced internal discord concerning agrarian
reform. The Obregonista generals were rebelling against President Calles's
imposition of his successor: Portes Gil was not one of their own. Escobar
tried to influence Hoover by waving the anti-Communist banner: he accused Calles of having assassinated Obregón and applying "a grotesque
Bolshevism" against foreigners. The rebel general even slandered Morrow
as an unworthy ambassador "of the great country that he represents."[45]

President Hoover was kept well informed of the situation in Mexico and
declared that legally the rebels were "ordinary outlaws and bandits." He
helped the Mexican government defeat the rebels by shipping arms and by
preventing the insurgents from obtaining provisions on the other side of the
border. For his part, Morrow sent Colonel McNab to Texas with several
Mexican officials to arrange shipments of important quantities of arms for
the army.[46] The rebels were defeated in less than three months.

The Aftermath of the Crisis

Former ambassador Sheffield wrote an acquaintance—who, in turn, con-
tacted the secretary of state—that it had been a mistake to have assisted
Mexico during its recent mess. By coming to its rescue, the United States
indirectly let the Mexican government know that Washington would not
oppose its policies, even if they hurt U.S. interests. For Sheffield, there was
no difference whatsoever between the defeated Escobar, Carranza, Obregón, and the victorious Calles. He reiterated what he had said many times:
he was confident that the day would come when "the better elements"
would rebel and overthrow those in power.[47]

Following the Escobar rebellion, the U.S. consuls believed that the political situation was worsening in Mexico. From Durango, a diplomat reported
that the peasants, led by "red insurgents," had refused to surrender the arms
that the government had provided to fight the military rebels. Another
consul, reporting from Tampico, described a May Day demonstration, during which the workers insulted the government as their "worst enemy"
because it had fulfilled only half of what it had promised them. He added
that the governor was incapable of controlling the state of Tamaulipas,
where peasant activists supposedly "no longer needed the government to
take land."[48] On the other hand, the Division of Eastern European Affairs of
the U.S. State Department reported to the Justice Department that a new

labor-peasant union had been formed in Mexico. According to Division Chief Kelley, everything indicated that a new revolutionary center had been established in Mexico.[49]

Morrow, meanwhile, relayed an appreciation of the situation radically different from what the consuls were reporting to the State Department. The Mexicans with whom the ambassador had spoken conveyed to him their fear that if the government fell, another revolution could erupt. Moreover, in their opinion, the United States would gain less by selling destructive arms to Mexico than by making good business in a country at peace.[50] After the Escobaristas were defeated, Morrow was a witness to the continuance of the political renewal interrupted by the Obregón assassination and the military insurrection.

In 1929, Pascual Ortiz Rubio was the PNR presidential candidate, basically because he did not represent any of the important political factions. Absent from the country during most of the decade, the candidate had few enemies, it was said, and his discreet ties made him an ideal conciliator between the different conflicting groups. Ortiz Rubio's election also corresponded to the need to avoid feeding accusations that Calles had imposed the candidate or that he wanted to remain in power. Appearances aside, the selection of Ortiz Rubio allowed the jefe máximo to put the agrarian reform on a more conservative course. By then, Calles had concluded that Mexico would not be able to develop on its own. Agricultural productivity had to grow in order to pay for imports of manufactured goods from the United States and to gradually prepare the country for industrialization.[51] To attract foreign investors, Mexico had to do its part to guarantee that the good neighbor policy was successful.

When Arthur Bliss Lane arrived in Mexico in September 1930 as the new U.S. embassy press secretary, the Mexican foreign minister explained that the government had to decide between two broad projects. One, pursued by Portes Gil, was scandalously radical and was ruining the country; the other was the course chosen by the government, based on law and order. A military intelligence agent agreed that the revolutionary experiment came to an end once Luis León and Marte R. Gómez were removed from the government, and the agrarian and labor laws were expected to follow the same conservative course. Even in its foreign relations, Mexico was changing direction. When in January 1930 the headlines in the Mexican press announced that relations had been broken with the Soviet Union, the U.S. newspapers and the diplomatic corps received the news with satisfaction.[52]

The Balance Sheet on Morrow's Diplomacy

Morrow resigned his post in Mexico in September 1930, leaving behind mixed feelings on the work he had done as ambassador. Shortly before leaving, he commissioned Diego Rivera to paint a mural in the Palace of Cortés in Cuernavaca. The painting was to be a farewell gift to the authorities in the state of Morelos. As its theme, Rivera chose the history of Mexico from the Spanish conquest to the present. Graphically describing the cruelty that the conquerors and the clergy had inflicted on the Indians, the mural represented the conflict between Spanish colonialism and the resistance offered by the indigenous civilization. Genaro Estrada, the foreign minister, warned Morrow that Rivera's work might arouse resentment against him. In fact, when completed, the mural did spark certain public indignation: the left denounced Rivera for having collaborated with a capitalist ambassador; the right criticized Morrow for having supported a mural that criticized the church and the Spanish government.[53]

In drawing a balance sheet, some Americans felt that Morrow had served Mexico better than the United States. After Morrow left Mexico, the giant oil companies and their political backers again centered their hopes on the marines overthrowing the Mexican government. On the other hand, banks, small businesses, small oil companies, and the AFL continued to insist that more could be won with a carrot than a stick. Businessmen were more concerned with profits, stability, and the safety of their investments than with ideology. These goals motivated the business community to make an effort to adapt to the demands of Mexican nationalism. Not less important in their thinking was the conviction that only through prosperity could Bolshevism be kept at bay in the Western Hemisphere.

Most Mexican government officials were pleased with the style and results of Morrow's diplomacy. During his tenure, business between the United States and Mexico expanded severalfold more than what it had been before the ambassador's arrival. Corporations such as Ford, J. G. White, and International Telephone and Telegraph (ITT) had set up shop before Morrow's arrival, but with the ambassador's assistance, many others learned to conduct business in Mexico and respect the country's laws. For example, in 1929 the world's largest private bank, National City Bank of New York, opened a branch office in Mexico, its one hundredth office abroad. The United Fruit Company began to invest in Veracruz and Oaxaca, and Mexico became an attractive market for the aviation industry and Electric Bond &

Share Company. By 1930, it was home to the largest number of subsidiaries of U.S. manufacturers in all of Latin America.[54]

But Morrow was also accused of having applied excessive pressure on Mexico to undermine the revolution's program. For example, Eyler N. Simpson, a specialist on ejido farmland in the 1930s, argued that "It may well be that the revolutionary movement has already run its course. On the other hand, it may be that the kindly, sympathetic, well-intentioned, subtly flattering former Morgan partner, by trying to help Mexico to put her house in order and to settle everything up in ship-shape, business-like fashion, succeeded in putting the brakes on the only real reform movement in the history of the country."[55] Was Morrow able to put the breaks on the revolution's momentum? Was the *Nation's* assertion correct—that Mexico had conceded exactly what the United States wanted? What should one make of the article in the *New Republic* that charged Mexico with betraying its social programs?[56]

Somewhat related to all this controversy, an interesting incident occurred at the end of 1930. At the request of the U.S. Congress, the Mexican government agreed to collaborate with a special committee formed to investigate Communist activities in the United States, as well as in Mexico. The committee was headed by Congressman Hamilton Fish from New York, who had made a political career of witch-hunting persons with leftist reputations, even though the political climate in the United States had changed since the time of the red scare in the aftermath of World War I. Fish sent Ulysses Grant-Smith to Mexico to consult with officials and "exchange information regarding Communist activities."[57]

Minister Estrada promised to cooperate with the committee on the condition that the investigation be informal and be conducted among officials and police agents without becoming an official government activity. Grant-Smith could meet with Mijares Palencia, head of the Mexico City police, but with no one else. However, the collaboration between the two governments leaked out and the *Washington Post* published an optimistic article on the assistance President Ortiz Rubio was willing to provide to the U.S. police. Irritated, the Mexican government withdrew from the deal.[58]

However, some information was exchanged before the collaboration ended. The U.S. congressional committee suspected one Lulinsky, an employee of the Amtorg Trading Corporation in the United States. This Soviet-American company, in charge of importing and exporting raw materials and manufactured goods between the United States and the USSR, was also known as a cover for espionage activities. The Mexican police already had a file on Lulinsky, and Ambassador Téllez handed it over to the State Department but at the same time requested that no further emissaries from the committee be sent to Mexico because such visits would be badly viewed.[59] In February 1931 the intelligence division of Mexico's Interior Ministry officially communicated to the U.S. congressional committee that it had concluded its own investigation and lacked further evidence concerning individuals accused of being Communists.[60]

It is true, of course, that by the end of the decade the Mexican government seemed resigned to accepting the country's geopolitical reality, but it rejected Americans' intolerance and contempt. Since the end of the nineteenth century the political elite had sought to put relations with the United States—characterized by material inequality and cultural differences—on a level of respect and, where possible, of mutual benefit. In the 1920s, Mexico continued to be a poor country, but it now had a state apparatus strengthened by resistance to seven years of war, the military uprisings of 1923–1924 and then of 1929, and a latent conflict aborted before it erupted into a full-blown dangerous crisis in 1927.

Although Morrow could settle political differences between the United States and Mexico thanks to his diplomatic savoir faire and the change in State Department policy, his efforts were also made possible because the Mexican government had been intimidated by the ten previous years of animosity and belligerence. The success of the Americans was also due to the Mexican government's fear that if it continued to resist the pressures, the government could lose the reins of power to the mercenaries of the United States, given Mexico's political instability and increasing economic weakness. It is against this background that Mexico welcomed Dwight Morrow's good neighbor representation of U.S. government and business interests, notwithstanding his meddling in the country's internal affairs.

Chapter 8

THE IDEOLOGICAL
EXCESSES OF
THE COMINTERN

One of the Bolshevik government and party's main objectives was to industrialize Russia, convinced as they were that socialism could not be built without transforming Soviet society into a modern industrial nation. Lenin's original plan to introduce electric power to the entire country and to develop metallurgy, metalwork, the tool and dye industry continued its course, albeit slowly throughout the 1920s, and filled the Soviet leaders with confidence that it was possible to achieve economic development based on their own resources and through society's own efforts. In fact, the phrase "socialism in one country" expresses this strategy in a nutshell. It also meant that Russia did not need the European revolution as a jumping off point to be able to carry out its own proletarian revolution, nor did it need the goodwill of foreigners to be able to construct Soviet power.[1]

The most dynamic industrial spurt began with the First Five-Year Plan (1928–1932) and was accompanied by forced collectivization of agriculture. The strategy for socioeconomic development—based on national self-sufficiency if necessary—sought to overcome Russia's backwardness and overtake economic levels achieved by the capitalist countries. Both processes were carried out as if the country were in a state of war because of the setbacks in foreign policy experienced in 1926 and 1927. The break in diplomatic relations with Great Britain, the massacre of the Chinese Communists by the Kuomintang, and the assassination of the Soviet ambassador in Poland shook the leaders' confidence in international cooperation and convinced them that the West was preparing for war to wipe out the Bolshevik government. Some feared that the loss of authority abroad could provoke domestic disturbances. As a consequence of this concern, the Soviet government's defensive capacity was strengthened by bolstering the armed forces.[2] Added to this, the party began to attack the private sector created by the New Economic Policy (NEP), the middle class, well-off peasants, and the specialists who had come from the ranks of the bourgeoisie. The NEP was liquidated by 1929, when any possibility for the survival of independent producers, traders, and artisans was canceled.[3]

According to Stalin's premise that the Soviet Union was in a transitional stage from a bourgeois to proletarian state, in 1928 the Comintern adopted the so-called "third period" thesis. Although in economic terms the notion signified that capitalist stabilization had ended and the system was about to collapse, on a political level it meant that the Soviet government anticipated a renewed revolutionary wave equal to, it was thought, what had been expected after the First World War. All forms of workers' struggles should assume the character of an attack on the existing system and should oppose any form of collaboration with the organs propping up capitalist rule. An increasingly intense struggle was required against the social democracy. Coalitions with democratic parties and reformist trade unions ceased to be acceptable. To the degree that the building of socialism in a single country progressed, the "motherland of the international proletariat" —that is, the USSR—would be strengthened. In view of the favorable perspectives for socialism and the death sentence passed on capitalism, the Communist parties of the entire world should join forces to protect the Soviet Union from its enemies. The leaders of the Comintern sharpened their fighting tactics with the slogans "class against class," "united front from below," and "social fascism,"[4] and they exhorted the Communist parties to apply the slogans in their respective countries. Based on their obsessive fear of an imminent war in Europe, the Soviets also changed their foreign policy.

Alexandr Makar's Embassy

After Alexandra Kollontai left Mexico in June 1927, the Soviet embassy remained vacant, and the new Russian ambassador would not arrive and occupy the offices on Eliseo Street until March 1928. With a doctorate in sciences and medicine, Alexandr Makar had matured politically under the Czarist regime, and his temperament was forged during the revolution. With several arrests and escapes from Czarist prisons under his belt, he, along with Lenin, returned to Russia from exile in April 1917. Since 1923 he had been in the Soviet foreign service, first in Italy and then in Norway. The British ambassador to Oslo described him as "a short, fattish fellow, with a slimy green complexion and pronounced features," and referred to him as an ingrate.[5]

Makar hosted Carleton Beals several times at the embassy. The writer observed the zeal with which the ambassador and his wife, "a fine, large, placid woman," entertained their guests.[6] Makar continued with his predecessor's custom of serving tea and showing Soviet films. For the tenth anniversary of the revolution, Eisenstein produced the movie *October* (1927), the most propagandistic of his revolutionary trilogy. When Makar invited members of the diplomatic corps and Mexican officials to the screening, this time Minister Estrada accepted the invitation, but Calles, as on all previous occasions, declined.[7]

In Mexico, Makar adopted a discreet approach, by all accounts. The only rumor circulating at the time had it that he referred to his shoe-shine boy as "comrade" and his wife treated the laundry woman as her equal.[8] According to Beals, the embassy limited "all official contacts to government and upper-class circles," and avoided liaisons with "local radical labor elements." Makar "scarcely allowed Mexican Communists to step inside the embassy, or if he did so, very secretly."[9] This view coincided with the local British embassy's opinion. Even though the British had stopped attending social events at the Soviet embassy after Great Britain broke off diplomatic relations with the USSR, they continued to keep a close eye on what transpired there. On one occasion, the British ambassador informed the Home Office that Makar did not engage in any propaganda activities and that in the diplomatic milieu he had the reputation of being "a person of moderate opinions" who "does not exercise any undue influence over the Mexican government."[10] On the contrary, the British embassy referred to the strenuous Soviet efforts to promote trade between the two countries. The Soviet government purchased lead and henequen from Mexico and sold films, handicrafts, cereals, and lumber to Mexico.[11] Beals attributed Makar's cautiousness to his "great personal ambition" to ingratiate himself to Dwight Morrow and obtain the latter's support for U.S. diplomatic recognition of the Soviet Union. At the time, it was said that Morrow favored an end to Washington's policy of isolating the Soviet Union, and that after he served in Mexico, he wanted to go to Moscow to try to crack the other tough nut.[12] The Narkomindel hoped Morrow's appointment as U.S. ambassador to

Mexico would favor normalization of relations between the USSR and the United States. If Makar, who had experience in the Soviet foreign service and in party work, was named as ambassador, it was because the Narkomindel hoped that at his new post he would help prepare the groundwork for such an eventuality.[13]

On the surface, Makar strictly adhered to diplomatic protocol and tried to allay Mexican and foreign diplomats' fears that the USSR was committed to extending the flames of revolution worldwide. However, no matter how hard he tried, he could not avoid the reputation of his predecessors as radical. These fears intensified in 1928 when the Soviet government changed its foreign policy from allowing a "peaceful coexistence" to preparing to repel the capitalist attack it felt was on the verge of being launched against the USSR.

One of the consequences of Moscow's perception of an imminent attack to topple Soviet power was the intensification of its state of alert, including an expansion of its espionage services. Although there is no evidence to indicate that the Soviet embassy in Mexico served as an intelligence center before 1928, after Mexico broke off diplomatic relations with the USSR in 1930, a raid on the embassy revealed that several diplomats were spies and that Makar was part of an intelligence network in Mexico and in the northern border area. The raid gave the Mexican authorities clues as to which individuals had been participating in such activities. Unlike Makar, his family, and the embassy secretary, some individuals—those involved in espionage activities in Mexico after relations had been severed—wanted to remain in the country. One of them, Alexandr Lishagin, offered to become a police informant. According to Beals, Lishagin "bought the tolerance of the authorities to be able to reside in the country and in exchange offered himself to denounce all Russian communists whom he had known, a task he performed well."[14] In addition to giving information to the police, however, Lishagin was interrogated concerning his own past in Russia and his activities in Mexico. The other Soviet embassy official accused of espionage was Sergei Granovsky. To round out their information, the police interrogated each one concerning the other's activities. What Lishagin told the police about Granovsky and vice versa should be viewed with some skepticism because both wanted to exonerate themselves of any guilt and turn the tables on the other to avoid a jail sentence and deportation.

Interrogated by a secret agent from the Interior Ministry, Lishagin accused Granovsky of being "an agent and spy" for the Soviet government since 1922 and of being on embassy payroll when Makar was ambassador. Lishagin's testimony included information, for example, that Granovsky was in charge of distributing Soviet propaganda along the U.S.-Mexico border and collecting information about the Mexican police because he spoke Spanish well. He supposedly belonged to an espionage network whose ramifications Lishagin did not divulge. Lishagin concluded his declaration concerning Granovsky by saying that he had decided to testify because he wished "to be useful to the Mexican government."

In his own declaration, Granovsky said he had escaped Bolshevik persecution in the Ukraine in 1920 and arrived in Mexico in May 1922. He explained that Lishagin's negative testimony was an act of personal revenge because he owed Lishagin money. He also denied ever having distributed Communist propaganda in Mexico. In defending himself, he tried to paint Lishagin as having an equally colorful and compromising past and made him appear as a person who did not merit Mexican authorities' confidence. According to Granovsky, Lishagin was anti-Bolshevik and had been jailed and sentenced to death because of his counterrevolutionary activities. To save his skin, he had changed sides and become a Soviet spy, denouncing the government's enemies. In 1928, he was sent to Mexico to head up intelligence at the embassy.

According to Beals, the authorities obtained as much information from Lishagin as they needed, then had him arrested. Once in jail, he stopped talking. It is not known what became of him. Granovsky, on the other hand, was reportedly expelled from Mexico.[15]

From everything that can be thus far determined, the Mexican Communist Party was not aware of the Soviet government's clandestine activities in the country. Thus, the distance Makar maintained from the Communists was not due to any separation between the government's foreign policy and the activities of the Comintern, as diplomats in other foreign embassies in Mexico wrongly believed. Rather, he prudently maintained this distance from the Mexican left and a closeness with the bourgeoisie and the official circles in Mexico as the best cover so that he would not be suspected of being involved in illegal activities.

The Comintern "Discovers America"

Given that the Bolsheviks expected an imminent attack on the Soviet Union, Stalin delineated a policy that was laid down to the Communist parties during the Sixth Congress of the Comintern in the summer of 1928.

This new line required the parties to fight both fascism and social democracy, viewed as the main enemies of the international Communist movement. The policy also involved strengthening the revolutionary movements in regions in which the Comintern expected imperialism to suffer setbacks due to the anticipated debacle facing the capitalist system.

The Comintern conceived the slogan "class against class" as a reflection of a heightened class polarization that subsumed all other social questions and that inevitably would lead to a struggle for power. The tactic of the "united front from below" was designed as a response to sentiments for unity among Communist and socialist workers, which would at the same time exclude the socialist leadership from any coalition efforts. Lozovsky, the Profintern leader, sustained that the reformist unions were allies of the bourgeois state, however, and that their leadership would be toppled only when the state itself was overthrown.[16]

The other line that the Comintern forced the Communist parties to adopt was the struggle against "social fascism." The Comintern argued that the social democracy, like fascism, was a pillar of the capitalist system and that both served the cause of counterrevolution. Therefore, the bourgeoisie, together with imperialism, should be resisted by worker-peasant blocks in a class war fought on a global, not strictly national, scale. The imminent collapse of the world capitalist system would provoke civil wars in which the Communist parties would be placed in positions that would enable them to seize state power.[17]

These theories, ideas, and exhortations were presented to Communist delegates when they arrived in Moscow in 1928 to participate in the Profintern and Comintern congresses. This time, the Soviet leaders paid more attention to the Latin American delegates than they had at any previous congress because both Lozovsky, as well as Dmitry Manuilsky—who would soon replace Nikolai Bukharin at the head of the Comintern—had just "discovered America."

The burgeoning importance of Latin America for the Soviet Union's global strategy was the result of the realization that the United States had become a world economic center and that the "dollar republic" was now the world's "exploiter."[18] On numerous occasions, both the prominent economist Eugen Varga as well as party theoretician NiKolai Bukharin underlined the importance of the U.S. economy as an example of capitalist stabilization. Bukharin postulated the idea that the revolutionary wave would emerge not from capitalism's decline, but from its advance. However, by the end of the decade, a prosperous and expanding U.S. capitalism clashed with the Marxist theorem of capitalism's failure, called "rotten stabilization" by party general secretary Stalin. The Man of Steel himself challenged Bukharin's position and predicted the end of capitalist stabilization with the system's collapse and subsequent revolutionary insurrections.[19] Varga, the main advisor to the Comintern on economic questions, had to write the official position (Stalin's), which was presented to the Sixth Congress as a directive and which demonstrated that the end of capitalist stabilization was a consequence of high productive levels and the replacement of workers by the technological revolution. In other words, "capitalism never was and never could be stable."[20]

At a special conference with the delegates from Latin America, Lozovsky presented a diagnosis of Anglo-American imperialism and warned that it was preparing an attack on the USSR. Based on the prognosis that the capitalist system was reaching its end, the Comintern assigned concrete tasks for the Latin American Communists to carry out on their return from Moscow: form worker-peasant blocs to fight the bourgeoisie and imperialism, and at the same time defend the Soviet Union.[21]

To be sure that the Latin American Communist parties would strictly toe the Comintern's line, as well as to improve communications between the central leadership and the national sections, the Comintern launched for the first time ever, as of September 1928, a Spanish-language magazine directed to the workers and peasants of the New World, *El Trabajador Latinoamericano*. To oversee the Latin American regional movement, the Comintern organized a conference of the workers movement in Montevideo, Uruguay, in May 1929, from which the Latin American Trade Union Confederation emerged. In June the Communists met in Buenos Aires, Argentina, to cement the Latin American movement, at all times under the watchful eye of the Comintern.

The Comintern and the MCP

Neither in 1928 nor before had the Comintern ideologues who belonged to the Communist International's secretariat been of one mind in terms of how to appreciate world developments and what political line to follow. Although Stalin increasingly had the final word, in 1928 the Comintern was still far from monolithic. The deliberations of the secretariat illustrated how divided its members' opinions were. These divisions reflected the factionalism inside the Comintern, as well as the fragmentation of the national Communist movements. In reality, each party had its allies and adversaries within the Comintern. The Mexican Communist Party (MCP) was no exception.

Among the MCP's allies in Moscow were some high-ranking officials— Alfred Stirner, Sen Katayama, and former ambassador Stanislav Pestkovsky.[22] The three understood better than any other ideologue in the leadership of the Bolshevik Party and the Comintern the reality of the Mexican situation and the difficulties involved in building a Communist party and a workers movement independent of the state in a country that, for better or for worse, had had its own revolution. Stirner and Katayama belonged to the Executive Committee of the Comintern, whereas Pestkovsky worked in the Peasant's International. From their high positions the three could influence the Comintern's policies as well as defend Mexican comrades' positions and, especially, the reputation of one or another Communist leader. This necessity arose each time the results of the work done by the Mexican Communist leaders were not in tune with the expectations of Moscow, or when the factional struggle within the party became a knockdown-drag-out affair that periodically came to the attention of the leaders of the Third International.

Because Comintern ideologues dealt with Mexico according to the theory that dominated Bolshevik thinking at the time, those with knowledge of the country did not take pains to adjust reality to fit the prevailing dogma, but at the same time avoided being tagged as heretics. This very problem occurred, in fact, in Moscow in the discussion in the first months of 1928 on whether the MCP should support Obregón's candidacy. The question that arose was how to present the party line to the masses so that they would not only follow it, but also understand that it was a tactical move, not a betrayal vis-à-vis the state, and that Obregón was not one of their own. Opposition to Obregón's candidacy, Katayama argued in an oversimplified manner, could be interpreted as support for U.S. capitalism, inasmuch as the Sonoran politician was seen as its enemy. In addition, the majority of Mexicans would vote for Obregón. If the MCP did not support him, it would isolate itself and expose itself to repression. Voting for Obregón, then, would mean uniting with the masses.

Pestkovsky, alias Banderas, also felt that Obregón was the best option for the Mexican revolutionary movement because not casting a ballot for Obregón was in essence ceding a vote to the landowners or imperialism. After all, Obregón had backed Calles's changes to the agrarian and oil legislation.

Meanwhile, Stirner defended MCP support for Obregón not because the party had the "erroneous, opportunist and dangerous" illusion that he would defend the interests of the working class, but because he was anti-imperialist and pro-peasant. This last argument weighed in the party's political orientation because the organization enjoyed considerable influence in the National Agrarian League that it did not want to lose, although it would have to share this influence with reformist leaders such as Adalberto Tejeda.[23]

Among the "Mexicanists" in the Executive Committee of the Comintern, Victorio Codovilla, the Argentine Communist leader, was against such a line and opposed any compromise with the reformists, be it in the unions or government. Codovilla's position flowed not only from ideological orthodoxy, but also from a desire for the Comintern to center its activities and resources in the Southern Cone, instead of in Mexico. The Argentine Communist's opinion had a certain weight in the Comintern and made top leaders Otto Kuusinen and Bukharin waver in approving the MCP position as recommended by Katayama, Pestkovsky, and Stirner. Codovilla argued that Mexican Communists should not support Obregón solely on the basis of his commitment to agrarian reform and the peasant movement; he also criticized Stirner for idealizing the Mexican government's land distribution policies. Idealizing the policies was the equivalent of validating "opportunism": the government distributed the land, but the peasants had to abandon it because they lacked the means and resources for farming. The party should have its own political line and make it clear that it would support Obregón in exchange for political benefits for the working class. The road forward was to form a worker-peasant bloc as an electoral front in which the workers would lead the peasants toward an eventual overthrow of the bourgeois government and its replacement by a workers state.[24]

The Party Toes the Line

The Mexican delegates to the Sixth Congress of the Third International—held from July 17 to September 1, 1928—tried to defend the position put forward by Katayama, Pestkovsky, and Stirner in the highest leadership bodies of the Comintern. So as not to deviate from the official Comintern line, they affirmed that the renewed U.S. imperialist penetration in Latin America had created a revolutionary situation. However, with the Obregón candidacy a new conjunctural situation had emerged. Charles Phillips, alias Ramírez, who had presented himself as the intermediary between the MCP and the Communist Party of the United States at the beginning of the 1920s, spoke in the name of the Mexicans. He presented the Mexican Revolution as a chain of internal conflicts in which all sectors of society had participated and which had provided the working class with some reforms and a "nice" constitution, but which at the same time had strengthened the bourgeoisie. This class was adverse to reactionary dictatorships and so shared common ground with the workers. The workers movement, divided along the same territorial lines as the country, lacked the capacity to launch an independent struggle for power, unless the struggle were to be organized on a national level. Given the country's panorama, and in view of the fact that reaction and the clergy were seeking to overthrow the petty bourgeois government, the Communist Party not only had to support the government[25] but had to continue its policy of drawing forces away from the state unions and winning them to Communist organizations.

This position was different from that of the Comintern, which at the time considered the reformist unions as "schools of capitalism" and "extension[s] of the apparatus of the bourgeois state within the working class." It also considered the reformist governments as close to, if not the same as, fascist regimes.[26] The Comintern expected all the national sections to strictly adhere to its line.

Initially, Rafael Carrillo the MCP general secretary, was in disagreement with the Comintern's line and defended the party's work in the reformist trade unions—work that was aimed at influencing their membership from within and attracting them to Communism. Bertram Wolfe, who in Moscow also spoke for Mexico, was in agreement with the Comintern that the Latin American proletariat was weak. But by forming a bloc with the peasantry, the working class component would wind up not being strengthened, but "peasantized" because the peasants would have a majority and would dominate the front.[27]

After the Sixth Comintern Congress, the MCP would adhere to the political line with some vacillations. But while the MCP delegation was still in Moscow, its candidate was assassinated in Mexico, and the Communists' principal rival in the labor movement, the CROM, was losing the government's sympathy as Morones's power slipped. The party, or a faction of it supervised by Orestes, the pseudonym of the Profintern representative, took advantage of the opportunity to create a Communist-led labor confederation with the Mexico City unions leaving the CROM, with independent unions, and with organizations under Communist influence. From these currents, in January 1929 the Confederación Sindical Unitaria de México (United Trade Union Confederation of Mexico [CSUM]) was founded, with David Alfaro Siqueiros, the avant-garde muralist, as its leader. Among the new confederation's demands were defense of labor against imperialism, but also "the open struggle against national governments that exploit and oppress the workers of Latin America."[28]

The other faction in the party, with General Secretary Rafael Carrillo at its head, opposed the creation of the CSUM and was thus bitterly criticized by the Comintern representative and accused of sabotaging the party's line and being on the side of the petty bourgeoisie.[29] This internal division in the party—sparked by the adoption of the Comintern's antigovernment position and by the support offered to a government split as a result of the assassination—coincided with the insurrection headed by General José Gonzalo Escobar.

Together with the CSUM, the party and the powerful National Agrarian League formed the worker-peasant bloc as an electoral front, which months later was to run its own presidential candidate.[30] The Comintern organ *Inprecorr* reported that the bloc had grown organically out of the new revolutionary situation unfolding in Mexico, in which the peasants no longer obeyed their petty bourgeois leaders and were joining the unions under communist leadership.[31] This assertion was nothing but propaganda because the same peasants who had joined the Communist-led bloc now enlisted in the government's armed forces to fight the "reactionary" military insurrection. As a result, the peasants' participation on the side of the government deepened the division between the Communists.

According to the Comintern, the participation of the peasants on the government's side against the military insurgents was an error due to the domination of the Mexican Communist Party by its "right wing"—that is, the leadership headed by Rafael Carrillo. In a manifesto sent to the party after the rebellion, the Comintern equated support of the government by the worker-peasant bloc with support of imperialism.[32] In the final analysis, according to the dogmatic position of the Third International's officials, the military rebellion was financed by British capitalists to overthrow the Mexican government, which they considered a puppet of their rival, the United States.

Most likely the orders to the MCP to cease its support for the government came from the Comintern. According to Siqueiros, the party sent peasant leader José Guadalupe Rodríguez, member of the MCP Central Committee and the National Agrarian League, to the northern state Durango "with orders to organize the peasants and provide arms and horses" to fight the federal army. In the heat of the events and believing that the hour for a general insurrection had arrived, Rodriguez played a major role; "his activity was extraordinary, but somewhat ostentatious, even branding the horses with the hammer and sickle." After he was taken prisoner by the government, Siqueiros, on his own initiative, cabled the other leaders in Durango "not to surrender the arms and if they try to disarm you, resist and take to the mountains."[33] The peasant troops, armed with what the government had provided for its defense, obeyed these instructions and demanded that the federal government be purged and that "the enemies of the working class" be replaced with candidates from the masses.[34]

José Guadalupe Rodríguez and another peasant leader, Salvador Gómez, were executed on May 14, 1929. The commander of military operations in Durango, Manuel Medinaveitia, informed President Portes Gil that Calles, minister of war, had authorized the executions because it had been proven that the two leaders were involved in acts of "subversion and agitation" against established institutions and had encouraged other peasant leaders to follow them.[35] It was true that the party had exhorted Ursulo Galván, the peasant leader from Veracruz, and his followers to respond to the Communist call to overthrow the government, but Galván refused and publicly broke with the party. The Veracruz peasants also refused to renounce their alliance with the government when Moscow condemned it. Later that same year, Galván even tried to ban circulation of *El Machete* and sabotaged the Communist presidential election campaign in Veracruz, a state that the Communists considered a party bastion.[36]

In mid-1929 and during the following year, the government persecuted the Communist Party until it forced the organization underground. The question that still has never been satisfactorily answered is if, in reality, there was an MCP insurrectionary plan induced by directives from the Comintern, of which the government was aware and which motivated its reprisals, first against the party and later against the Soviet government. No evidence has been found in either Mexican or Soviet archives to confirm unequivocally the existence of such a plan. Orestes, Moscow's trade union representative in Mexico, was familiar with a circular that the Profintern had sent to CSUM branches concerning the military rebellion, but he never revealed its content.[37] It can be deduced from the testimony of Siqueiros and of two additional sources—one, Comintern activist Vittorio Vidali, and the other, repentant MCP member Bernardo Claraval—that instructions from the Comintern had been issued to turn the insurrection against the military rebels into a revolt against the government.

For Vidali, conspiracy and discretion were second nature, as they were for most Communist activists, which is why the Comintern envoy left only scraps of information from which to reconstruct the events surrounding the supposed Communist insurrection against the government in 1929. During the Escobar rebellion, Vidali went to Jalisco to "participate in the resistance against the generals' anti-government rebellion." But he himself admits that this was only one of two fronts. The other purpose of the Communists' struggle was to overthrow the government. According to Vidali, "we had the illusion we could seize power. And it was, on the contrary, a defeat that cost the life of my friend, José Guadalupe Rodríguez." Vidali did not indict any particular person for the failure of the Communist strategy, but pointed out that "insurrections cannot be decided sitting around a table. They'd either fall flat or lead to a massacre."[38] Was this perhaps an allusion to an insurrectional plan hatched by the Comintern in anticipation of a revolutionary wave on a world scale?

Another Communist militant who worked with Vidali left a somewhat different account of the climate in which the insurrectional plan was conceived. As opposed to Vidali, who affirmed that the Communists decided to fight on two fronts at the same time, Bernardo Claraval sustains in his book that fighting the rebel generals was only a tactical ploy aimed at turning the military rebellion into a civil war against the government. The call to arms came from the Comintern representatives—Vidali, Alfred Stirner, and the mysterious "Pedro," pseudonym of an emissary from Moscow.[39] From the three testimonials, it can be deduced that the party, probably under instructions from the Comintern, did give the order to turn the struggle against the rebel generals into an uprising against the government, with the same arms that Portes Gil had provided to the peasants to defend the government.

The government answered the Communists' aborted insurrection with a ferocious repression. In addition to executing the two peasant leaders in May, the police ransacked MCP headquarters from top to bottom in June 1929, carting away propaganda and the printing presses and locking up any Communists who did not speedily go into hiding. The government repression in Mexico provoked a reaction from the Executive Committee of the Comintern. In several special sessions, the Third International's standing commission concluded that in response to the repression, a protest campaign was necessary. A statement was prepared and sent to both the Comintern press and the Communist parties:

> The assassination of our two heroic comrades Rodríguez and Gómez, who fell under the fire of the executioner, and the most shameful and cynical terror launched against the Mexican workers and peasants, together with the dissolution of the Communist Party, the prohibition of the workers and peasants' revolutionary press, and the arrest of the best militants active in the consistent struggle against imperialism completely unmasked the self-styled 'revolutionary' government of Portes Gil, Calles & Company, showing the whole world that the Mexican government has become an openly fascist government and an agent of North American imperialism.[40]

The Comintern then issued a call to the Mexican workers: "Do not hand over your arms to the exploiters who will use them to crush you!" The declaration also urged the workers in the rest of Latin America to "vigorously protest against the threat from the fascist government of Mexico that, if not stopped, will affect the entire Communist and anti-imperialist movement of the workers and peasants of Latin America."[41] The Communists responded to the Comintern's call to organize protest demonstrations in front of Mexican embassies, not only in Latin America, but also in main European and U.S. cities.

In January 1930 the Mexican government broke off diplomatic relations with the USSR, citing the Communist demonstrations organized from Moscow as its principal reason. The public never found out, however, that intelligence agencies in the United States, Europe, and Cuba used for their own ends the change in Soviet foreign policy and then the Mexican government's malaise over the Communist street demonstrations. One of their objectives was precisely to get Mexico to break with the USSR and draw closer to the United States as a geopolitical and historical inevitability.[42]

The Soviet Interpretation of the Break in Relations

When the Mexican government attributed the break in diplomatic relations to the Soviet Union's betrayal of its revolution, Moscow couched its interpretation in similar terms—that is, the Mexican government's betrayal of its own revolutionary process. And just as the Mexican government minimized the importance of relations with the USSR, the Soviets dismissed Mexico as an irrelevant partner in international affairs because it had become "a pawn" in Washington's hemispheric policy.

The Soviet account of the break between Mexico and the USSR coincided with the First Five-Year Plan. After the initiation of the process of accelerated industrialization and collectivization in agriculture, the dramatic achievements of the Soviet economy appeared to demonstrate the superiority of Marxism-Leninism over all other political theories.[43] This confidence added weight to the explanation offered by Soviet ideologues concerning Mexico's political transformation:

> In the international world, the Mexican Republic does not carry much weight, and if five years ago we openly greeted with establishment of relations with that country, the chief reason was that up till that time Mexico had been carrying on the fight against foreign imperialism against the oil kings of the U.S.A. and the internal landlords and feudal aristocracy.
>
> The present-day decision of the Mexican government interests us in another way, that is, in its relation to American politics. It is all very well for the American Minister of Foreign Affairs to state that the Americans did not give Mexico any advice, and was in fact ignorant of Mexico's intentions. The working masses of the [Soviet] Union know the value of such oaths.
>
> At the present moment it is beyond doubt that America is the guiding hand in Mexico. The part now played by American imperialism in the affairs of Mexico means the betrayal of the small bourgeois block in Mexico into the hands of the foreign capitalists, the landowners and the feudal aristocracy.[44]

According to the Soviets, the Americans demanded that Mexico break off relations with the USSR. The United States "was going through a serious economic crisis" and feared the revolutionary movement of the proletariat, who were indignant that the U.S. government had taken upon itself the role of world policeman and head of the united capitalist plan to attack the USSR. The Mexican government's charge that the Soviets had engaged in hostile propaganda against their country was nothing but a smoke screen erected to hide the true motivation behind the break in relations.[45]

At a press conference on February 1, 1930, the commissar for foreign affairs, Maxim Litvinov, feigned surprise at the Mexican government's decision. Pretending to be in the dark as to Mexico's reasons, Litvinov told the journalists that bilateral relations had been harmonious and that the Mexican ambassador left Moscow for personal, not political, reasons.[46] This claim was, of course, not true, because the Mexican embassy in Moscow on several occasions had protested the Comintern's disparaging campaign against Mexico. Litvinov told Esmond Ovey, the British ambassador who maintained a heightened interest in Mexico after having been posted there, that he did not regret the break in relations because "there were practically no Mexican-Soviet common interests. The Soviet diplomatic representation in Mexico had been a mere 'gesture.' "[47]

An analyst at the Commissariat of Foreign Relations interpreted the break in relations as the result of the growing influence of foreign capital in Mexican domestic politics. In *Mezdunarodnaia Zhizn'*, the commentator identified the first half of the 1920s—when the Mexican petty bourgeoisie in the government had struggled against "feudal-clerical reaction" and against the expansion of imperialist "appetites"—with the reestablishment of diplomatic relations between Mexico and the Soviet Union. But in this process, the analyst continued, the petty bourgeoisie had divided up land among itself and had become an intermediary between foreign companies and Mexican resources and labor. This transformation had diverted the government from the revolutionary course it had initially undertaken. At that point it declared an end to land distribution and allowed foreign companies to purchase land in states where the agrarian reform had advanced. Codifying government arbitration in labor disputes, the labor law (under discussion in 1929–30 and promulgated in 1931) was an imposition on the trade unions. The domination of capital was preventing the government from negotiating with the unions. The government made concessions to the church and the clergy by once again allowing religious services to be held. All in all, Mexico's anti-Soviet policy was subordinated to foreign influence and was consistent with the continued imperialist threat to the Soviet Union.[48]

The Comintern press took the same position, but expressed it in more aggressive terms: "Mexico became more openly a U.S. colony and the U.S. imperialists ordered the break."[49] Another article expressed the categorical opinion that the domination of U.S. capital had left the Mexican petty bourgeois government with two alternatives: "either to stand with determination on the side of the masses, or to sell out to imperialism and to proceed, together with the big landed proprietors and the Church, against the growing revolutionary mass movement in order to annihilate it." The petty bourgeoisie, fearing the masses, acted like it had in China and other colonial countries when it betrayed the fight for independence in order to serve its own class interests.[50]

By the end of the decade, and to the degree that the intellectual climate changed in the Soviet Union from a relative plurality of opinion to an unequivocal commitment to the officially sanctioned position, the Comintern showed little compassion for the Mexican Communist Party. In explaining the reasons for the party's failure to guide the masses toward the overthrow of the bourgeois regime, the Soviet ideologues resorted to the argument, common at the time, that reformist and anarchist influences prevailed in the popular movements, which the party and its "opportunist" leadership were unable to take on successfully. For lack of a "correct" revolutionary theory to guide the party, the movement fell into the hands of a "kulak organization"—that is, the National Agrarian League and its opportunist leadership personified by Ursulo Galván and Adalberto Tejeda.[51]

The Soviet interpretation of the break in relations and the reinterpretation of the history of the Mexican Revolution were not totally off the mark. It erred in attributing to the United States the order for Mexico to break relations with the USSR. But it was not far from the truth in viewing the need to attract foreign capital as the underlying factor in the closer relations between Mexico and the United States and the Mexican government's retreat from its social policies. Where the Soviet interpretation also went wrong, however, was in not seeing the negative economic and political consequences for Mexico when it tried to resist hegemonic attempts by the United States to dictate its decisions and programs. In addition, the Soviet ideologues never recognized their own contribution to the failure to foster an alliance acceptable to Mexico. By hurling a challenge at the Mexican government through the medium of the Communist Party, the Soviets themselves contributed to the creation of the conditions that motivated the Mexican government to break diplomatic relations with the USSR.

After the United States finally recognized the Soviet government in 1933, President Abelardo Rodríguez tried to reestablish diplomatic relations with the USSR. Litvinov then answered the Mexican initiative with a request that first the government should provide a satisfactory explanation of why it had broken off diplomatic relations with the USSR in 1930. The Mexican government responded that it had no explanations or apologies to offer because it had been branded with the insulting appellative *fascist*.[52] After 1933, when real fascism reared its dangerously racist and anti-Communist character, the Soviets abandoned their hostility and began to seek alliances with bourgeois governments. Once the popular front line of government coalitions between left and center parties was adopted in 1935, the Soviets no longer demanded any explanations from Mexico on why it had proceeded as it did in 1930.[53] With Lázaro Cárdenas in the presidency at that time, relations were about to be reestablished. After all, the Mexicans shared with the Soviets both sympathy and material aid for Republican Spain. However, diplomatic ties were not immediately reestablished because Cárdenas himself had chosen to grant political asylum to Leon Trotsky rather then seek relations with the USSR. Thus, it was not until 1943 that diplomatic relations with the USSR were renewed. Trotsky was assassinated in 1940, and by then the United States had become an indispensable ally of the Soviet Union, which had launched a crusade against Hitler and for its own survival. During the Second World War, Mexico, with its enormous natural resources, joined with the United States. Subsequently, there was no longer any obstacle to block the reestablishment of relations with the USSR.

Chapter 9

THE BREAK

IN RELATIONS

BETWEEN MEXICO

AND THE USSR

At the end of 1926, former president Alvaro Obregón reached the arrogant conclusion that his reelection in 1928 would be the best option for safeguarding Mexico's interests. Even though his decision violated one of the main tenets of the Mexican Revolution—"effective suffrage, no reelection" —the caudillo felt that he enjoyed enough support in the country to be able to get away with a constitutional amendment to allow a second term in office. At a banquet organized in his honor following his successful election campaign in July 1928, however, he was assassinated.[1]

The caudillo's death polarized the Mexican political elite. Some, such as Marte R. Gómez and Ramón P. de Negri, said in private that the removal of Obregón from the scene presented the ideal opportunity to recover the revolution from the decadence to which it had succumbed during the second half of the Calles presidency. Gómez lamented Obregón's death because only he had the moral stature, the experience in governing, and the vision to dominate the up-and-coming caudillos, the caudillejos.[2] Gómez and the other radical intellectuals close to Obregón believed themselves to be the inheritors of the mantle of the fallen caudillo, with the right to continue his social policies.

The generals who had fought with Obregón on the battlefield, and who later were to benefit from the cushy jobs and other perks the new government bestowed on them, felt themselves to be the caudillo's legitimate descendants. The CROM leadership had opposed Obregón's reelection, and when accused of plotting his assassination, they rapidly lost hopes of making it to power. The animosity toward Morones was so great that Calles, who had promoted the labor leader, did not oppose moves by loyal Obregón and Calles supporters to replace him as minister. Nor did Calles prevent the removal of another powerful CROM leader, Celestino Gasca, from his position as head of Mexico City government.[3]

It was a stroke of good luck that the U.S. ambassador, Dwight Morrow, was to be involved in resolving many of the Mexican government's numerous financial and political problems precisely at the moment when the foundations of the country's political system were shaken by Obregón's death. Morrow's goodwill mission had given the Mexican government the necessary breathing room in its relations with the United States and opened up the possibility of beginning to resolve the new political crisis without adverse U.S. interventions. Although it was true that national security was not threatened from the north thanks to the favorable disposition of the United States toward its neighbor in the south, Mexico had more adversaries than allies.

A Plot against Mexico: Gerardo Machado's Intrigue?

Fear that the virus of the Mexican Revolution would infect Latin America and the Caribbean had been prevalent since the beginning of the revolution. Encouraged by American and anti-Mexican propaganda, the governments of the Central American countries and Cuba viewed Mexico as a beachhead and breeding ground for Bolshevism in the Western Hemisphere. The Central American elites, entrenched in oligarchical regimes, feared an outbreak of peasant unrest. The rural landlords were not willing to share with the working classes the benefits of the relative prosperity of the agro-export economies. In their world view, *agrarianism*, the agrarian reform process as practiced in Mexico and protected by President Calles, was equivalent to Communism.[4]

At the end of 1927, for example, the Mexican ambassador in San Salvador sent the following telegram to the Foreign Relations Ministry in Mexico City:

> Panic is so intense and so firm is this government's belief that all Mexicans are Bolsheviki, that the Interior Ministry had come to inform me that the printed propaganda that is circulating arrives in the diplomatic pouches this legation receives. In reality, this allegation has its roots in the Yankee press and diplomatic campaign in Central

America against Bolshevik Mexico and since we do not have adequate means at our disposal, we cannot counteract it.[5]

The impact of the Mexican Revolution in the area was inevitable, especially after the revolutionaries had declared their victory over the old regime and the principles of the 1917 Constitution became the envy of the left and liberal forces in neighboring countries. As the local oligarchies and dictatorships suppressed the workers and peasants' demands, the number of popular movements and Communist parties grew, and they intensified their activities. In addition, in the mid-1920s the Comintern increased its flow of human and financial resources to Central American and Caribbean opposition groups to enable them to work within and orient the labor movement. Books by Bukharin and Lenin circulated in condensed and inexpensive Spanish-language editions. Political instructors arrived from Mexico, Venezuela, and Peru to assist workers in adapting the significance of Communist doctrine to Latin American reality.[6]

Like the Central American governments, the Cuban regime was nervous about Mexican "Bolshevism." President Gerardo Machado's concern grew after a group of Cuban Communists, persecuted by the government, found refuge in Mexico in 1926. Their leader was the legendary Julio Antonio Mella, whom Machado had jailed in 1925 but had to release due to the protests his imprisonment provoked both in Cuba and abroad. Mella made no secret of his hatred for "the tropical Mussolini" and from Mexico attacked Machado in *El Machete* and *El Libertador*, denouncing the social conditions that prevailed in Cuba and the dictatorship in power in Havana. Shortly after Mella arrived in Mexico, it became known that he and his followers were planning the overthrow of the Cuban regime.[7]

The first time Cuban authorities lodged a protest with the foreign relations minister, Aarón Sáenz, was in April 1926 concerning the refusal of the Mexican government to prevent the Cuban exiles in Mexico from publicly denigrating the Machado regime. In a veiled threat, the Cuban authorities insinuated that if the Mexican government did not put a halt to Mella's activities, they would take it upon themselves to do so. In response, the Mexican government tried to calm the Cubans, arguing that there was nothing to fear because Mella was unknown in Mexico. However, Havana continued its pressure on the government, which at each juncture tried to placate the Cubans' concerns.[8] But far from curtailing his campaign against the dictatorship, Mella intensified the barrage of propaganda against Machado. In 1927 he founded the Association of New Revolutionary Immigrants from Cuba and launched its press organ, *¡Cuba Libre!* [9]

The Cuban secret police trailed Mella's every move and kept Machado informed on his political activities, as well as on the content of the articles he wrote. The police must have known that in 1927 Mella attended the First World Anti-Imperialist Congress organized by the Comintern in Brussels and from there went on to Moscow.[10] Cuban intelligence knew that upon returning to Mexico, he would be preparing an expedition to Cuba to assassinate Machado. Although the full details are still not available, it is known that the expedition failed due to betrayal by one of its members.[11]

Having failed in his attempts to persuade Mexican authorities to expel Mella, Machado may also have tried to pressure the Mexicans to banish the Cuban student leader by fabricating a Communist plot that supposedly threatened the Mexican government itself. Following Obregón's assassination in the summer of 1928, the unsettled political climate was ripe for the circulation of documents that detailed an alleged Comintern master plan to assassinate President Calles, the war minister, and the head of the police, as well as to organize an uprising against the government. Although there is no conclusive proof, it is believed possible that the documents were part of a Machado stratagem to accomplish what he could not achieve by pressuring Mexican authorities.[12]

In July 1928 the foreign relations minister, Genaro Estrada, received from the Mexican consul in Antwerp, Belgium, a list of eighty names of supposed "agents of the Third International's overseas action and propaganda committee." According to the report, these agents were at that moment on their way "through various European ports to Mexico for the purpose of organizing communistic agitation in this country in view of the political conditions believed to exist in Mexico since the death of Obregón and for the further purpose of establishing a center of communistic propaganda and agitation in Mexico with particular reference to the United States and other countries of this continent."[13] The Mexican consul in Antwerp obtained the list from someone very "close to President Machado's general staff." Estrada turned the information over to Ambassador Morrow, who in turn sent it to the State Department. Estrada explained to Morrow that he was not concerned with the political strength of the Mexican Communists, but that Obregón's death could be used to spread even more confusion than already existed in Mexico. The government had reason to believe in such an eventuality, Estrada told Morrow, because it had uncovered evidence that Communist literature produced by the Comintern had been received in Mexican homes, "above all by people of the lower class."[14] After receiving the list, he warned all Mexican customs officials of the danger that undesirable Communists would be arriving through the country's ports. Morrow alerted the U.S. government in case suspicious individuals tried to cross the border into Mexico from the United States. Secretary of State Kellogg was pleased by the Mexican foreign minister's vigilant attitude and requested further information on persons, ships, and landing ports that could throw light on the subversive plan— information that Estrada provided in October.[15]

There is almost no doubt that all the documents Estrada received and shared with Morrow were forgeries. The list of activists was made up of a melange of eighty Jewish, Russian, Czech and Polish names in keeping with the commonly held (anti-Semitic) conception that most Bolsheviks were Jewish and Eastern European. The individuals on the list were described as possessing false passports and having pockets filled with counterfeit money. Thirteen of the activists on the list were supposedly members of the Central Committee of the Mexican Communist Party returning from the Comintern congress.

The content of the documents circulating in 1928 could not be anything but spurious. True, the Comintern congress had been held that summer, and the delegates in attendance there discussed how to apply methods of revolutionary struggle in Latin America to overthrow the bourgeois governments. But the Comintern plan described in one of the documents vastly exceeded the Third International's real goals. The individuals depicted in the list were portrayed as terrorists, and because the members of the MCP Central Committee supposedly traveled with this unsavory crew, they were also identified as bomb-throwers.[16]

The Mexican government accepted the documents as genuine but did not make them public. Nor did it prevent Mella and the Communists from conducting their propaganda activities. According to the government's perception, based on its own experience, the Communists were inoffensive, their criticisms against the government and imperialism limited to the strength of their pens or paint brushes and occasionally expressed through street demonstrations. When a critical juncture arose, such as the Delahuertista rebellion or the other political crises that shook Mexico during the 1920s, the Communists caved in on the government's side. For that reason, Calles ignored the Cuban demand that the government put an end to Communist propaganda against the Machado dictatorship.

Faced with his failure to achieve Mella's expulsion from Mexico, Machado plotted his opponent's assassination. On January 10, 1929, at nine o'clock in the evening, Mella was gunned down in downtown Mexico City. Gravely wounded, he nonetheless managed to accuse Machado of responsibility for his imminent death.[17] The following day, the Communists took to the streets and demanded an investigation into the crime. The police and the press tried to cover up the political motive behind the murder, labeling it in newspaper headlines as a "crime of passion." At his side at the time of the murder, Mella's companion, Tina Modotti, was accused of the crime and arrested. Police brutality against the demonstrators and the shabby treatment of Modotti in prison convinced provisional president Emilio Portes Gil to order the gendarmes to allow the street protests to take place and to ease the pressure on Modotti in jail.[18]

If the Mexican government did not respond to Machado's request to expel the Cuban oppositionist, it was because while he was alive, he posed no threat to Mexico's stability, even after the assassination of Obregón. But once Mella was killed and the Communists took to the streets demanding that those guilty be punished, the government reached the limits of its tolerance toward a vociferous opposition at the precise moment when the elites were committed to unifying the political forces fractured by Obregón's murder.[19] The government's awareness of its own fragility apparently prompted it to lend credence to the forged documents and later to incorporate them into its archive on enemy activities of the USSR in Mexico.

Calles Takes Care of Obregón's Orphans

The creation of a state ruling party, the Partido Nacional Revolucionario (National Revolutionary Party [PNR]) was Calles's principal instrument for unifying the political factions divided by the loss of Obregón. Conceived in the fall of 1928, the party was founded in March 1929.[20] Proclaimed the "national united front," the PNR in reality narrowed the political spectrum in existence before its creation. Obregón's balancing act and Calles's politics of conciliation now became obsolete as new rules of the political game were established. It was legitimate to undertake political activity within the party, but illicit to do so outside its structure. In addition, authority was transferred from the state and local governments and mass organizations to the new party. One year after the PNR was founded, the government introduced modifications in the way the Chamber of Deputies was elected. Instead of one congressional deputy per 70,000 inhabitants, henceforth it would be one per 150,000. Thus, the number of congressional deputies would be reduced from 270 to 150. In other words, the state was consolidated through the party, but at the cost of political participation. It appears that the party even assumed part of the presidency's prerogatives.[21]

In the fall of 1928, Calles, through Congress, appointed Portes Gil as interim president with the aim of reaching a compromise with the civilian wing of the Obregonista forces before general elections were called for 1929. However, the designation of Portes Gil was considered a rebuff to Obregón's military allies and to the more conservative Calles supporters. General Escobar, one of Obregón's orphans, called Portes Gil a passive instrument of Calles, whereas foreign minister, Estrada—a holdover from the Calles administration—feared his radicalism.[22]

In March 1929, a sector of the military launched an armed uprising against the government. Led by General Gonzalo Escobar, the rebels included almost thirty thousand well-equipped soldiers (twenty thousand less than had participated in the Delahuertista rebellion). Escobar, the supreme commander of the Ejército Renovador (Renovating Army), wanted to reestablish the principle of forbidding reelection and to revoke the laws regulating religious worship. He sent his negotiators to the United States to seek U.S. government recognition for their cause. However, the cooperation established and firmly cemented between Calles and Morrow two years previously turned out to be tremendously helpful to Portes Gil. The Mexican government could purchase airplanes, arms, and ammunition in the United States without any problem, and by May the rebels were defeated. Although crushing this military uprising was easier than dealing with the rebellion of 1923–1924, the government had to spend considerable funds to do so, and the cost to the country in civilian lives was high. Some railway lines and trains were destroyed in the conflict, and several banks were robbed.[23] The defeat of the pro-Obregón military forces allowed the civilian wing, legitimized by the victory, to surpass the moderate social program Obregón had projected.

As president, Portes Gil turned out to be much more than just a compromise with the Obregonistas. Although he was not as independent of Calles as he would have liked, he was also not Calles's puppet, which in fact was a widely held view of him at the time.[24] The new president had his own agenda. First and foremost, he wanted to break the alliance between the state and the CROM, to re-create the government-labor movement axis, and eliminate the CROM leaders' practice of creating enclaves of power within

the administration. In December 1928 Portes Gil told foreign correspondents that "the great majority of the workers of the Republic are not with
the CROM. These workers are convinced that the goals that motivate my
government benefit the proletarian classes without sowing hatred and discord among them."[25] He also let it be known that the new labor law would
be enacted without the CROM's interference. Only the federal government
could arbitrate labor disputes.[26]

Portes Gil gave a new lease on life to the agrarian reform, which sur-
passed Calles's expectations that this interim president would be merely a
"stand-in." Portes Gil declared, for example, that he would veto any Supreme Court decision concerning land grants that did not favor the peasants. He believed that justice for Mexico's rural population would be
achieved only through the peasants' recovery of their land. Marte R. Gómez
said in private that he would prefer to distribute land together with credits,
water, and seeds and provide the peasants with agricultural schools, but if
the government could not pay for the entire package, it would be enough to
give them land until more resources could be made available. The human
aspect of the agrarian reform was thus considered more important than
technical considerations.[27]

By 1929 this position was held by a minority within the political elite.
Many officials in Calles's cabinet argued that agrarian reform was holding
down the pace of economic recovery and development, and in fact was
ruining the country. The opinion that uncertainty regarding land ownership was discouraging landowners from investing and that once productive
haciendas were becoming unproductive in the hands of the peasants was
common among the governing elite. It was further claimed that agrarian
reform was deterring foreign capital investment in Mexico.

After the Escobar rebellion, the country was in dire straits. The government's coffers were empty; capital was needed as never before. The magic
incantation, "the revolutionary cause," acquired a new meaning. Consolidating the revolution seemed to depend less on the quantity of land distributed and more on the number of tons of grain produced. In addition, the
experience of the previous ten years demonstrated that the government had
been destabilized not by peasants, but by the military, the church, and the
United States. To weaken the military and bring the religious war to an end,
Mexico had to recover economically and to that end needed foreign capital.
Investments would not flow into the country unless it cleaned house. Peace
had to be bought. According to Fernando de la Fuente, chief justice of the

Supreme Court, the goodwill of the United States toward the Mexican government was largely due to the completion of the social revolution, and Washington accepted the validity of the reforms it had opposed for so many years. This goodwill, which had been so costly for Mexico to win, had to be preserved. Another spate of radical agrarian reform would endanger it.[28] But moderation and caution also emerged at the end of the 1920s from the other side of Mexico's ideological rainbow.

The Radical Elite's Awakening

Whereas the conservative governing elite saw the need to accept the inevitability of neighborly relations with the United States and the consequences of the latter's economic superiority, the leftist elite grew disillusioned with the Soviet Union and its influence over the Mexican Communists. The attacks by the Soviet press on the Mexican government offended those who once admired the Bolshevik Revolution and were inspired by the accomplishments they thought it had achieved. For example, Eduardo Villaseñor, trade attaché in London, visited the Mexican ambassador in Moscow in the summer of 1929. Before the trip, Villaseñor had said that he still held the illusion that by expanding beyond the borders of the Soviet Union, the Bolshevik Revolution could rectify the course taken by the Mexican Revolution. When he returned from the USSR, he wrote Marte Gómez concerning the trip: "Extremely interesting. Above all, because of the prejudices I abandoned along the way."[29] His disillusionment can be attributed to his recognition that the "world revolution" he thought would tear down the barriers holding back a socialist revolution in Mexico was no longer on the Soviet agenda. In its place, he argued, the Bolsheviks sought the subordination of their allies to Moscow's own political interests, with no consideration for the welfare of the world's peoples. There was nothing left to do but to seek an accommodation with the Mexican style of politics: "We cannot be Communists subservient to Moscow, nor agents of New York or Washington, or *slow-motion* socialists like the English. Historic, geographic, even climatic conditions force us to be different. Let's be disciples of Marx, but not agents of Moscow."[30] Villaseñor predicted the birth of a new generation of Mexican socialists who would bravely enter the turbulent waters of Mexican politics. In the meantime, he wrote nostalgically to his friend: "Goodbye to hopes that the natural process of the world will resolve our problems! We cannot but rely on ourselves."[31]

In a different way, Marte R. Gómez lost his sympathy for the Soviet

Union as a result of the introduction of the First Five-Year Plan and of forced collectivization. He dedicated his entire life to agrarian questions, and the plight of the peasants became his own. When in 1929 Calles declared *urbi et orbi* that the agrarian reform had ended in Mexico and Portes Gil's interim presidency was over, Gómez lost his job as agriculture minister. He then packed his bags and, thanks to a stipend from the government, went to Europe until the antiagrarian storm had blown over in Mexico. Reflecting on the agrarian question in the Mexican Revolution, he agreed with Calles that the period of the expropriations should have been shorter, but added that it had lasted as long as it did because of formidable opposition. He knew from his own experience that the same government had slowed down or prevented land from being distributed to the peasants in order to safeguard other interests. But he was not an oppositionist and never criticized Calles in public; his personal creed was "be silent and wait."[32] Although the absence of further land distribution in Mexico upset him, the fervor of the forced collectivization in the Soviet Union, launched in 1929, did not satisfy him either because the peasants who had wanted to own a parcel of land were forced to give it up as a result of the restructuring of rural property. At the time, as during his entire life, Gómez recalled a phrase attributed to Lenin: "Peasants have the right to err; we have no right to contradict their aspirations."[33]

Another admirer of the Bolshevik Revolution was Jesús Silva Herzog, who, like Juan de Dios Bojórquez, belonged to a generation that had politically matured during the 1910–1920 revolution. In the following decade they played a role in the process of reconstructing Mexico's political and cultural life. In December 1928 Silva Herzog asked President Portes Gil to assign him to the post of ambassador in the USSR so that he would be able to experience the Russian Revolution firsthand.[34]

With no previous diplomatic experience or preparation, Silva Herzog arrived in Moscow in February 1929. The first three months of his diplomatic career were exciting as he met the leading Soviet personalities—such as Anatoli Lunacharsky, commissar for education and the arts, party ideologue Bukharin, Comintern president Zinoviev, and the poet Vladimir Mayakovsky, with whom he dined one night. Silva Herzog had the illusion of opening the embassy to Soviet visitors to exchange ideas and experiences, and hoped that, in return, the doors of Soviet institutions would be open to him. To his dismay, few people visited the Mexican embassy, and out of all the Soviet institutions, he was invited only by the International

Agrarian Institute, where he presented three lectures on Mexico. The press commented on the first lecture and ignored the others. Later, Silva Herzog learned that the institute's director was reprimanded for having allowed a representative from a "petty bourgeois" country to speak at a Communist institution. The ambassador was also displeased to learn that Mexican painter Xavier Guerrero, who studied at the Lenin School—where Communist cadre were trained—had been discouraged from maintaining any contact with him. Thus, Silva Herzog's social world was limited to other members of the diplomatic corps, whom he found terribly tedious.[35]

Silva Herzog kept himself intellectually alive through an intensive study of the Soviet economy and the few trips he was able to make outside of Moscow. He was initially impressed by workers' living conditions, which were better than those of Mexican workers. The educational system seemed excellent. He considered the Gosudarstvennoe Politicheskoe Upravlenie (GPU)—that is, the political police, or precursor of the KGB—to be an "unpleasant" institution, albeit necessary to consolidate and defend the Soviet government. But what most impressed him was the social role played by the army. After two years in military service, a soldier was molded into a Communist and returned to his village as a "civilizing agent." The ambassador was so impressed by this practice that in a letter to the Foreign Relations Ministry he urged its adoption by Mexican authorities: "It would be good for a well-prepared and honest Mexican military official to come here and study these things. The experiment being carried out in Russia is one of the most important episodes in history. The immediate future of all nations depends on its success or failure. One would have to be blind to deny the social, economic and political significance of what is occurring here."[36] In addition, Mexico could take advantage of the Soviet experience in organizing consumer and production cooperatives, as well as educational institutions that spread mass culture. In general, Silva Herzog was impressed by the Soviets' daring push to industrialize their country outside the confines of the capitalist system, "thus trying to modify the evolution of world economic history."[37]

If Silva Herzog had a limited social life before May 1929, he was totally ostracized by Soviet institutions after José Guadalupe Rodríguez and Salvador Gómez were executed in Mexico.[38] The anti-Mexican articles published daily in the Soviet press offended him. Pestkovsky himself contributed to this campaign with an article in *Pravda* that the ambassador considered an affront to Mexican authorities. To top it all, the Comintern issued a manifesto to the Mexican, Latin American, and entire world proletariat that characterized the Mexican government as fascist and called for protests in the streets of Mexico and important international cities. Silva Herzog sent protest letters to Litvinov, who tried to minimize the seriousness of the matter. Hiding behind the facade of a nonexistent democracy, the commissar responded that the Soviet government was not responsible for what appeared in the press, just as Moscow felt "that the anti-Soviet articles published in the Mexican press do not express the government's point of view." Litvinov wanted the ambassador to believe that the Comintern press was independent of the government and that it represented the point of view of the Communist parties "of almost all countries."[39] Silva Herzog was not fooled.

Shortly thereafter, the Mexican ambassador reported that his mail was being intercepted and the embassy was under surveillance—to the degree that each time he needed to communicate with Mexico, he had to pay a messenger to take correspondence to Berlin and dispatch it from there. It was precisely during these turbulent days that Silva Herzog's old friends, Eduardo Villaseñor and Juan de Dios Bojórquez, both close to Calles, visited him in Moscow. The ambassador gave them the Comintern manifesto to show to Calles, whom they were to meet in Paris. Thus, the jefe máximo read the Soviet condemnation of the Mexican government several days after it was issued and a few days before he returned to Mexico to lead the upcoming presidential election campaign. In the race, the Communists would present General Pedro Rodríguez Triana as their choice to seize state power and build a workers government.[40]

After all these latest developments, Jesús Silva Herzog felt deceived and began to reflect on his role in the USSR, the significance of Soviet-Mexican relations, and the two revolutions. Like many other Mexicans, he had believed that the Soviet Union sympathized with Mexico's efforts to improve the economic and political conditions of the proletariat and that it shared the Mexican government's progressive ideology. He also thought that Mexico's "disinterested and generous gesture" in recognizing the Soviet Union, despite the tense relations at the time between Mexico and the United States, should have inspired respect in the Soviet Union. But such was not the case. Mexico had made a mistake—committed "an error that we should have recognized a long time ago." The countries that maintained embassies in the USSR were its neighbors or had large-scale trade relations with the Soviets. Mexico was in neither category. The Comintern attacked the Mexican

Communists for being lukewarm and opportunist, but it sent them instructions and material aid. Silva Herzog knew very well that the antigovernment campaign of the Mexican Communists was inspired by Moscow.[41]

By December 1929, after ten months in Moscow, Silva Herzog was depressed. The Soviet Union, governed by the Communist Party, had converted the dictatorship of the proletariat into a dictatorship of the Central Committee—in fact, the dictatorship of Stalin himself. The Russian people had benefited from some accomplishments, "but more has been said about it than done. The propaganda books that we read in Mexico with pathetic good faith are one hundred percent exaggerations."[42] Silva Herzog analyzed the first results of the Five-Year Plan. He was impressed with the method known as Stakhanovism,[43] used to increase production, but he also observed the growing cult of Lenin and the punishments meted out to directors and workers of factories that did not meet the assigned goals. Popular discontent was kept in check by the much feared GPU. In its foreign policy, the USSR maintained economic and political relations with countries that it truly deplored and fought against by means of the Comintern. This policy, which seemed irrational to foreign countries, fit into the Russians' logic and convenience: capitalism's success meant the ruin of the Soviet Union, whereas capitalism's ruin meant the Soviets' success.

Viewed from this vantage point, why maintain relations between Mexico and the Soviet Union at all? The Soviet embassy in Mexico achieved its goal of becoming a center for Communist propaganda. By contrast, life in the Mexican embassy in Moscow was boring and precarious. The diplomatic mission could do nothing constructive due to the hostile environment and the obstacles placed in the way of its activities. The Mexican ambassador in Moscow was nothing but a passive observer: the Soviet government prevented its people from learning about other cultures and denied the validity of other methods of improving the lives of the majority. In short, Mexico and the Soviet Union failed in developing significant ties due to the lack of a common racial, historical, and linguistic base. As he had previously observed, Silva Herzog believed "that deep down they smile at our noble yet somewhat romantic attitude of keeping a costly mission in Moscow without having any material interests to defend."[44]

The ambassador said that not then or in the future would the two countries share any economic interests. Russia exported what it could, which was not much, and purchased little. Whereas Soviet companies could move freely in Mexico, Mexican firms could not do the same in the Soviet Union due to the existence of a state monopoly on foreign trade. The ideology of the Russian Revolution was different from that of the Mexican Revolution: Russia's abolition of private property and its internationalism contrasted with the Mexican ideology of private property, nationalism, and democracy. The Mexican Revolution was built on the country's cultural heritage, whereas the Russians sought to create a totally new culture. Silva Herzog concluded that comparisons made between the two revolutions were false, explainable only by Mexican ignorance of Soviet reality. The Mexican mission in Moscow was superfluous.

Just as Silva Herzog had requested his post the previous year, he now asked to be relieved as ambassador. He and his family left Moscow for Berlin on January 5, 1930. On January 24 during the intermission at the Berlin opera, Primo Villa Michel, the Mexican ambassador in Germany, showed Silva Herzog a telegram that had just arrived from Mexico: "Inform Silva Herzog that today we have broken relations with the Soviet Union."[45]

Mexico Lowers Its Flag in Moscow

President Portes Gil had also reached the conclusion that the Mexican and Bolshevik Revolutions were incompatible. His vantage point was political economy. Interviewed by the London *Times* in September 1929 on his ideas and governmental program, Portes Gil made it clear that Mexico, barely industrialized, could not be anticapitalist because it enjoyed abundant natural resources that required capital investments in order to be exploited. Nor could Mexico follow the Marxist road to development: "On the other side of the border is the world's richest and strongest country, a capitalist country par excellence, conscious of its economic strength, in the middle of a period of expansion. Would it look indifferently on a war to the death against capital at its very doorstep?"[46] Portes Gil reiterated that given Mexico's geopolitical situation, it needed to develop domestic capital formation and make certain that foreign capital did not enjoy privileges in exploiting its resources when national capital did not have the same capacity to do so.

The view that domestic capital was superior to foreign investment was a return to the notion introduced by Calles during his 1924 presidential campaign, a notion that *Excélsior* was now trying to refute. In an editorial, the newspaper rejected the concept that capital had either benign or malignant qualities depending on its origin; either it flowed freely or its movements were obstructed, as in the USSR. The essential choice was between progress, achieved by the United States, or poverty, in which Mexico would continue to be submerged if it did not change.[47] The country needed to define its economic and foreign policy.

Given the demands made by national and foreign investors and businessmen that the government clearly define which road it wished to follow, the influential daily, or the interests it represented, once again began publishing alarmist reports about Communist conspiracies, hatched abroad and aimed at undermining the Mexican government. The news reports were another "red scare," fabricated to twist the government's arm for a change in political direction. Once again, it is difficult to pinpoint the source of the new wave of supposed threats to the established order. In October, for example, *Excélsior* published a report about how the Communists "shamelessly" stopped workers at factory gates to hand them leaflets "in the hope that [they] might accept and practice Bolshevik theories." The newspaper also warned that a new group of Communist agitators was about to enter the country and that its presence could frighten away foreign investors.[48] Two months later, in December, it reported that another group of international terrorists, complete with bombs and Communist propaganda, had just been discovered in the Mexican capital. Thanks to the timely intervention of the military and civil authorities "the extremely serious danger that was closing in on the country's inhabitants was averted on time."[49]

What *Excélsior* printed was a leak from reports that in the preceding weeks had reached the Interior and Foreign Relations Ministries from Mexican embassies and consulates in Europe. These reports, probably invented and then circulated to give rise to the rumors, provided lurid details on the maneuvers of Russian conspirators to establish centers of agitation and subversion throughout Mexico. Thus, from Berlin, Hamburg, and Stockholm, the Mexican government received separate reports that a "Ivan Tetarishvilli" and a "Grigor Servaliev"—"both very dangerous sectarians"—were on their way to Mexico with large quantities of money at their disposal to provoke political incidents between Mexico and its northern neighbor. These individuals were allegedly plotting the assassination of important political leaders and planning to stockpile weapons in cities considered of strategic importance—such as Chihuahua, Monterrey, and Tampico. The report claimed that one of their objectives was to turn Puebla into a center for Soviet espionage and a rendezvous point for revolutionaries. Moreover, the entire country was allegedly being targeted for Soviet subversion: "Moscow desires at all costs and by any means to overthrow the Mexican government," read a telegram from Hamburg. From Stockholm came the news that the Soviets had recalled Kollontai from Norway to put her in charge of a government political department that dealt exclusively with Mexico.[50]

The Mexican ambassador in Berlin, Primo Villa Michel, supplied the source for all this information: a person by the name of Caputo claimed to work for the intelligence division of the U.S. Treasury and Interior departments in Europe. In fact, the information Caputo supplied to Villa Michel was the same that the U.S. embassy in Mexico had furnished to Estrada, the foreign relations minister.[51] As it turns out, this same person, namely Caputo, had provided the information to the two different Mexican government sources.

Just as it had in 1919 and 1928, the government accepted the validity of the documents and acted in accordance with the gravity of the sinister goals detailed by the news reports because they tended to coincide with the self-proclaimed intentions of the Communist Party to overthrow the government and the well-known global objectives of the Comintern. In addition to the evidence the Interior Ministry already had, however, in the fall of 1929 it received reports concerning "a great number of individuals of Russian nationality agitating among the masses and planning to provoke difficulties for the government."[52] Thus, all the information together at government disposal—the documents probably fabricated on Machado's orders in July 1928 alleging Comintern conspiracies in Mexico; the manifesto of the Comintern to the workers of Mexico and Latin America urging protests against the Mexican government and calling on the Mexican workers to overthrow the petty bourgeois "fascist" regime; Silva Herzog's letters from Moscow questioning the very reason for relations between Mexico and the USSR; and finally, the MCP's goal of subverting the existing order—was enough proof for the Mexican government to accuse the Soviets of sedition and interference in its internal affairs.

However, an assessment of the rhetoric behind and the political handling involved in the break in relations with the USSR demonstrates that the Mexican government was aware of the negative consequences that breaking off diplomatic relations could have among the workers and peasants who sympathized with the Communist Party. When the government made the decision to break off relations—an intention never announced publicly —it simultaneously prepared the groundwork to soften the decision's impact on the Mexican public. Several days before the measure was announced, the PNR newspaper addressed the workers in an apologetic tone to explain the reasons why the Communist leaders had been imprisoned during the previous weeks: "not because they are Communists, but because they exploit the workers"; not because of the ideas they believed in, but because they were not engaged in "honest" labor. In addition, the newspaper continued, the protests orchestrated by the Comintern in the capital cities of Europe and Latin America against the persecution of the Mexican Communists and the expulsion of their foreign comrades were part of a slanderous "campaign that some Communists were carrying out abroad against the Mexican Revolution, which has shown with practical acts the social and economic improvement of the working people in our country."[53]

On the day relations were broken off *El Nacional Revolucionario* revealed that the conspiracies detected and repressed in December had been backed by the Soviet Union, which sought to destabilize the Mexican political and social system. In addition, the conspiracies betrayed Mexican magnanimity: even though maintaining ties would imply risks, the government had established relations with the USSR because it considered Russia "a nation that has traditionally suffered in seeking its own freedom." However, not only did the USSR fail to appreciate "this generous attitude," but it also headed up Communist propaganda efforts in Mexico and published insulting manifestos abroad. The Soviet Union had hurt Mexico's pride because it maintained better relations with fascist Italy, where Communists were persecuted, than with Mexico, which had been one of its few friends.[54] This conduct was due to the fact that the Bolshevik Revolution had lost its bearings:

> Communism, which was destined to evolve after 1921 under the leadership of its great and inspiring leaders, headed by Lenin, during the most difficult period of its crisis fell into hands of well-known figures of second and third rank who have become entangled with not knowing what to do with the proletarian dictatorship and winding up in the most vulgarly ambitious way with a supreme tyranny in comparison with which the Czarist autocracy was a broad and liberal government.[55]

With Trotsky, Alexei Rykov, Mikhail Tomsky, and other outstanding Bolshevik leaders eliminated, the revolution "was left at the mercy of a fierce and rough provincial," Stalin, "with a brutal fist and a deficient brain." Recent news on the execution of peasants "for an insurrection against Communism" during the first phase of forced collectivization, when they refused to hand over their harvests, contributed—according to the government's official organ—to Mexico's being obligated to disassociate itself from the Soviet regime. Mexico "has not wanted to expose its decorum to the uncivilized treatment of such men and therefore has removed the national flag from our legation's flagpole in the red city of Moscow."[56]

Although through the press the government claimed it was justified in breaking relations because it was responding to Soviet and Communist provocation, in the political world it was really unleashing a witch-hunt to eliminate any obstacle to the transmission of presidential power from Portes Gil to Pascual Ortiz Rubio in February 1930. The government claimed to have information concerning sinister plans that could disrupt an orderly transition.

The Anti-Red Witch-Hunt of 1930

Once news of the break in relations became known, the Comintern organized a new campaign of protests against the Mexican government in the main cities of Europe and the United States. Simultaneously, sensationalist information, by all accounts forged, continued reaching the Mexican Foreign Relations Ministry. Since January, authorities had news that President-elect Pascual Ortiz Rubio would be assassinated, and on the day of his inauguration, February 5, 1930, an attempt was in fact made on his life. The president escaped with minor injuries, but the government unleashed an unprecedented wave of repression to apprehend those responsible.[57] Authorities quickly moved to imprison numerous Communists and expelled several foreign radicals from Mexico. One of those deported was Tina Modotti. Vittorio Vidali managed to evade the police and in disguise was able to get on the same boat as Modotti. Alexandr Makar was ready to sail from Veracruz to Europe but was detained and interrogated, and his belongings were searched, despite his diplomatic immunity. According to the *Times* (London) one of Makar's aides was arrested, the seals on the ambassador's trunks were broken and some documents removed. Carleton Beals noted that the embassy archives were returned to Mexico City to be reviewed by the police and military, in what the writer characterized as a hysterical anti-red witch-hunt. The embassy itself was raided and evidence of Soviet espionage in Mexico uncovered, with some of the documentation shared with the U.S. government.[58]

The red scare climate continued in the months following the break in relations with the USSR, even though many Communists had been banished to the Islas Marías island prison in the Pacific and their foreign comrades expelled from the country. Once again, while one arm of the government was putting Communists behind bars, another was mitigating the effects their persecution had on labor. Dr. Puig Casauranc, mayor of Mexico City, addressed the unions to explain that the detention of the Communists had nothing to do with the government's confidence in workers as law-abiding citizens.[59]

In March the government freed some of the Communist prisoners, who took to the streets to protest against unemployment, imperialism, and the break in relations with the USSR even before they returned to their homes. "More energy, more fighting spirit, more action against the new blows of Mexican fascism" was the party call to which the Communists responded. When the demonstrators marched from downtown Mexico City to the U.S. embassy, they were intercepted by armed police. The skirmish ended in more Communists being sent to jail, some for the second time in ten months.[60]

It was probably Portes Gil, the interior minister, who was behind the suppression of the demonstrators. In an article in *El Nacional Revolucionario*, however, the minister himself tried to minimize the importance of the Communist demonstrations, which he declared could not overshadow the achievements of revolutionary nationalism. The organizers of the demonstrations believed themselves to be the disciples of Marx and Lenin, and as such wanted to transform the world through cataclysmic upheavals. Such methods, which Lenin had upheld before 1921, were obsolete even in the Soviet Union, according to Portes Gil. Instead of redeeming the proletariat, Stalin "killed off peasants on both sides of the Volga River." Although in Russia the revolution had failed, in Mexico the revolutionary program was being carried out to the letter.[61] Despite the rhetoric of nonviolence, the police repression continued. In August the offices of International Red Aid were ransacked, and in December the headquarters of the Communist United Trade Union Confederation (CSUM) were seized.[62]

The witch-hunt was out of proportion to reality, according to Luis Cabrera, one of the most keen and lucid commentators on Mexican politics. He was appalled by the government's overreaction. In his opinion, Communism in Mexico was an ideology of despair adhered to by men and women who had suffered from want, misery, and ignorance, which the government was unable to alleviate. The Mexican Communists were innocuous. They would meet to exchange ideas, distribute simplistic leaflets, and sing "The

Internationale." Their existence, and especially their imprisonment, reflected the government's failure to resolve the social problems that had
sparked the revolution. It was regrettable that the government could not
face an adversary except by use of force.[63]

Indeed, the government had lost a sense of perspective after Obregón's
death and the Escobar rebellion. Through the PNR it wanted not only to
institutionalize the revolution, but to monopolize power when faced with
challenges to its political hegemony. The government's determination to
do so was made clearer during the presidential election campaign of 1929.
The PNR openly proclaimed itself the party of ideological unity and representative of all social classes, and invited the opposition into its ranks.[64]
Both the Communists as well as opposition candidate José Vasconcelos
ignored the PNR's call. In doing so, however, they lost the right to participate openly in the nation's political life.

Right before election day, *El Machete* published the Communists' position: "Naturally, we do not believe in democracy. Today, only bourgeois
democracy exists, which is, in the final analysis, the dictatorship of the
bourgeoisie. The Communist Party struggles not to win public office in a
bourgeois regime, but to destroy it and replace it with a workers government."[65] Because the bourgeoisie would not peacefully hand over power,
"we shall have to take it by force." The Communists also wanted to ensure
that the workers did not vote for the pro-government candidate: "We need
to promote the independence of the working masses, separate them from
the bourgeois and petty-bourgeois elements that have thus far led and utilized them to advance their own political ends."[66]

The PNR did not believe in "bourgeois" democracy either, and its response to the Communist strategy corresponded to its own interest in winning the masses the CROM was losing and the CSUM wished to win over.
Because of the PNR's stance—whoever was not with them was against them
—neither Vasconcelos nor Rodríguez Triana was able to participate in a fair
election campaign. The harsh treatment they received at the hands of local
governments and the police during the campaign was a clear sign that the
federal government was not willing to tolerate any opposition to Pascual
Ortiz Rubio's election. Thus, the November 1929 elections produced the
results the government wanted to achieve: Ortiz Rubio won with 1,825,732
votes, 93.5 percent of the total. Vasconcelos received 105,655 votes, 5.4
percent, and Rodríguez Triana obtained only 19,665 votes, or one percent.[67]

There can be no doubt that both Rodríguez Triana as well as Vasconcelos were victims of the government's need to restore stability to the country after Obregón's assassination and the Obregonista insurrection. At the same time, it must be remembered that Rodríguez Triana's election campaign was linked to the Communist plan to overthrow the government and that the authorities' repressive response was due to their conviction that the plan came from the Soviet Union. Because of the political challenges that the government had to face at the end of the 1920s, it lost the capacity to distinguish between real dangers and imaginary evidence that supposedly threatened its stability. Hence, the persecution of the Communists was one of the consequences of the loss of political equilibrium: the concocted plots touched sensitive nerves in a government that feared the fulfillment of conspiracy prophecies. As a result, the wave of indiscriminate repression launched in 1929 and 1930 served as a preemptive strike.

FINAL REFLECTIONS

Mexico established diplomatic relations with the Soviet Union out of solidarity—because it believed they shared a common destiny and hope of achieving mutual advantages. When in 1925 and 1926, Ambassador Pestkovsky helped organize the rail workers strike, and in 1929 when the Comintern advised and possibly led the Mexican Communist Party in its attempt to overthrow the government, the Soviets not only violated norms of diplomatic conduct, but offended Mexico's deep-felt sense of national sovereignty and dignity. Thus, Soviet internationalism clashed with Mexican nationalism as it had with U.S. imperialism.

At the time, it appeared as if the United States had influenced Mexico to distance itself from the Soviet Union. Perhaps under the table Washington could have contributed to Mexico's decision by providing, or even planting, false information in decisive moments to undermine the Mexican government's confidence in its ability to rule. Because the Comintern's objective was to extend its revolutionary activities to Latin America and the United States, it is not farfetched to think that the anti-Bolshevik organizations and interest groups of the United States wanted to prevent the Communist enemy from approaching its shores. With this end in mind, they could have induced the break in relations between Mexico and the USSR.

However, the reason Mexico clashed so forcefully with both the United States and the Soviet Union should be attributed, in the final analysis, to the incompatibility of the faith displayed by each of the two world powers in the universality of their respective ideologies as well as to their attempts to convince the world of the advantages of their systems and of their extension worldwide. The Americans' confidence in the free interplay of market forces, promoted through the unrestricted expansion of capital investment, had the same roots as the Soviet faith in the benefits of the socialist economic system, promoted through world revolution. Both countries believed they were invested with a mission to regenerate the world: in the case of the United States, the backward and underdeveloped countries; and in the case of the Soviet Union, the oppressed and exploited.

Mexico had no such sense of national grandeur or its special mission in the world. Unlike the Bolsheviks, the Mexican revolutionaries did not aspire to create a utopia in power, but to resolve the country's major economic, political, and social problems. They would have preferred to have more liberal governments south of their own border, but did not see exporting their revolution as a viable endeavor, especially because it would clash —as it in fact did in Nicaragua in 1926 and 1927—with the powerful interests of the United States. In reality, by 1930 Mexico felt trapped between the two economic and political systems and between the two world powers —unable to influence either.

An additional element that influenced Mexico's estrangement from the Soviet Union was its perception that the Bolshevik Revolution had gone astray. The radical elite in the Mexican government had identified with the Bolshevik goal of empowering the workers and peasants. However, during the course of the decade the intellectuals in the government came to realize that the Soviet state was losing contact with the Russian masses and was becoming a dictatorship. Mexicans had identified with Lenin, the New Economic Policy (NEP), and Trotsky. But Lenin had died, the NEP was abandoned, and Trotsky was defeated. Extremism prevailed over moderation and Stalin symbolized tyranny. In contrast with this turn of events, the Mexican government believed it could harmonize the social forces that had emerged from its own revolutionary upheaval better than the Bolsheviks had.

Unlike Stalin's determination to industrialize a gigantic country through its own efforts and to subject Soviet society to a dictatorial elite, the Mexican government at the end of the 1920s decided to come to terms with the country's dependence on foreign capital, technology, and markets. To develop the country's natural riches and productive energy, the government subordinated the dispersed and diverse social forces to the authority of a single party in order to consolidate the country politically and to create a climate of peace that would attract foreign investments to industry and agriculture.

However, when all of a sudden the Soviet economy began to churn out astonishing achievements as a result of the First Five-Year Plan, but at the same time the capitalist world plummeted to the depths of depression following the 1929 crash and the shock waves of the crisis rocked the entire system, the new generation of Mexican progressive politicians began to think anew about the Soviet Union. While Soviet furnaces produced tons of steel, and capitalist production stood still for lack of markets; while fifteen million unemployed wandered the cities of the United States, and more than a quarter of a million Mexicans had to return from the other side of the border, the old dilemma resurfaced: Mexico was caught between the socialist ideal and the capitalistic reality—between an idealized Soviet Union and the real United States. And this dilemma would continue to reappear, although in different forms, right up until the fall of the Berlin Wall.

NOTES

1 The United States in Search of Its Mexican Policy

1 Nell Irvin Painter, *Standing at Armageddon: The United States, 1877–1919* (New York: W. W. Norton, 1987), p. xi.

2 Richard Hofstadter, *The Paranoid Style in American Politics and Other Essays* (New York: Alfred A. Knopf, 1965), pp. 2–40; David Brion Davis, ed., *The Fear of Conspiracy: Images of Un-American Subversion from the Revolution to the Present* (Ithaca, N.Y.: Cornell University Press, 1971), pp. xiii–xxiv; Phillip Knightley, *The Second Oldest Profession: Spies and Spying in the Twentieth Century* (New York: W. W. Norton, 1986), p. 78.

3 M. J. Heale, *American Anticommunism: Combating the Enemy Within, 1830–1970* (Baltimore and London: Johns Hopkins University Press, 1990), pp. xi–xiv; Richard M. Fried, *Nightmare in Red: The McCarthy Era in Perspective* (New York and Oxford: Oxford University Press, 1990), pp. 3–16; Lars Schoultz, *National Security and United States Policy toward Latin America* (Princeton, N.J.: Princeton University Press, 1987), p. 119.

4 William E. Leuchtenberg, *The Perils of Prosperity, 1914–1932* (Chicago: University of Chicago Press, 1958), p. 204; Betty Miller Unterberger, "Woodrow Wilson and the Russian Revolution," in Arthur Link, ed., *Woodrow Wilson and a Revolutionary World, 1913–1921* (Chapel Hill: University of North Carolina Press, 1982), p. 50; Alan Singer, "Communists and Coal Miners: Rank-and-File Organizing in the United Mine Workers of America during the 1920s," *Science and Society* 55, no. 2 (summer 1991), pp. 132–57; David Montgomery, *The Fall of the House of Labor: The Workplace, the State, and American Labor Activism, 1865–1925* (Cambridge: Cambridge University Press, 1987), pp. 330–32, 388–93; Robert K. Murray, *The Harding Era: Warren G. Harding and His Administration* (Minneapolis: University of Minnesota Press, 1969), pp. 82–89.

5 Montgomery, *Fall of the House of Labor*, p. 389.

6 Peter Filene, *American Views of Soviet Russia, 1917–1965* (Homewood, Ill.: Dorset, 1968), p. ix; Josephus Daniels, *The Wilson Era: Years of War and After, 1917–1923* (Chapel Hill: University of North Carolina Press, 1946), p. 546; Edward Herman and Noam Chomsky, *Manufacturing Consent: The Political Economy of the Mass Media* (New York: Pantheon Books, 1988), p. 32; Peter H. Buckingham, *America Sees Red: Anti-Communism in America, 1870s to 1980s* (Claremont, Calif.: Regina Books, 1988), pp. 11–22.

7 Cited by John Lewis Gaddis, *Russia, the Soviet Union and the United States: An Interpretive History* (1978; reprint, New York: McGraw-Hill, 1990), p. 113; Montgomery, *Fall of the House of Labor*, p. 434, Filene, *American Views of Soviet Russia*, p. 157 and pp. 173–85; Theodore Draper, *American Communism and Soviet Russia* (New York: Viking Penguin, 1960; reprint, New York: Vintage Books, 1986), chap. 9.

8 Michael H. Hunt, *Ideology and U.S. Foreign Policy* (New Haven: Yale University Press, 1987), p. 115; Filene, *American Views of Soviet Russia*, pp. 160–61.

9 Walter Duranty, *I Write as I Please* (New York: Simon and Schuster, 1935), p. 72;
John Hohenberg, *Foreign Correspondence: The Great Reporters and Their Times*
(New York: Columbia University Press, 1964), p. 229.

10 Robert W. Desmond, *Crisis and Conflict: World News Reporting between Two
Wars, 1920–1940* (Iowa City, Iowa: University of Iowa Press, 1982), pp. 229–30,
271, 329; Duranty, *I Write as I Please*, pp. 86–104.

11 Walter Lippmann and Charles Merz, "Test of the News, An Examination of the
N.Y. Times Reports on the Russian Revolution," *New Republic*, 4 August 1920,
cited by Neno Lovenstein, *American Opinion of Soviet Russia* (Washington,
D.C.: American Council on Public Affairs, 1941), p. 31 and p. 173, n. 10; Malcolm
Carroll, *Soviet Communism and Western Opinion, 1919–1921*, ed. by Frederic
B. M. Hollyday (Chapel Hill: University of North Carolina Press), 1965, pp. 6–8;
Desmond, *Crisis and Conflict*, p. 31.

12 Alexander F. Kerensky, *The Catastrophe: Kerensky's Own Story of the Russian
Revolution* (New York: D. Appleton, 1927); Grigory Besedovsky, *Revelations of a
Soviet Diplomat* (Westport, Conn.: Hyperion, 1931); Gordon Brook-Shepherd,
The Storm Petrels: The Flight of the First Soviet Defectors (New York: Harcourt
Brace Jovanovitch, 1977); Knightley, *Second Oldest Profession*, pp. 9–17.

13 Cited by Gaddis, *Russia, the Soviet Union and the United States*, p. 105.

14 Cited by Peter Filene, *Americans and the Soviet Experiment, 1917–1933* (Cambridge, Mass.: Harvard University Press, 1967), pp. 51–52.

15 "United States Inquiry into Bolshevism: Lenine-Trotzky Regime in Russia Described by Eye Witnesses-Views of Sympathizers," *New York Times Current History* 10 (April–September 1919), pp. 128–144.

16 Raymond Robins "did say some kind words for the Bolsheviki, but he denounced
the movement as a menace to the whole world, and said that any man who
agitated for the overthrow of the Government of the United States should be
arrested, tried and jailed. Lenine himself had told him, Colonel Robins said, that
one of the ambitions of the Bolsheviki was the overthrow of the American form of
government and the substitution for it of the rule of the proletariat along the lines
such as prevail in Russia." *Ibid.*, pp. 134–35. In addition, see, "Lenine and Trotzky:
Two Character Sketches by the *London Times*," *Current History* 10 (September
1918–April 1919), pp. 208–272.

17 Rhodri Jeffreys-Jones, *American Espionage: From Secret Service to CIA* (New
York: Free Press, 1977), pp. 146–53.

18 Lincoln Steffens, *The Autobiography of Lincoln Steffens* (New York: Harcourt, Brace and Company, 1931), p. 735; Donald James Manning, "Soviet-American Relations, 1929–1941: The Impact of Domestic Considerations on
Foreign Policy Decision-Making," Ph.D. diss., Michigan State University, 1978),
pp. 38–39.

19 Lloyd C. Gardner, *Safe for Democracy: The Anglo-American Response to Revolution, 1913–1923* (New York: Oxford University Press, 1984), p. 203; Joan Hoff
Wilson, *Ideology and Economics: U.S. Relations with the Soviet Union, 1918–1933* (Columbia: University of Missouri Press, 1974), pp. 5–6.

20 Hunt, *Ideology*, pp. 108–11, 116–23; Mark Gilderhus, *Diplomacy and Revolution: U.S.-Mexican Relations under Wilson and Carranza* (Tucson: University of
Arizona Press, 1977), p. xii; William Appleman Williams, *Empire as a Way of Life*
(Oxford: Oxford University Press, 1980), p. 148.

21 Michael L. Krenn, *U.S. Policy toward Economic Nationalism in Latin America, 1917–1929* (Wilmington, Del.: Scholarly Resources, 1990), pp. 40–41.

22 Henry Lane Wilson to Philander Knox, Indianapolis, 15 May 1918, National Archives, Records of the U.S. Department of State Relating to the Internal Affairs of Mexico, 1910–1929, RG 59 (hereafter identified by reel and file number 812), reel 62, file 812.00/21435; Robert Freeman Smith, *The United States and Revolutionary Nationalism in Mexico, 1916–1932* (Chicago: University of Chicago Press, 1972), pp. 128–32. Felix Díaz was the nephew of the deposed president Porfirio Díaz and coveted the presidency.

23 Cited in Unterberger, "Woodrow Wilson and the Bolshevik Revolution," p. 75.

24 Friedrich Katz, *The Secret War in Mexico: Europe, The United States and the Mexican Revolution* (Chicago: University of Chicago Press, 1981), p. 539.

25 Undersecretary to secretary of state, 30 July 1919, National Archives, Records of the U.S. Department of State Relating to Political Relations between the United States and Mexico, 1910–1929, RG 59, series 711.12 (hereafter identified by reel, decimal file, and number), reel 2, file 711.12/216. British embassy to Foreign Office, Washington, D.C., 18 April 1919, Public Record Office, Foreign Office (hereafter PRO and FO) 371/3828; Gardner, "Woodrow Wilson and the Mexican Revolution," in *Woodrow Wilson and a Revolutionary World, 1913–1921*, ed. Arthur Link (Chapel Hill: University of North Carolina Press, 1982), pp. 27–30; Fletcher to Wilson, Mexico City, 18 August 1919, reel 2, file 711.12/187.

26 David H. Stratton, ed., "The Memoirs of Albert B. Fall," *Southwestern Studies* 4, no. 3 (1966), p. 3; Ramón P. de Negri to the Secretaría de Relaciones Exteriores (SRE), 11 October 1919, Archivo de la Secretaría de Relaciones Exteriores (hereafter ASRE), 17-17-170.

27 N. Stephen Kane, "Corporate Power and Foreign Policy: Efforts of American Oil Companies to Influence United States Relations with Mexico, 1921–1928," *Diplomatic History* 1, no. 2 (spring 1977), pp. 174–75.

28 William Gates, "The Four Governments of Mexico," *The World's Work* (April 1919), in PRO, FO, 371/3828.

29 From the *New York Times:* "Russian Reds in Mexico," 21 October 1918; "Say Bolsheviki Dominate Mexico," 12 March 1919; "Find Russian Reds Work in Mexico," 15 November 1919; and "Washington Sets Time Limit For Carranza to Comply," 4 December 1919.

In addition to home-spun articles, some Porfiristas who had settled in the United States after the revolution added a sting to the campaign; thus, a former minister of interior, Jorge Vera-Estañol published in Los Angeles *Carranza and His Bolshevik Regime* (Los Angeles: Wayside Press, 1920).

30 Francis Dyer to secretary of state, Nogales, 16 May 1919, reel 65, file 812.00/22711.

31 Marsh to secretary of state, Progreso, 21 October 1918, reel 65, file 812.00/22315.

32 Douglas Little, "Antibolshevism and American Foreign Policy, 1919–1939: The Diplomacy of Self-Delusion," *American Quarterly* 35 (fall 1983), pp. 380–81.

33 Arthur Thomson, *The Conspiracy against Mexico* (Oakland, Calif.: International, 1919). Other works written by the league members were: Samuel Guy Inman, *Intervention in Mexico* (1919); J. K. Turner, *Hands Off Mexico* (1920); Leander J. de Bekker, *The Plot against Mexico* (1919); see Mark T. Gilderhus,

"Senator Albert B. Fall and 'The Plot against Mexico,'" *New Mexico Historical Review* 48, no. 4 (October 1973), pp. 302–3 and p. 310, n. 10.

34 Lorenzo Meyer, *México y los Estados Unidos en el conflicto petrolero (1917–1942)* (Mexico City: El Colegio de México, 1972), pp. 124–27; Emilio Zebadúa, *Banqueros y revolucionarios: La soberanía financiera de México, 1914–1929* (Mexico City: El Colegio de México and Fondo de Cultura Económica, 1994), chap. 3.

35 "Bolshevist Agents Seized in Tampico," "Reds Claim Aid of Mexican Heads," *New York Times*, 4 and 12 January, 1920.

36 Richard Gid Power, *Secrecy and Power: The Life of J. Edgar Hoover* (New York: Macmillan, 1987), p. 56; Jeffreys-Jones, *American Espionage*, pp. 49–53.

37 Kosterlitzky to Bureau of Investigation, Los Angeles, 20 July 1919; Richmond Levering to Bureau of Investigation, New York, 15 October 1919; Gus T. Jones to Bureau of Investigation, El Paso, Texas, 25 September 1919. In Records of the Federal Bureau of Investigation, investigative case files, 1907–1923 (hereafter FBI), reel 867; see also, Cornelius C. Smith, *Emilio Kosterlitzky: Eagle of Sonora and the Southwest Border* (Glendale, Calif.: Arthur H. Clark, 1970), p. 172. "Memorandum," Mexican embassy, Washington, D.C., 10 June 1919, reel 65, file 812.00/22800.

38 Jacob Spolansky, *The Communist Trail of America* (New York: Macmillan, 1951), pp. 172–175; U.S. Military Intelligence Reports, General Intelligence Bulletin, Mexico City, 4 September 1920, p. 14.

39 The informant signed his letters with the initials E. O. and sent them to the U.S. embassy where the military had an office. See Military Intelligence Division (hereafter MID), "Political, Radical and Labor Activities," U.S. National Archives, U.S. Military Intelligence Reports: Mexico, 1919–1941, RG 165, box 2290. Barry Carr, *Marxism and Communism in Twentieth-Century Mexico* (Lincoln: University of Nebraska Press, 1992), pp. 20–21; Paco Ignacio Taibo II, *Bolshevikis: Historia narrativa de los orígenes del Comunismo en México (1919–1925)* (Mexico City: Joaquín Mortiz, 1986), pp. 45–46.

40 R. M. Campbell to the director of military intelligence, Mexico City, 26 May 1920, MID, box 2290.

41 Edgar Burr, major of cavalry, Mexico City, 25 August 1919, U.S. MID, reel 1, p. 1280; 10 September 1919, p. 1658.

42 Jeffreys-Jones, *American Espionage*, p. 155.

43 Department of State to U.S. embassy in Mexico City, Washington, D.C., 27 March 1920, reel 90, 812.0013/2; Department of State to U.S. consul in Veracruz, Washington, D.C., 23 April 1920, reel 70, file 812.00/23663. From Veracruz, Consul Foster wired back: "Conditions growing better. American warships have not arrived and will probably not be necessary unless a change in condition occurs." Foster to secretary of state, Veracruz, 8 May 1920, reel 71, file 812.00/23880.

44 Mr. Lindsay to Foreign Office, Washington, D.C., 23 January 1920, PRO, FO 371/4490/157. Pablo González had been Carranza's chief of military operations in several states and in 1920 had the ambition to succeed him as president of Mexico. Felix Díaz, nephew of Don Porfirio, had been plotting against the revolutionary government ever since his uncle's departure from Mexico in 1911.

45 Cunard Howard Cummins to Lord Curzon, Mexico City, 15 March 1920, PRO, FO 371/4491.

46 Cited by Wilson, *Ideology and Economics*, p. 17.

47 *New York State Legislative Joint Committee Investigating Seditious Activities*, vols. 1 and 2 (New York, n.p., 1920), v. 1, p. 494, and v. 2, pp. 1770–71.

48 W. Hanna to secretary of state, Mexico City, 26 October 1920, reel 73, file 812.00/24759.

49 Albert Fall to the National Association for the Protection of American Rights in Mexico, Washington, D.C., 19 January 1921, PRO, FO 371/5580/57–60.

50 Meyer, *México y los Estados Unidos*, pp. 165–77; Smith, *The United States and Revolutionary Nationalism*, pp. 190–94.

51 George D. Beelen, "The Harding Administration and Mexico: Diplomacy by Economic Persuasion," *The Americas* 41, no. 2 (October 1984), pp. 181–83; "Mexico under a New President," *New York Times Current History* 13 (October 1920–March 1921), pp. 112–14.

52 See Roger W. Babson, "Mexico Reaching a Crisis," prepared by Babson's Statistical Organization, Massachusetts, 29 March 1921, reel 74, 812.00/933–6.

53 "Un mes de intercambio con México es más importante que varios años con Rusia," *Excélsior*, 19 February 1921. See also John Hays Hammond, *The Autobiography of John Hays Hammond*, 2 vols. (New York: Ferrar and Rinehart, 1935), vol. 2, pp. 748–753.

54 Gregory A. Andrews, "Toward a Consensus on U.S. Hegemony in Latin America: American Labor and U.S. Officials View the Mexican Revolution," paper presented at the Southwestern Social Science Association, Austin, Texas, March 1991, p. 12; Harvey A. Levenstein, *Labor Organizations in the United States and Mexico: A History of Their Relations* (Westport, Conn.: Greenwood, 1971), pp. 94–95 and 100–101; Ronald Radosh, *American Labor and United States Foreign Policy* (New York: Random House, 1969), p. 353.

55 Smith, *The United States and Revolutionary Nationalism*, pp. 194–201.

56 Jeffreys-Jones, *American Espionage*, p. 111.

57 "Spy Uses Ocean Greyhound to Uncover Soviet Secrets," *New York American*, 11 October 1925; Bertram D. Wolfe, *A Life in Two Centuries: An Autobiography* (New York: Stein and Day, 1981), pp. 163–64; Theodore Draper, *American Communism*, p. 175.

58 "Toda una vasta conspiración Comunista fue fraguada en México por dos audaces y peligrosos aventureros,"*Excélsior*, 21 September 1925; "Soviet Spy Worked Way into U.S. Secret Service," *New York American*, 4 October 1925.

59 Jeffreys-Jones, *American Espionage*, pp. 155–56.

60 "Super Spy Tells 'How I Faked the Constitution of the Red Army in Mexico to Scare the U.S,'" *New York American*, 27 September 1925.

61 *Ibid.*

62 Unsigned "Memorandum," Department of State, 13 April 1921, reel 90, file 812.00B/52.

63 *Ibid.*

64 Unsigned "Memorandum" to the Department of State, 13 April 1921, reel 90, file 812.00B/52; MID, General Intelligence Bulletin, 30 April 1921, p. 26.

65 "Lo que piden a México los E. Unidos," *El Universal*, 5 May 1922.

66 Smith, *The United States and Revolutionary Nationalism*, pp. 197–214.

67 Robert Hammond Murray, *The Harding Era: Warren G. Harding and His Administration* (Minneapolis: University of Minnesota Press, 1955), p. 331; Wilson, *Ideology and Economics*, pp. 59–60.

68 "Summary of the Principal Factors Menacing the Obregón Administration in Mexico and Biographical Sketch of Principal Leaders Involved," 4 March 1922, MID, reel 1; Paul Foster to secretary of state, Veracruz, 27 April 1922, reel 78, file 812.00/25590; Hanna to secretary of state, Washington, D.C., 16 and 20 June 1922, reel 73, file 812.00/26029 and 26060; "American-Mexican Special Commission," 12 May 1923, MID, reel 1, file 3895 and 2 June 1923, file 3935.

2 Mexico in Soviet Calculations

1 "Bibliograficheskii ukazatel' periodicheskoi i neperiodicheskoi literatury o strannakh Latinskoi Ameriki," *Revoliutsionnyi vostok*, nos. 3–4 (1932–1934), pp. 346–359; J. Gregory Oswald, "México en la historiografía soviética," *Historia Mexicana* 14, no. 3 (January–March 1965), pp. 691–706; Eugenia Scarzanella, "La imagen de América Latina en la prensa y en los debates de la III Internacional, 1929–1935," *Estudios Latinoamericanos*, 6 (1980), pp. 193–213; Teddy J. Uldricks, *Diplomacy and Ideology: The Origins of Soviet Foreign Policy* (London: Sage, 1979), p. 36 and p. 144.

2 As part of its ostentatious turning of the back on traditional "bourgeois" practices, the Bolshevik regime in 1917 renounced the use of terms such as *cabinet, ministry, minister,* and *ambassador*. The former ministries were rebaptized "people's commissariats" and those in charge of them "people's commissars." Ambassadors became "plenipotentiary representatives" of the USSR.

3 Peter Kenez, *The Birth of the Propaganda State: Soviet Methods of Mass Mobilization, 1917–1929* (Cambridge, England: Cambridge University Press, 1985), pp. 39–44; Jeffrey Brooks, "Public and Private Values in the Soviet Press, 1921–1928," *Slavic Review* 48, no. 1 (spring 1989), pp. 16–19; Oded Eran, *Mezhdunarodniki: An Assessment of Professional Expertise in the Making of Soviet Foreign Policy* (Israel: Turtledge, 1979), pp. 9–25.

4 Mark W. Hopkins, *Mass Media in the Soviet Union* (New York: Pegasus, 1970), p. 69; Aino Kuusinen, *The Rings of Destiny: Inside Soviet Russia from Lenin to Brezhnev* (New York: William Morrow, 1974), p. 43.

5 "Bibliograficheskii ukazatel'," p. 348; Henryk Szlajfer, "Review Essay: *Latin America and the Comintern:* An Interesting Book with Many Mistakes," *Boletín de Estudios Latinoamericanos y del Caribe* 46 (June 1989), pp. 110–18; Eran, *Mezhdunarodniki,* p. 31; León Trotsky, *The Third International after Lenin* (New York: Pioneer, 1957), pp. 6–7.

6 Articles about the labor movement: "Pis'mo k meksikanskim rabochim," *Krasnyi Internatsional Profsoiuzov*, no. 1 (30 August 1921), pp. 330–31; "Meksika. Profesional'noe i politicheskoe dvizhenie," *ibid.,* no. 6 (20 October 1921), pp. 247–49; "Meksika. Kongress Vseobshchei Konfederatsii Rabochikh," *ibid.,* no. 10 (11 December 1921), pp. 484–85 and 534; Luis Fraina, "Meksika. Bor'ba za prisoedinenie k Krasnomu Profinternu" and "Rost bezrabotnitsy," *ibid.,* no. 1 (12 January 1922), pp. 60–63; A. Nin, "Meksika. Rabochee dvizhenie v Meksike," *ibid.,* no. 1 (January 1923), pp. 90–95; "Meksika. Sovremennoe polozhenie rabochikh organizatsii i bor'ba za edinnii front," *ibid.,* nos. 5–6 (May–June 1923), pp. 875–77; "II-i Kongress Vseobshchei Konfederacii rabochikh," *Mezhdunarodnoe Rabochee Dvizhenie,* no. 12 (April 1923), p. 8; "Meksika. Raboche-profesional'noe dvizhenie," *ibid.,* no. 40 (November 1923), pp. 9–10;

Articles and books about the oil question and the United States: Ali Ferid, "Die Petroleumrevolution in Mexiko," *Inprekorr*, no. 15 (1 February 1922), p. 1537; "Istoshchnenie meksikanskikh neftianykh istoshchnikov," *Mezhdunarodnaia Zhizn'*, no. 8 (8 June 1922), pp. 46–47; Communist International, *Ezhegodnik Kominterna* (Petrograd and Moscow: Communist International, 1923), pp. 760–64.

An article about the Mexican peasant movement's joining the Krestintern, the Comintern's peasant front organization, can be found in *Krest'ianskii Internatsional*, no. 1 (April 1924).

7 "Soedinennye Shtaty i Meksika," *Mezhdunarodnaia Zhizn'*, no. 12 (1926), pp. 34–42.

8 Eugen Varga, "Meksika," *Planovoie Khoziaistvo*, no. 9 (September 1926), pp. 137–54.

9 Robert Service, *Lenin: A Political Life*, 2 vols. (Bloomington: Indiana University Press, 1991), vol. 2, p. 157; V. I. Lenin, "Preface to the French and German editions," 26 April 1920, in E. Varga and L. Mendelsohn, eds., *New Data for V. I. Lenin's Imperialism, the Highest Stage of Capitalism* (London: Lawrence and Wishart, n.d.), p. 6. Lenin wrote his book on imperialism in 1916. In 1920 Varga and Mendelsohn updated his work, including new economic data on Latin America.

10 *Ibid.*, pp. 180–88.

11 Leon Trotsky, *The First Five Years of the Communist International*, 2 vols. (New York: n.p., 1945), vol. 1, p. 22; Executive Committee of the Communist International, *Strategy of the Communists: A Letter from the Communist International to the Mexican Communist Party* (Chicago, Illinois: Workers Party of America, 1923), pp. 6–7.

12 Gabriel Gorodetsky, *The Precarious Truce: Anglo-Soviet Relations 1924–1927* (Cambridge, England: Cambridge University Press, 1977), pp. 1–6.

13 Georgi Chicherin, "La politique exterieure des Deux Internationales," *L'Internationale Communiste*, no. 6 (October 1919), pp. 853–864, and "Address by USSR People's Commissar of Foreign Affairs G. V. Chicherin at the Fourteenth Congress of the VKP (b) (1925)," in *Russian Studies in History* 31 (spring 1993), pp. 84–85.

14 Aldo Agosti, "World Revolution and World Party of the Revolution: The Evolution of Two Concepts"; Kirill Shirinia, "The Comintern: A World Party and its National Sections"; papers presented at the International Scientific Conference, *History of the Comintern in the Light of New Documents*, Moscow, 20–22 October 1994.

15 Eric Hobsbawm, *Age of Extremes: The Short Twentieth Century, 1914–1991* (London: Michael Joseph, 1994), p. 69.

16 R. Edward Glatfelter, "Borodin," in Joseph L. Wieczynski, ed., *The Modern Encyclopedia of Russian and Soviet History* (Gulf Breeze, Fl.: Academic International, 1976), pp. 140–41. Borodin became a legendary figure in China, where he acted as the Soviet advisor to Kuomintang between 1923 and until Chiang Kaishek brutally put an end to the Communist-nationalist collaboration in 1927. Following his return to Moscow, Borodin fell into obscurity. He was arrested in Moscow in 1949 during the anti-Jewish purges and died in prison in 1952 while he was interrogated. See Pavel Sudoplatov and Anatoli Sudoplatov, *Special*

Tasks: The Memoirs of an Unwanted Witness—A Soviet Spymaster (Boston: Little Brown, 1994), p. 334, n. 7.

17 Teddy J. Uldricks, *Diplomacy and Ideology*, pp. 15–24; Adam B. Ulam, *Expansion and Coexistence: The History of Soviet Foreign Relations, 1917–1967* (New York: Praeger, 1968), pp. 92–93; Linda Killen, "The Search for a Democratic Russia: Bakhmetev and the United States," *Diplomatic History* 2, no. 3 (summer 1978), p. 253.

18 M. N. Roy, *Memoirs* (Bombay: Allied, 1964), pp. 196–203.

19 Spolansky, *The Communist Trail of America*, p. 173; Roy, *Memoirs*, pp. 187–97; Branko Lazitch and Milorad D. Drachkovitch, *Lenin and the Comintern* (Stanford: Hoover Institution Press, 1972), pp. 143–64; Lydia Holubnychy, "Michael Borodin and the Chinese Revolution, 1923–1925" (Ph.D. diss., Columbia University, 1979), p. 45.

20 Manuel Gómez, "From Mexico to Moscow," *Survey*, no. 53 (October 1964), p. 36. Manuel Gómez was one of Charles Phillips's pseudonyms; the others were Frank Seaman, Jesús Ramírez, and Charles Shipman, under which his autobiography was published. See Charles Shipman, *It Had to Be Revolution: Memoirs of an American Radical* (Ithaca, N.Y.: Cornell University Press, 1993), p. 82.

21 Roy, *Memoirs*, p. 22.

22 *Ibid.*, pp. 23–29, Roy cited on p. 43.

23 *Ibid.*, p. 201.

24 Shipman, *It Had to Be Revolution*, p. 84.

25 Roy, *Memoirs*, p. 210.

26 Shipman, *It Had to Be Revolution*, p. 85.

27 Taibo, *Bolshevikis*, p. 41; Carr, *Marxism and Communism*, p. 24.

28 Roy, *Memoirs*, p. 211; Shipman, *It Had to Be Revolution*, p. 89.

29 Lazitch and Drachkovitch, *Lenin and the Comintern*, pp. 165–66 and pp. 182–89.

30 Dan N. Jacobs, *Borodin: Stalin's Man in China* (Cambridge, Mass.: Harvard University Press, 1981), p. 81; Roy, *Memoirs*, pp. 125 and 346.

31 Shipman, *It Had to Be Revolution*, p. 118.

32 *Second Congress of the Communist International: Minutes and Proceedings*, 2 vols. (London: New Park, 1977), vol. 1, p. 125.

33 Brian Pearce, ed., *Congress of the Peoples of the East: Baku, September 1920* (1920; London: New Park, 1977), p. 86.

34 Shipman, *It Had to Be Revolution*, p. 119 and 123.

35 Reiner Tosstorff, "The Red International of Labour Unions," in Jürgen Rojahn, ed., *The Communist International and Its National Sections* (Leiden: Peter Lang, 1998).

36 *Los cuatro primeros congresos de la Internacional Comunista* (Mexico City: Siglo XXI, *1981*; trans. from the French ed., Paris: Maspero, 1970), p. 143.

37 Shipman, *It Had to Be Revolution*, pp. 124 and 127.

38 José Allen to Edgar Woog, Mexico City, 29 April 1920; *Juventud Mundial*, organ of the Young Communist Federation, in the Archive of the Mexican Communist Party (hereafter RTsKhIDNI, by its Russian acronym), Russian Center for Preservation and Study of Documents of Contemporary History (formerly the Central Party Archive), fond 495, register 108, files 3 and 26; Taibo, *Bolshevikis*, p. 54.

39 *Ibid.*, pp. 129–130; *Nuestros Ideales*, 2 June 1922; Rosendo Salazar and José G.

Escobedo, *Las pugnas de la gleba*, 2 vols. (Mexico City: Editorial Avante, 1923), vol. 2, pp. 113–114.

40 *Ibid.*, pp. 120–121; Katayama to R (Roy?), Mexico City, 12 April 1921, AMCP, fond 495, register 108, file 11; Shipman, *It Had to Be Revolution*, p. 130.

41 Katayama to the Congress of the Labor Confederation in Puebla, 5 June 1921; Katayama to the CROM Congress in Orizaba, 25 June 1921, RTsKhIDNI , fond 495, register 108, file 10.

42 Taibo, *Bolshevikis*, p. 138.

43 Katayama to the comrades, Mexico City, 26 May 1921, RTsKhIDNI, fond 495, register 108, file 11.

44 American Agency of the Profintern to the Executive Committee of the Youth Federation, Mexico, 17 November 1921, RTsKhIDNI, fond 495, register 108, file 10.

45 American Agency of the Profintern to the Small Bureau of the Executive Committee of the Communist International (ECCI), Mexico City, n.d., RTsKhIDNI, fond 495, register 108, file 11.

46 Louis Fraina to the Small Bureau of the ECCI, Mexico City, 2 January 1922, RTsKhIDNI, fond 495, register 108, file 21.

47 *Ibid.*, and Esther Corey, "Passage to Russia," *Survey*, no. 55 (April 1965), p. 108.

3 Soviet Russia in Mexican Politics

1 "León Trotski quiere renovar la lucha contra Alemania," *El Universal*, 20 March 1918; "Se habla de la restauración de la monarquía en Rusia," *El Universal*, 22 March 1918; "Se considera inevitable la Caída del Primer Ministro Ruso Lenin," *El Universal*, 28 March 1918; "Ha sido derrocado el gobierno Bolsheviki," *Excélsior*, 29 June 1918; "Alemania quiere intervenir en Rusia para sostener el gobierno de Lenine," *Excélsior*, 30 June 1918; "Los Bolsheviques fusilaron al ex zar," *El Universal*, 27 June 1918; "Estado de sitio en Moscú," *El Universal*, 10 June 1918; "Kerensky en Paris que el pueblo Ruso del lado de Aliados," 11 July 1918. From *Excélsior*: Herman Bernstein, "La libertad roja," 8 September 1918; "Protesta diplomática por ejecuciones en masa de civiles y militares, opositores del régimen Bolshevique," 9 September 1918; "Estados Unidos protesta contra el salvajismo que está imperando en Rusia," 22 September 1918; "Un Golpe de Estado en Omsk," 22 December 1918; "Llegaron a Paris Ex-Ministro Miliukov y Ex-Embajador Nicolás Fedeko," 23 December 1918; "La entente discute el arduo problema Ruso," 24 December 1918.

2 Stanley R. Ross, ed., *Fuentes de la historia contemporánea de México: Periódicos y revistas* (Mexico City: El Colegio de México, 1965), p. 247.

3 In *El Demócrata*: "Kerensky Cayó: Transferencia de poder sin derramamiento de sangre," 9 November 1917; "El gobierno de los Bolsheviky se consolida con gran rapidez," 9 November 1917; "Obreros y campesinos controlarán el gobierno," 10 November 1917; "Combates callejeros en Moscou, Petrogrado en llamas," 16 November 1917; "Se hacen grandes elogios de la sangre fría de N. Lenine," 15 November 1917; "La cuestión de la Asamblea Constituyente Rusa adquiere carácter en extremo grave," 25 November 1917; "Bajo los mejores auspicios comenzaron las negociaciones para el concierto de la paz entre los imperios centrales y Rusia," 26 November 1917; "La suspensión de la Asamblea Constituyente

puede dar lugar a un serio conflicto en Rusia," 28 November 1917; "Una man-
ifestación en Petrogrado de civiles y militares para la inmediata convocatoria a
Asamblea Constituyente," 22 November 1917; "Lenin anuncia pacto de armi-
sticio," 24 November 1917; "Discurso del canciller Alemán Richard von Kuehl-
mann ante Reichstag," 4 December 1917.

4 From *Excélsior:* "El golpe de estado en Rusia," 9 November 1917; "Fracasa sis-
tema de gobierno de fábricas implantados por Trotsky y Lenine," 24 December
1918; "El robo es la divisa del gbno. Bolsheviki," 30 December 1918. From *El
Universal:* "Los Bolsheviki han capturado varias ciudades," 21 January 1919;
"Disminuye la fuerza de los Bolsheviki," 25 January 1919; "Trotzky, el ministro
Bolsheviki de la guerra ha sido capturado," 27 January 1919; "La recaptura de la
Ciudad de Nerva exige Lenine," 29 January 1919. From *Excélsior:* "El pueblo ruso
perece a millares atacado por el hambre y la peste," "Esta dolorosa situación se
debe a la epoca de terror Que predomina originada por los Bolsheviki, Lenine y
Trotzky," 7 March 1919; "Levantamiento de obreros en Petrogrado," 23 April
1919; "Ha sido arrestado Nikolai Lenine, jefe del gobierno de los Soviets Rusos,"
9 October 1919.

5 Bertrand Russell, "El fracaso del Comunismo en Rusia," *El Demócrata*, 1 November 1925. In addition to publishing news put out by press agencies, Mexican
newspapers published articles from sources such as the *New York Times*, the
New York Herald Tribune, the *Chicago Tribune*, the Philadelphia *Public Ledger*,
New York American, and occasionally from the London *Times*. In 1924 *El Demócrata* published a series of thirty-four articles written by the American Communist Bertram Wolfe, who was living in Mexico at the time. Wolfe visited the
Soviet Union in 1924, and his articles reflected his enthusiasm for Soviet socialism. *El Demócrata* also published the Communist senator Luis Monzón's
proselytizing articles on behalf of the Soviet Union. See Luis Monzón, *Algunos
puntos sobre el Comunismo* (Mexico City: Soria, 1924).

6 Lorenzo Meyer, *Su Majestad Británica contra la Revolución Mexicana, 1900–
1950: El fin de un imperio informal* (Mexico City: El Colegio de México, 1991), p.
199; Alan Knight, *The Mexican Revolution*, 2 vols. (Lincoln: University of Nebraska Press, 1990), vol. 2, p. 427.

7 "El Bolshevismo en la América del Sur toma incremento," *Excélsior*, 22 December 1918; "Varios Rusos pretendieron derrocar a los gobiernos de Argentina y
Uruguay," *El Universal*, 13 January 1919; "Se teme que IWW en comunicación
con sociedades obreras en Veracruz," *El Universal*, 8 February 1919.

8 "Los Bolsheviqui han cruzado la frontera," *El Universal*, 27 December 1919;
"Aires de primavera del Bolshevismo en México," *El Universal*, 18 January 1919;
"Terribles vaticinios para México," *Excélsior*, 27 August 1919.

9 "En Tampico va en aumento la idea Bolsheviki," *Excélsior*, 6 May 1919; "Excélsior Señaló a Tampico como un Centro Bolsheviki," *Excélsior*, 10 June 1919. See
Lief Adleson, "Coyuntura y conciencia: Factores convergentes en la fundación de
los sindicatos petroleros de Tampico durante la década de 1920," in Elsa Cecilia
Frost, Michael C. Meyer, and Josefina Vázquez, eds., *El trabajo y los trabajadores
en la historia de México* (Mexico City and Tucson: El Colegio de México and
University of Arizona Press, 1979), p. 635.

10 "Muy activa propaganda Bolsheviki," *Excélsior*, 25 August 1920; "Se descubre la
cuna del Bolshevismo," *Excélsior*, 27 August 1920.

11 "Los Alemanes introducen el Bolshevismo en México," *El Universal,* 19 February 1919; "Propaganda Bolsheviki en México," *Excélsior,* 10 October 1919; "La gestión Bolsheviki en México," *Excélsior,* 31 August 1920; "Nuestros campesinos ante los agitadores," *El Universal,* 13 September 1920; "No ha prosperado la campaña Bolchevique en México," *El Universal,* 4 September 1920; "Fracasó la propaganda sindicalista entre los trabajadores de los campos," *El Universal,* 13 September 1920.

12 Enrique Krauze, *Caudillos culturales en la Revolución Mexicana* (Mexico City: Siglo XXI, 1976); Robert E. Quirk, *The Mexican Revolution, 1914–1915* (New York: W. W. Norton, 1960), p. 10; Knight, *The Mexican Revolution,* vol. 2, pp. 472–73; Susana Quintanilla, "Los intelectuales y la política mexicana: Estudio de casos," *Secuencia,* no. 24 (September–December 1992), pp. 47–73.

13 Marte R. Gómez to José Vasconcelos, Chapingo, 22 September 1924, in Marte R. Gómez, *Vida política contemporánea: Cartas de Marte R. Gómez* (Mexico City: Fondo de Cultura Económica, 1978), p. 40.

14 Sheldon B. Liss, *Marxist Thought in Latin America* (Berkeley: University of California Press, 1984), p. 209.

15 Manuel Gómez Morín to Vasconcelos, Mexico City, 7 June 1926, Archivo de Manuel Gómez Morín, vol. 589, file 1976.

16 Carr, *Marxism and Communism,* p. 4.

17 John W. F. Dulles, *Yesterday in Mexico: A Chronicle of the Revolution* (Austin: University of Texas Press, 1967), p. 98; José Vasconcelos, *Memorias: El desastre* (1938; reprint, Mexico City: Fondo de Cultura Económica, 1982), p. 19; Mary Kay Vaughan, *The State, Education, and Social Class in Mexico, 1880–1928* (DeKalb: Northern Illinois University Press, 1982), pp. 249–51.

18 Henry Fletcher to SRE, Mexico City, 21 September 1918; General Aguilar to Manuel Troncoso, Mexico, 1 October 1918, ASRE, 17-5-26; and Enrique Arriola Woog, ed., *Sobre Rusos y Rusia: Antología documental* (Mexico City: Lotería Nacional para la Asistencia Pública, 1994), pp. 195–96.

19 Leopoldo Ortiz to SRE, Berlin, 29 December 1919, ASRE, 17-15-4. Similarly, the Argentine representative was arrested three times for different reasons. See Mario Rapoport, "Argentina and the Soviet Union: History of Political and Commercial Relations (1917–1955)," *Hispanic American Historical Review* 66, no. 2 (1986), p. 241; Aldo César Vacs, *Discreet Partners: Argentina and the USSR Since 1917* (Pittsburgh: University of Pittsburgh Press, 1984), p. 3.

20 Ortiz to SRE, Berlin, 29 December 1919, ASRE, 17-15-4.

21 From *Excélsior:* "Desean iniciar una revolución mundial los Maximalistas," 14 March 1919; "La Política de Lenine y la dictadura del proletariado," 29 April 1919; "Bombardean a Petrogrado los Aliados," 28 May 1919; "Tchicherin informa sobre la verdadera situación en Rusia," 28 May 1919; "El peligro Bolsheviki vuelve a preocupar al Congreso de Paz," 3 June 1919; "Extensa región controlada por las tropas del Gral. Denikine," 13 June 1919; "Por negarse a combatir sus tropas, los maximalistas ya están evacuando Petrogrado," 28 August 1919; "Yudenich detenido por los Maximalistas a 7 millas de Petrogrado," 17 October 1919; "Los Bolsheviques ocuparon Omsk," 29 November 1919.

For the initial reaction to and rejection of the Soviet regime by the West, see Louis Fischer, *The Soviets in World Affairs: A History of Relations between the Soviet Union and the Rest of the World 1917–1929,* 2 vols. (London and New

York: Jonathan Cape, 1930), vol. 1, pp. 279–92; Sir Curtis Keeble, *Britain and the Soviet Union, 1917–89* (New York: Macmillan, 1990), pp. 58–61.

22 Carranza to Hermila Galindo, Mexico City, 29 June 1919, reel 68, exp. 812.00/23111; Hermila Galindo, *La Doctrina Carranza y el acercamiento Indo-Latino* (Mexico City: Secretaría de Relaciones Exteriores, 1919), p. 134.

23 Ricardo Corzo Ramírez, José G. González Sierra, David A. Skerritt, *Nunca un desleal: Cándido Aguilar, 1889–1960* (Mexico City: El Colegio de México and Gobierno del Estado de Veracruz, 1986), pp. 233–38.

24 Hilario Medina to Carranza, Mexico City, September 1919, ASRE, 17-16-63; Hanna to secretary of state, Mexico, 6 October 1920, reel 3, file 711.12/292. The treaty is mentioned in Gardner, *Safe for Democracy*, pp. 204–5. Alberto J. Pani, *Apuntes autobiográficos*, 2 vols. (Mexico City: Porrúa, 1950), p. 271.

25 Enrique Krauze, *El vértigo de la victoria: Alvaro Obregón* (Mexico City: Fondo de Cultura Económica, 1987), p. 74.

26 Roy, *Memoirs*, pp. 206–208.

27 Ramón P. de Negri to SRE, New York, 20 October 1919; undersecretary of foreign relations to Ramón de Negri, Mexico City, 21 November 1919, ASRE, 17-17-217.

28 Ramón P. de Negri to Hilario Medina, New York, 11 February 1920, ASRE, 17-17-336.

29 M. G. Prieto to SRE, Rotterdam, 18 February 1920, ASRE, 17-17-341.

30 Emile Dillon, *President Obregón, World Reformer* (Boston: Small, Maynard, 1923), p. 222.

31 Marjorie Ruth Clark, *La organización obrera en México* (Chapel Hill: University of North Carolina Press, 1934; reprint, Mexico City: ERA, 1984), p. 69.

32 John Womack, *Zapata and the Mexican Revolution* (New York: Alfred A. Knopf, 1970), pp. 365–66; Linda B. Hall, "Alvaro Obregón and the Politics of Mexican Land Reform, 1920–1924," *Hispanic American Historical Review* 60, no. 2 (1980), pp. 213–38; Heather Fowler Salamini, "Tamaulipas: Land Reform and the State," in Thomas Benjamin and Mark Wasserman, eds., *Provinces of the Revolution: Essays on Regional Mexican History, 1910–1929* (Albuquerque, N.M.: University of New Mexico Press, 1990), pp. 185–86.

33 *Discursos del General Alvaro Obregón* (Mexico City: Dirección General de Educación Militar, 1932), pp. 266, 289, and 392: "Discurso pronunciado en el banquete que le fue ofrecido por el Partido Socialista, en el Parque del Centenario," Yucatán, 9 September 1920; "Discurso pronunciado en Sodzil," Yucatán, 10 September 1920; "Discurso pronunciado por el C. General Alvaro Obregón, Presidente de la República, con motivo de la recepción que en su honor se verificó en Veracruz," 2 September 1920. Dulles, *Yesterday in Mexico*, p. 87.

34 Romana Falcón and Soledad García, *La semilla en el surco: Adalberto Tejeda y el radicalismo en Veracruz, 1883–1960* (Mexico City: El Colegio de México and Gobierno del Estado de Veracruz, 1986); Gilbert Joseph, *Revolution from Without: Yucatán, Mexico, and the United States* (Cambridge, England: Cambridge University Press, 1982), part 3; Thomas Benjamin, *A Rich Land, a Poor People: Politics and Society in Modern Chiapas* (Albuquerque: University of New Mexico Press, 1989).

35 Carrillo Puerto to Dora Carrillo Palma, Mérida, 12 October 1919 and 22 March 1920, letters displayed in the Museo de Felipe Carrillo Puerto in Motul, Yucatán. Falcón and García, *La semilla en el surco*, p. 310; "Testimonio del ingeniero

Marte R. Gómez," in Aarón Sáenz, *La política internacional de la Revolución: Estudios y documentos* (Mexico City: Fondo de Cultura Económica, 1961), pp. 114–20.

36 Hall, "Alvaro Obregón," p. 219.

37 Luis León, *Crónica del poder en los recuerdos de un político en el México revolucionario* (Mexico City: Fondo de Cultura Económica, 1987), pp. 139–41; José María Sánchez to Pani, Mexico City, 4 October 1922, ASRE, 18-5-59; "El General J. M. Sánchez como agente Soviet," *Excélsior*, 26 October 1922. For a comparison, see Dulles, *Yesterday in Mexico*, p. 268; Rafael Ramos Pedrueza to Obregón, Paris, 15 December 1923, Archivo General de la Nación, ramo Obregón/Calles (hereafter AGN, ramo O/C), file 809-R-209; Obregón to de Negri, Mexico City, 20 December 1923, AGN, ramo O/C, 609-R-26; Pedrueza to Obregón, Paris, 20 February 1924, AGN, ramo O/C, file 826-R-51; Obregón to the cashier of the National Palace, 29 April 1924, AGN, ramo O/C, 104-R-11; Rafael Ramos Pedrueza, *La estrella roja: Doce años de vida soviética* (Mexico City: n.p., 1929); Adolfo Mejía González, *México y la Unión Soviética en la defensa de la paz* (Mexico City: Novosti, 1986), pp. 23–24; Magdaleno Mondragón, *Cuando la Revolución se cortó las alas* (Mexico City: Costa-Amic, 1966), pp. 309–16.

38 Obregón to Pani, Mexico City, 15 May 1921, ASRE, 17-14-128; Obregón to the Congress, September 1921, Archivo Histórico de la Diplomacia Mexicana, *Un siglo de relaciones internacionales de México a través de las mensajes presidenciales* (Mexico City: SRE, 1935), p. 329.

39 Summerlin to secretary of state, Mexico City, 16 June and 25 August 1920, reel 90, exp. 812.00B/132; "Offer to Invest Millions in Mexico," *New York Times*, 23 July 1920; Emile Dillon, *Mexico on the Verge* (New York: George H. Doran, 1921), pp. 139–56.

40 Murray, *The Harding Era*, p. 329.

41 Attorney Myron Parker to Bainbridge Colby, Washington, D.C.: 24 May 1920, reel 71, file 812.00/24129; Harvey A. Levenstein, *Labor Organizations*, p. 103; Gregory A. Andrews, "American Labor and the Mexican Revolution, 1910–1924" (Ph.D. diss., Northern Illinois University, 1988), p. 193.

42 Gregory A. Andrews, "Toward a Consensus on U.S. Hegemony in Latin America," p. 12; Levenstein, *Labor Organizations*, pp. 94–95, 100–101; Ronald Radosh, *American Labor*, p. 353.

43 Dr. D. H. Dubrovsky to Obregón, New York, 11 February 1921, AGN, O/C, 805-R-101; Commission Mixte du Comité International de la Croix-Rouge et de la Ligue des Sociétes de la Croix-Rouge to SRE, Geneva, 5 August 1921, ASRE, 7-21-172; Dubrovsky to Obregón, Mexico, 23 January 1922, and Dubrovsky to Obregón, New York, 13 May 1922, AGN, ramo O/C, 205-R-103. As a footnote to the Mexican assistance to Soviet Russia it could be added that the ship that sailed from the Mexican wharf in June 1922 was still loaded in Riga in February 1923 because the Bill of Landing got lost. The ship was finally unloaded and the food distributed in April 1923.

44 Wright to secretary of state, London, 3 May 1921, in U.S. Department of State, Records of the Department of State Relating to Political Relations between Mexico and Other States, 1910–1929, RG 59 (hereafter cited by reel 2 and file), file 712.61.

45 Hughes to the U.S. embassy in Mexico (cyphered telegram), Washington, D.C., 7 July 1922, reel 2, file 712.61.

46 "México invitado a una conferencia internacional en Moscou" and "¿Sólo hay
    que confiar en cañones y bayonetas?" *El Universal*, 23 May 1922; "México en
    Moscou," *El Universal*, 24 May 1922; "México considerado como importante
    centro Soviet," *Excélsior*, 28 August 1922.

47 *Excélsior* published: "Puede asegurarse que Europa tiene ya reconocido al gobi-
    erno Sovietista Ruso," 1 January 1922; "El gobierno Soviet quiere que se le recon-
    ozca en Génova," 1 April 1922; "Las perspectivas del Soviet Ruso," 14 April 1922;
    "Los Aliados están redactando un ultimátum para los Rusos," 27 April 1922; "Lo
    que ofrecen 17 países a Rusia para que acepte las demandas de la conferencia," 30
    April 1922; "Si el Soviet no acepta el memorándum Aliado se suspenderán las
    negociaciones hasta que haya Otra forma de gobierno en Rusia," 3 May 1922;
    "Los delegados en La Haya dispuestos a discutir los créditos," 28 June 1922;
    "Acercamiento entre Rusia y Francia," 18 October 1922.
        El Universal published: "Rusia contesta el memorándum de los Aliados," 12
    May 1922; "Que pague Rusia para ser reconocida," 4 May 1922; "Rusia contesta
    el memorándum de los Aliados," 12 May 1922; "El Pacto de Rapallo, alma de la
    política del Soviet," 28 May 1922; "Fracasaron las conferencias de la Haya," 14
    July 1922; "El problema de Rusia no se resuelve ni con una docena de conferen-
    cias," 27 July 1922; "El gobierno Francés reconoce al Soviet," 11 February 1923.

48 Moshe Lewin, "The Civil War," in Diane Koenker, William Rosenberg, and
    Ronald Grigor Suny, eds., *Party, State and Society in the Russian Civil War:
    Explorations in Social History* (Bloomington: Indiana University Press, 1989), pp.
    404–9; Lewis H. Siegelbaum, *Soviet State and Society between Revolutions,
    1918–1929* (Cambridge, England: Cambridge University Press, 1992), ch. 2.

49 Basch to Dr. Alfredo Caturegli, Moscow, 5 October 1922, Arkhiv Vneshnei Pol-
    itiki Rossiiskoi Federatsii (Foreign Policy Archive of the Russian Federation,
    hereafter AVPRF), Office of Mexico, fond 110, register 1b, file 12, and register 1m,
    file 13.

50 *Christian Science Monitor*, January 1923.

51 Basch to SRE, Copenhagen, 17 July 1922; Basch to SRE, 4 August 1922; Basch to
    SRE, 8 November 1922; SRE to Basch, Mexico City, 29 November 1922, ASRE,
    31-22-22.

52 From *Excélsior:* "Rusia es un factor de importancia en la situación mundial," 21
    July 1923; "El reconocimiento de Rusia por el gobierno de los Estados Unidos," 23
    July 1923; "Parece que se ha reconciliado con el Comunismo Albert Fall," 30 July
    1923. M. R. Werner and John Starr, *Teapot Dome* (New York: Viking, 1959), p. 103.

53 Juan Manuel Alvarez del Castillo, *Memorias* (Mexico City: n.p., 1960), pp. 150–97.

54 *Ibid.*, p. 203.

55 *Ibid.*, pp. 203–4.

56 Alvarez del Castillo to Obregón, Berlin, 2 May 1923; Obregón to Alvarez del
    Castillo, Mexico City, 13 September 1923; Alvarez del Castillo to Obregón, Mex-
    ico City, 17 October 1923, AGN, ramo O/C, 104-R-7; Téllez to SRE, Washington,
    D.C., 20 September 1923, ASRE, 15-28-30; Héctor Cárdenas and Alexandr Siz-
    onenko, *Relaciones mexicano-soviéticas, 1917–1980* (Mexico City and Moscow:
    SRE and the Academy of Sciences, 1981), pp. 32–35; Ministerstvo Innostrannykh
    del SSSR, *Dokumenty Vneshnei Politiki SSSR* (Moscow: Gosudarstvennoe
    izdatel'stvo, 1962), vol. 7, p. 437 and 443.

57 Alvarez del Castillo, *Memorias*, p. 221.

58 Vito Alessio Robles in Sáenz, *La política internacional*, pp. 236–239; Dulles, *Yesterday in Mexico*, pp. 156–76; R. Guzmán Esparza, *Memorias de don Adolfo de la Huerta según su propio dictado* (Mexico City: Guzmán, 1957), p. 230.

4   The United States Challenges Mexico

1 Sheffield to Coolidge, Mexico City, 7 May 1926, reel 5, file 711.12/755.
2 Waldo H. Heinrichs Jr., *American Ambassador: Joseph C. Grew and the Development of the United States Diplomatic Tradition* (Boston: Little, Brown and Company, 1966; reprint, New York and Oxford: Oxford University Press, 1986), p. 100.
3 Arthur Schoenfeld to secretary of state, Mexico, 19 August 1924, reel 90, file 812.00B/79.
4 Schoenfeld to secretary of state, Mexico City, 5 September 1924, *ibid.*
5 See chapter 1.
6 Schoenfeld to secretary of state, Mexico City, 2 December 1924, reel 90, file, 812.00/85.
7 Cited by Gaddis, *Russia, the Soviet Union and the United States*, p. 105; Hunt, *Ideology*, p. 138.
8 "After the Election," signed by E., *Foreign Affairs* 3, no. 2 (15 December 1924), p. 176.
9 Sheffield to secretary of state, Mexico, 14 November 1924; Hughes to Sheffield, Washington, D.C., 14 November 1924, reel 82, file 812.00/27448.
10 "Mexicans Oust Bolsheviki," *New York Times*, 21 November 1924; "Ask Mexico to Oust Reds," *New York Times*, 2 January 1925; Alexander Weddell to secretary of state, Mexico City, 6 January 1925, reel 83, file 812.00/27495; report by G-2, 28 January 1925, MID, reel 1, file 27; Sheffield to secretary of state, Mexico City, 17 March 1925, reel 90, file 812.00B/89; Weddell to secretary of state, Mexico City, 21 May 1925, reel 83, file 812.00/27542.
11 Sheffield to secretary of state, Mexico, 6 April 1925, reel 83, file 812.00/27533; report by G-2, 2 April 1925, MID, reel 1, file 165.
12 Keith Allen Haynes, "Order and Progress: The Revolutionary Ideology of Alberto J. Pani" (Ph.D. diss., Northern Illinois University, 1981), pp. 110–28.
13 Kellogg to Sheffield, Washington, D.C., 12 June 1925, reel 4, file 711.12/546a.
14 Eduardo Moneda to Kellogg, Mexico City, 17 June 1925, reel 4, file 711.12/563.
15 Kellogg to Sheffield, Washington, D.C., 15 June 1925, reel 4, file 711.12/548.
16 Sheffield to secretary of state, Mexico City, 14 November 1924, reel 82, file 812.00/27448.
17 "What Lies Back of New Mexican Crisis," *New York Times*, 21 June 1925; Colonel James Reeves, "Memorandum for the Chief of Staff," 18 June 1925, MID, reel 1, file 592.
18 Mayor R. R. Burleigh, chief of the general staff to the military attaché, Washington, D.C., 23 June 1925, MID, reel 1, file 597; Captain James Bogart, "Memorandum for the Chief of Staff," Washington, D.C., 17 June 1925, MID, reel 1, file 607.
19 See chapter 5.
20 The *New York American*, 27 September 1925.
21 "Mexico and Communism: Series of Articles Dealing with the Hold That Com-

munistic Forces Have over Mexico and Its Present Government," 11 November
1924, PRO, FO 371, file 9563.
22 James Horn, "El embajador Sheffield contra el presidente Calles," *Historia Mexicana* 20, no. 2 (October–December 1978), pp. 266–84; W. Green to Kellogg,
Washington, D.C., 15 June 1925, reel 4, file 711.12/553.
23 Henry Lane Wilson to Senator George H. Moses, Indianapolis, 16 June 1925, reel
4, file 711.12/565.
24 Guzmán Esparza, *Memorias*, p. 283.
25 Joseph C. Grew, *Turbulent Era: A Diplomatic Record of Forty Years, 1904–1945*
(London: Hammond, 1953), p. 669.
26 Heinrichs, *American Ambassador*, pp. 109–10.
27 Arthur Schoenfeld to secretary of state, 2 July 1925 and 10 September 1925, reel
90, file 812.B/95; John Q. Wood to secretary of state, Veracruz, 12 September
1925, reel 90, file 812.00B/96.
28 Sheffield to Nicholas Murray Butler, 17 November 1925, in Robert H. Ferrell,
Frank B. Kellogg and Henry L. Stimson, vol. 11 of Robert H. Ferrell, ed., *The
American Secretaries of State and Their Diplomacy* (New York: Cooper Square,
1963), p. 31.
29 Jonathan C. Brown, "Why Foreign Oil Companies Shifted Their Production from
Mexico to Venezuela during the 1920s," *American Historical Review* 90, no. 2
(April 1985), pp. 362–85; Dulles, *Yesterday in Mexico*, pp. 319–20.
30 Ethan L. Ellis, *Frank B. Kellogg and American Foreign Relations* (New Brunswick, N.J.: Rutgers University Press, 1961), p. 33.
31 G. M. Russell, military attaché, report by G-2, Mexico City, 18 January 1926,
MID, reel 1, file 740.
32 Sheffield to secretary of state, Mexico City, 26 January 1926, reel 5, file
711.12/671; Sheffield to secretary of state, Mexico City, 16 February 1926, reel 5,
file 711.12/685; Kellogg, "Memorandum of Conversation between the President
of the United States, the Secretary of State, and the Mexican Ambassador," Washington, D.C., 21 March 1927, reel 7, file 711.12/143, and "Forged correspondence," file 711.12/145.
33 John Page to Sheffield, Mexico City, 23 January 1926, and Sheffield to secretary of
state, 25 January 1926, reel 5, file 711.12/671.
34 "Un problema continental," *El Universal*, 22 January 1926; "La responsabilidad
de México ante el pueblo de América," *El Demócrata*, 23 January 1926; "De
nuevo la diplomacia del dólar," *Excélsior*, 26 January 1926.
35 Tannenbaum's statements were published in Mexican newspapers *Excélsior*, 26
January 1926, *El Demócrata*, 23 January 1926, and *El Universal*, 22 January 1926;
they were translated into English and sent to the Department of State, reel 5, file
711.12/667–668.
36 Grew to Weddell, Washington, D.C., 6 February 1926, reel 5, file 711.12/711;
Division of Mexican Affairs to secretary of state, 15 February 1926, reel 5, file
711.12/695; Grew, *Turbulent Era*, p. 667.
37 *Ibid.*, p. 670.
38 "Siniestros planes de los Soviets," *Excélsior*, 26 April 1926.
39 Sheffield to Coolidge, Mexico City, 5 April 1926, reel 5, file 711.12/744, and Sheffield to secretary of state, Mexico City, 4 May 1926, reel 5, file 711.12/753 1/2.
Sheffield to secretary of state, Mexico City, 29 June 1926, reel 90, file 812.00B/122.

40 "Tirantez mexicana-EU por la supuesta ingerencia de México en Nicaragua," *Excélsior*, 6 December 1926.

41 Kane, "Corporate Power," p. 183; Smith, *The United States and Revolutionary Nationalism*, p. 236; Richard V. Salisbury, *Anti-Imperialism and International Competition, 1920–1929* (Wilmington, Del.: Scholarly Resources, 1988), p. 77; Jürgen Buchenau, *In the Shadow of the Giant: The Making of Mexico's Central American Policy, 1876–1930* (Tuscaloosa: University of Alabama Press, 1996), ch. 7.

42 Frederic Lewis Propas, "The State Department, Bureaucratic Politics and Soviet-American Relations, 1918–1938" (Ph.D. diss., University of California at Los Angeles, 1982), p. 53.

43 Cited by H. G. Chilton to Foreign Office, Washington, D.C. 11 November 1926, PRO, FO 371, file 11780.

44 Sheffield to secretary of state, Mexico City, 9 December and 18 December 1926, reel 90, files 812.00B/135 and 812.00B/138.

45 Ellis, *Frank B. Kellogg*, p. 38.

46 William S. Howell Jr., "Memorandum: Radical and Socialistic Influences in Mexico," Division of Mexican Affairs, Department of State, Washington, D.C., 14 December 1926, reel 90, file 812.00B/134; *Excélsior*, 9 January 1927.

47 Cited by Harold Nicholson, *Dwight Morrow* (New York: Harcourt, Brace and Company, 1930), p. 307.

48 Propas, "The State Department," pp. 18–134; Peter H. Buckingham, *America Sees Red*, pp. 36–38; Little, "Antibolshevism," p. 379.

49 F.W.B. Coleman to secretary of state, Riga, Latvia, 17 September 1925, reel 90, file 812.00B/97; Propas, "The State Department," p. 53.

50 Kelley to secretary of state, Washington, D.C., 17 December 1925, reel 90, file 812.00B/103.

51 Kelley to Olds, Washington, D.C., 6 December 1926, reel 90, file 812.00B/195; Ellis, *Frank B. Kellogg*, p. 40.

52 Richard A. Melzer, "Dwight Morrow's Role in the Mexican Revolution: Good Neighbor or Meddling Yankee?" (Ph.D. diss., University of New Mexico, 1979, p. 88; "Acuerdo Presidencial," 1 January 1927, reel 5, file 711.12/929 3/4. From the *New York Times:* "Kellogg Explains Red Mexico Report," 4 January 1927; "Coolidge Sends More Ships to Nicaragua," 7 January 1927; "Mexico Denies Charge Made by Kellogg," 14 January 1927; "Says Mexicans Fight Reds," 15 January 1927.

53 Dudley Dwyre to Sheffield, Guadalajara, 3 February 1927, reel 85, file 812.00/28232; Sheffield to secretary of state, 4 February 1927, Mexico City, reel 85, file 812.00/28223.

54 Sheffield to secretary of state, Mexico City, 7 February 1927, reel 90, file 812.00B/158.

55 George Seldes, *You Can't Print That: The Truth behind the News, 1918–1928* (New York: Payson and Clarke, 1929), p. 384.

56 Melzer, "Dwight Morrow's Role," pp. 66–70; Alex Legge to Kellogg, International Harvester Company, Chicago, 16 February 1927, reel 6, file 711.12/984.

57 Cited by H. G. Chilton to Foreign Office, Washington, D.C., 11 November 1926, PRO, FO 371, file 11780.

58 Ferrell, *Frank B. Kellogg*, pp. 33–34.

59 Ricardo Treviño to Kellogg, Mexico City, 13 January 1927, reel 6, file 711.12/855.
60 Cordell Hull, *The Memoirs of Cordell Hull*, 2 vols. (New York: Macmillan, 1948), vol. 2, p. 128.
61 Melzer, "Dwight Morrow's Role," pp. 29–33 and 45–65.
62 Kellogg to Sheffield, Washington, D.C., 14 April 1927, reel 6, file 711.12/1042a; Friedrich Katz, "El gran espía de México," *Boletín del Fideicomiso Archivos Plutarco Elías Calles y Fernando Torreblanca*, no. 20 (September–December, 1995), pp. 1–31.
63 "Address of President Coolidge before the United States Press Association," April 1927, in *Foreign Relations of the United States, 1927*, vol. 3 (Washington, D.C.: U.S. Government, 1941), p. 209.
64 Kane, "Corporate Power," pp. 181–86; Meyer, *México y los Estados Unidos*, pp. 255–256.
65 Schoenfeld to secretary of state, Mexico City, 20 October 1927, reel 6, file 711.12/1109.
66 Weddell to secretary of state, Mexico City, 20 October 1927, reel 6, file 711.12/1110.

5 The Soviets Misunderstand Their Mexican Friend

1 Robert Conquest, *Stalin: Breaker of Nations* (London: Weidenfeld, 1993), p. 70.
2 Stanislaw Pestkowski, *Wspomnienia revolucjonisty* (Lodz, Poland: Wydawnictwo Lodzkie, 1961).
3 Robert Vincent Daniels, *The Conscience of Revolution: Communist Opposition in Soviet Russia* (Cambridge, Mass.: Harvard University Press, 1960), pp. 95 and 114; Dmitri Volkogonov, *Stalin: Triumph and Tragedy*, trans. Harold Shukman (London: Weidenfeld and Nicolson, 1991), pp. 101–16.
4 Pestkowski, *Wspomnienia*, pp. 137–138; Witold S. Sworakowski, *The Communist International and Its Front Organizations* (Stanford: Hoover Institution Press, 1965), p. 444; Wolfe, *A Life in Two Centuries*, p. 341.
5 Pestkovsky to Ella Wolfe, June 1926, Bertram D. Wolfe Collection, Hoover Institution Archives, box 8, file 29; Executive Committee of International Red Aid, *Ten Years of International Red Aid in Resolutions and Documents, 1922–1932* (Moscow: n.p., 1932), p. 255.
6 See chapter 2.
7 Krestinsky to Litvinov, Berlin, 8 February 1924, AVPRF, Office of Mexico, register 4, file 1, p. 101.
8 Chicherin to Zinoviev, Moscow, 4 July 1924, AVPRF, Office of Mexico, register 4, file 1, p. 76; Chicherin to Stalin, Moscow, 26 July 1924, *ibid.*, p. 54.
9 "El excmo. sr. ministro de la Rusia Soviet presenta hoy sus credenciales," *El Demócrata*, 7 November 1924. See also AGN, ramo O/C, 104-R-28, and *Excélsior*, 8 November 1924.
10 Diego Rivera, *My Art, My Life* (New York: Citadel Press, 1960), p. 130; Bertram D. Wolfe, *The Fabulous Life of Diego Rivera* (New York: Stein and Day, 1963), pp. 134–40; Diego Rivera, *Arte y política*, ed. Raquel Tibol (Mexico City: Grijalbo, 1979), pp. 49–50.
11 Pestkovsky's speech was published under the title, "Estamos creando un Mundo Nuevo," *El Demócrata*, 8 November 1924.

12 Pestkovsky to Litvinov, Mexico City, 25 November 1924, AVPRF, Office of Mexico, register 4, file 1.

13 H.K.V., "Report on Propaganda," n.d., reel 90, file 812.00B/119.

14 Carleton Beals, *Glass Houses: Ten Years of Free-Lancing* (New York: J. B. Lippincott, 1938), p. 338.

15 Pestkovsky to Litvinov, Mexico City, 25 November 1924, AVPRF, Office of Mexico, register 4, file 1.

16 Voline (pseudonym of Vsevolod Eichenbaum), *The Unknown Revolution, 1917– 1921* (New York: Free Life Editions, 1975), pp. 541–710.

17 Wolfe, *A Life in Two Centuries*, pp. 343–348; Alexander Weddell to secretary of state, Mexico City, 31 March 1925, reel 83, file 812.00/27518; the office of the president to Haykiss, 10 November 1926, AGN, ramo O/C, 205-R-35; Torreblanca to Pestkovsky, Mexico City, 6 October 1927, AGN, ramo O/C, 205-R-44.

18 On 1 March 1925, Pestkovsky began to write his diary, *Dnevnik Polpreda*. The diary covers the following year and a half of his stay in Mexico and ends in Berlin after he was forced to leave the country. See AVPRF, fond 110, register 5, file 101.

19 William G. Rosenberg, ed., *Bolshevik Visions: First Phase of the Cultural Revolution in Soviet Russia* (Ann Arbor, Mich.: Ardis, 1984), p. 366; Kenez, *The Birth*, pp. 206–16.

20 Pestkovsky to Narkomindel, Mexico City, 15 July 1925, AVPRF, Office of Mexico, register 4, file 1.

21 Litvinov to Pestkovsky, Moscow, 11 February 1925. In a letter to Trotsky, Litvinov complained that Pestkovsky had no regard for proper diplomatic behavior and that the commissariat had to keep on teaching it to him; Litvinov to Trotsky, Moscow, 13 October 1925, AVPRF, Office of Mexico, register 4, file 1.

22 D. N., or Ramón P. de Negri, was a government official and Pestkovsky's closest friend in Mexico. Pestkovsky, *Dnevnik Polpreda*, n.d., p. 7.

23 *Ibid.*, pp. 7 and 20–21.

24 *Ibid.*, pp. 9–10.

25 Weddell to secretary of state, Mexico City, 11 February 1925, reel 83, file 812.00/27508; Robert J. Alexander, *Communism in Latin America* (New Brunswick, N.J.: Rutgers University Press, 1957), p. 326.

26 Vadillo to SRE, Moscow, 30 April 1925, ASRE, 18-22-86; Stephen Clissold, ed., *Soviet Relations with Latin America, 1918–1968* (London: Oxford University Press, 1970), p. 87.

27 *Ibid.*

28 Pestkovsky, *Dnevnik Polpreda*, pp. 11–12.

29 *Ibid.*, p. 12. See chapter 4.

30 *Ibid.*, p. 13.

31 Wolfe, *A Life in Two Centuries*, p. 350.

32 *Ibid.*

33 A report on the MCP and its Third Annual Congress, 7–13 April 1925, by M. Gómez, AMCP, fond 495, register 108, file 48.

34 Wolfe, *A Life in Two Centuries*, pp. 352–59.

35 Victor Emanuel Villaseñor, *Memorias de un hombre de izquierda*, 2 vols. (Mexico City: Biografías Gandesa, 1976), vol. 1, p. 280; Jean Meyer, Enrique Krauze, and Cayetano Reyes, *Historia de la Revolución Mexicana, 1924–1928: Estado y sociedad con Calles* (Mexico City: El Colegio de México, 1981), pp. 159–66;

Enrique Krauze, Jean Meyer, and Cayetano Reyes, *Historia de la Revolución Mexicana, 1924–1928: La reconstrucción económica* (Mexico City: El Colegio de México, 1981), pp. 83–97.

36 Amosov to Elías Barrios, Moscow, 22 March 1927, Profintern archive in the Russian Center for Preservation and Study of Documents of Contemporary History (hereafter RTsKhIDNI), fond 534, register 6, file 107.

37 Elías Barrios, *El escuadrón de hierro* (Mexico City: Cultura Popular, 1978), pp. 111–65. Barrios was one of the strike leaders. Wolfe, *A Life in Two Centuries*, p. 352; Clark, *La organización obrera*, pp. 111–15.

38 "To the Minister of Russia in Mexico City," cited by Clissold, ed., *Soviet Relations with Latin America*, p. 12.

39 Sheffield to secretary of state, Mexico, 21 April 1926, reel 90, file 812.00B/115.

40 Pestkovsky to President Calles, n.d., and Torreblanca to Pestkovsky, Mexico City, 6 October 1926, AGN, ramo O/C, 205-R-44.

41 See chapter 6.

42 Gorodetsky, *The Precarious Truce*, pp. 145–79; Keeble, *Britain and the Soviet Union*, pp. 102–8.

43 Barbara Evans Clements, *Bolshevik Feminist: The Life of Alexandra Kollontai* (Bloomington and London: Indiana University Press, 1979), pp. ix–xii; Marcel Brody, "Alexandra Kollontay," *Preuves*, no. 14 (April 1952), p. 23.

44 "The Intervention of the United States in Nicaragua and Mexico," *Inprekorr*, no. 12 (4 February 1927), p. 230; Wicks, "Die jüngsten Intrigen der Vereinigten Staaten in Mexiko," *Inprekorr*, no. 107 (1 November 1927), p. 2311; Loewen, "Der Oelfrieden zwischen den Vereinigten Staaten und Mexiko," *Inprekorr*, no. 33 (30 March 1928), p. 616. For a comparison, see Enrica Collotti-Pischel and Chiara Robertazzi, *L'Internationale Communiste et les problèmes coloniaux, 1919–1935* (Paris: Mouton, 1968).

45 "Madame Kollontay se siente feliz por su viaje a México," *Excélsior* 16 October 1926; "La Diplomacia Moderna no es ya de Intriga," *Excélsior*, 19 October 1926.

46 Kollontai to Litvinov, Mexico, 1 June 1927, AVPRF, Office of Mexico, register 4, file 1, p. 101.

47 Kollontai to Litvinov, Paris, 18 November 1926, AVPRF, Office of Mexico, register 1-z, file 2, p. 12.

48 "Diplomacia con Antifaz," *Excélsior*, 20 October 1926. Enrique Santana to SRE, Prague, 13 October 1926, and Lázaro Basch to SRE, Copenhagen, 10 December 1926, ASRE, 41-26-27; Beals, *Glass Houses*, pp. 340–42. D. V. Kelly to Sir Austin Chamberlain, 27 July 1927, PRO, FO 371, file 12003.

49 An entire dossier in the archive of Mexico's Foreign Ministry archive comprises articles and opinions both favorable and adverse to Kollontai. See ASRE, 41-26-27.

50 "No había manifestaciones para la Señora Kollontay," 7 December 1926; "En Rusia se tiene grande simpatía por México y se admira a nuestro pueblo," *Excélsior*, 8 December 1926.

51 "Mme. Kollontai presentó sus credenciales," *Excélsior*, 25 December 1926.

52 "Meksika. Ocherednoi s'iezd KROM," *Mezhdunarodnoe Rabochee Dvizhenie*, no. 21 (May 1926), pp. 13–15. From *Excélsior*: "El Comunismo no existe en nuestro país," 5 January 1927; "El Bolshevismo no aparece aún en esta nación," 23 March 1927; "Dinero de los Rusos para los huelguistas," 26 March 1927;

"Dinero Soviet enviado a los ferroviarios," 27 March 1927. "Contra la Sra. Kollontay," *El Universal*, 12 April 1927.

53 Torreblanca to Kollontai, 3 February 1927, AGN, Mexico City, ramo O/C, 205-R-35. Report by the Soviet ambassador in Mexico, AVPRF, Office of Mexico, register 6, file 2, p. 102. Interview with Ella Wolfe, Palo Alto, California, 24 July 1990.

54 Kollontai to Litvinov, Mexico, 30 January 1927, *Dokumenty vneshnei politiki*, vol. 10, p. 34.

55 Kollontai to Chicherin, Berlin, 3 June 1927, AVPRF, Office of Mexico, register 6, file 2, p. 102.

56 Brigitta Ingemanson, "The Political Function of Domestic Objects in the Fiction of Aleksandra Kollontai," *Slavic Review* 48, no. 1 (spring 1989), p. 74.

57 Beals, *Glass Houses*, p. 342; Clements, *Bolshevik Feminist*, p. 229.

58 Cited by Esperanza Tuñón Pablos, *Mujeres que se organizan: El Frente Unico pro Derechos de la Mujer, 1935–1938* (Mexico City: UNAM and Porrúa, 1992), p. 28.

59 Vadillo to SRE, Moscow, 11 November 1927, ASRE, 7-17-115. Cárdenas and Sizonenko, *Relaciones*, p. 74.

60 Representación Comercial de la U.R.S.S., *U.R.S.S.: Anuario para 1927* (Mexico City: Representación Comercial de la URSS, 1927), pp. 74–82.

6 Mexico at the Crossroads

1 From *Excélsior:* "Triunfo de Lenine en el Congreso Soviet," 5 January 1921; "Es publicado en Londres el convenio preliminar entre Rusia y la Gran Bretaña," 25 January 1921; "Es inevitable la caída del actual régimen Soviet," 1 February 1921; "La insurrección de los campesinos contra el régimen de los Soviets," 1 February 1921; "Propaganda de los Bolsheviki," 17 February 1921; "Hay desacuerdo entre Lenine y los extremistas," 25 February 1921; "El hundimiento de un régimen," 15 July 1921; "El Comunismo de los Soviets se declara vencido," 25 July 1921; "Llamamiento de Rusia a los capitalistas," 8 August 1921; "El Noveno Congreso de los Soviets aprobó la Nueva Política Económica anunciada por Lenine," 27 December 1921.

2 William G. Rosenberg, "NEP Russia as 'Transitional' Society," in Sheila Fitzpatrick, Alexander Rabinovitch, and Richard Stites, *Russia in the Era of NEP: Explorations in Soviet Society and Culture* (Bloomington: Indiana University Press, 1991), p. 3.

3 Alan M. Ball, *Russia's Last Capitalists: The Nepmen, 1921–1929* (Berkeley: University of California Press, 1987), pp. 10–11 and pp. 174–75, n. 42.

4 *Ibid.*, pp. 27–28; Leonard Shapiro, *The Communist Party of the Soviet Union* (New York: Random House, 1959; reprint, London: Methuen, 1978), p. 378.

5 Ingemanson, "The Political Function of Domestic Objects," p. 28.

6 E. H. Carr, *Interregnum 1923–1924* (New York: Macmillan, 1954), pp. 14–15 and 295–301.

7 From *El Universal:* "La NEP y cooperación exterior parecen una tregua," 12 April 1923; "En el Congreso Comunista Leonid Krasin abogó por créditos exteriores," 21 April 1923; "La realización de los idealismos de Lenin," 28 April 1923.

8 From *Excélsior:* "El Czarismo es opacado por los métodos Soviets," 8 September 1923; "Los Bolsheviki son peores que los capitalistas," 21 October 1923. From *El Universal:* "Primer paso para Poner en práctica los planes de Lenin," 1 February

1924; "La guillotina en lugar de la mazmorra al capitalista," 2 February 1924; "A pesar del reconocimiento de las grandes potencias, el Comunismo Ruso seguirá combatiendo contra la Burguesía," 29 February 1924. From *Excélsior:* "Ex-funcionarios de Rusia sentenciados a la pena capital," 8 May 1924; "Ha tenido buen exito el gno. de los Soviets," 19 June 1924; "Sólo en Rusia han aumentado los Comunistas," 20 June 1924.

9 From *Excélsior:* "El gobierno ruso se aparta de sus principios para dar mayor libertad al campesino," 9 January 1925; Luis Lara Pardo, "Las finanzas soviéticas," 11 March 1925; "La Tercera Internacional está por desaparecer," 26 March 1925.

10 From *El Universal:* "Se admite en Moscou que existe la insurrección," 28 July 1926; "No ha habido movilización de tropas del Soviet"; "La verdad que ni en Rusia se conoce la verdad," 9 August 1926. Also, "Peligra la Industria de los Soviets," 19 September 1926, *Excélsior.*

11 From *Excélsior:* "Inglaterra contra los Bolsheviki," 9 January 1926; "Los Soviets han fortalecido su posición en el Extremo Oriente," 23 January 1926; "Sinovieff pretendía sembrar la doctrina de los Bolsheviki en el norte de Africa," 11 February 1926; "Tendrán que salir de Berlin algunos comisionados Rusos," 16 February 1926; "En la primavera próxima estallará una nueva revolución Comunista en la rica región industrial del Valle del Ruhr," 23 February 1926. Henri Beraud, "En el País de los Soviets," *El Universal,* 4 January 1926. Also from *Excélsior:* "Huelga general en Gran Bretaña," 28 April 1926; "Los obreros ingleses rechazan a los rojos," 9 May 1926; Jesús Guisa y Azevedo, "El fracaso del socialismo en Europa," 12 May 1926; "No romperá ahora el gobierno Británico con el Bolshevique," 18 June 1926; "La propaganda Comunista hace peligrar las relaciones entre Alemania y Rusia," 5 June 1927; "Ministro ruso en Polonia Voikov asesinado," 9 June 1927; "El caos rojo en la República de los Soviets", 16 de June de 1927. "Negro Cuadro de la situación en Rusia: Asesinatos, fusilamientos de jefes militares y hasta suicidios," *El Universal,* 15 June 1927.

For a comparison, see E. H. Carr, *Foundations of a Planned Economy 1926–1929,* 3 vols. (London: Macmillan, 1976), vol. 1, pp. 64–65; Stationary Office, Great Britain, *Documents Illustrating the Hostile Activities of the Soviet Government and Third International against Great Britain* (London: HMSO, 1927); Gorodetsky, *The Precarious Truce,* pp. 134–68.

12 Moshe Lewin, *Political Undercurrents in Soviet Economic Debates* (Princeton: Princeton University Press, 1974), pp. 84–96; Ball, *Russia's Last Capitalists,* pp. 43–47.

13 "Trotzki está en relaciones con los monarquistas," *El Universal,* 21 February 1924; "¿Cuáles son las personalidades de la Rusia Sovietista?" *Excélsior,* 1 March 1924.

14 From *El Universal:* "La caída de Trotzky es peligrosa para los Rusos," 17 December 1924; "Trotzky es el blanco de formidables ataques," 24 December 1924; "Los tiranos Bolsheviquis han hecho de Rusia un país de esclavos," 31 December 1924. From *Excélsior:* "Temores por la vida del caído León Trotzky," 30 January 1925; "León Trotzky regresó otra vez a Moscow," 31 January 1925; "La literatura revolucionaria rusa según Trotzky y la literatura revolucionaria mexicana," 8 May 1925. Federico Gamboa, "El Espejo de Rusia," *El Universal,* 12 May 1925. From *Excélsior:* "Terrible lucha entre la autocracia y la democracia en Rusia," 17 October

1926; Max Eastman, "El testamento político de Lenin predice que una escisión en el Partido Matará al Soviet," 18 October 1926; "Han castigado ya a Trotzky, a Zinovieff y a sus partidarios," 24 October 1926; "Los Comunistas están reunidos," 28 October 1926; "Los Burgueses atacarán a la Rusia Soviet," 30 October 1926.

15 See Bertram D. Wolfe, "La Tumba de Lenin," *El Demócrata*, 17 October 1924.

16 Several decades later Wolfe admitted that he did not understand what was really going behind the scenes of this dramatic and magnificently staged congress, and that what impressed him most was the silence that surrounded Trotsky. See Wolfe, *A Life in Two Centuries*, pp. 307 and 323.

17 "Sobre la solución del problema agrario en Rusia"; "Una Nepman vista de cerca"; "El 'Bolsheviquismo' de Mexico y la 'NEP' rusa." In his autobiography Wolfe looks back at the articles he wrote and makes the comment that the material for them "was gleaned largely from handouts from the agitprop department of the Comintern concerning the wonders of the Socialism they were building" (*A Life in Two Centuries*, p. 332 and p. 572).

18 "El peligro Bolchevique," Vadillo to SRE, Moscow, 25 September 1925, ASRE, 39-3-13; Vadillo to SRE, Moscow, 20 November 1924, ASRE, 36-2-17; and *Izvestiia*, 19 November 1924 in ASRE, 21-5-177. Compare Héctor Cárdenas, *Historia de las relaciones entre México y Rusia* (Mexico City: SRE and FCE, 1993), pp. 171–175.

Basilio Vadillo was a rural teacher from Zapotitlán, Jalisco. From 1919 onward, he was an ardent supporter of Obregón, who in 1922 rewarded him for his loyalty with the governorship of Jalisco. However, their political enemies stripped him of this position, so the president compensated him with the post of ambassador—first in Oslo, Norway, and later in Moscow.

19 See the correspondence between Calles and Obregón in Carlos Macías, ed., *Plutarco Elías Calles: Correspondencia personal (1919–1945)* (Mexico City: Gobierno del Estado de Sonora, Instituto Sonorense de Cultura, Fideicomiso Archivos Plutarco Elías Calles y Fernando Torreblanca, and FCE, 1991), pp. 145–158.

20 Enrique Krauze, *Reformar desde el origen: Plutarco Elías Calles* (Mexico City: Fondo de Cultura Económica, 1987), p. 49; Haynes, "Order and Progress," p. 137.

21 Obregón to Calles, Navojoa, Sonora, 20 January 1925, in Macías, ed., *Plutarco Elías Calles*, pp. 146–147.

22 Calles in Washington Irving High School in New York, December 1924, as described in Beals, *Glass Houses*, p. 229.

23 José C. Valadés, *Memorias de un joven rebelde*, 2 vols. (Mexico City: Universidad Autónoma de Sinaloa, 1986), vol. 1, pp. 171 and 181.

24 "El señor ministro de Rusia no hará propaganda Soviet," *Excélsior*, 9 November 1924; "Propaganda Bolshevique se desarrolla en Mexico," *El Universal*, 29 December 1924, translation of an article from the *Herald Tribune*; see also the editorial "La esterilidad del Comunismo," *El Universal*, 30 December 1924.

25 Cited by Robert Hammond Murray, ed., *Mexico before the World: Public Documents and Addresses of Plutarco Elías Calles* (New York: Academy, 1927), p. 46, and originally published in *El Demócrata*, 18 April 1924. Murray was Calles's propagandist in the United States as Dillon had served Obregón.

26 "Guarantees to Foreign Capital and Betterment of the Conditions of the Mexican Workers," in Murray, *Mexico before the World*, pp. 35–36, originally published in *El Demócrata*, 22 April 1994.

27 Krauze, *Calles*, pp. 49–60.

28 Cited by Haynes, "Order and Progress," pp. 152–53.

29 "Intemperancias Bolshevistas," *Excélsior*, 5 May 1925.

30 Calles's speech in the National Palace, 4 May 1925, AGN, ramo O/C, 104-R-28; Manuel Becerra Acosta, "México no tolerará que se le tome de instrumento en política internacional," *Excélsior*, 5 May 1925.

31 Arthur Mackel, "Las declaraciones del C. Presidente se han recibido bien," *Excélsior*, 6 May 1925; "El ministro de la Rusia roja dio explicaciones ayer a nuestro gobierno," *Excélsior*, 8 May 1925.

32 "Mme. Kollontay presentó sus credenciales," *Excélsior*, 25 December 1926.

33 "Los Soviets no ayudan a Sacasa," 28 December 1926, *El Universal*; "Rectifica el Soviet a la Casa Blanca," *Excélsior*, 2 January 1927; "México no se aliará con Rusia" and "Ignorancia de los jefes de la Rusia roja," *Excélsior*, 18 and 19 January 1927.

34 At that same time, Calles sent Marte R. Gómez from Tamaulipas to the capital to organize a shipment of arms and ammunition from the secretary of war to the place in the Gulf region where the U.S. invasion was expected. See Marte Gómez to Portes Gil, Mexico, 7 January 1927, *Vida política*, p. 122.

35 "New Year Message to the Mexican People," 1 January 1927, in Murray, *Mexico before the World*, p. 156.

36 *Ibid.*, p. 157.

37 Calles, 1 September 1927, in Murray, *Mexico before the World*, pp. 173–78; Stephen H. Haber, "Assessing the Obstacles to Industrialization: The Mexican Economy, 1830–1940," *Journal of Latin American Studies* 24, part 1 (February 1992), pp. 1–2.

38 *Ibid.*, pp. 26–28.

39 Enrique Cárdenas, *La hacienda pública y la política económica, 1929–1958* (Mexico City: El Colegio de México, Fideicomiso Historia de las Américas, and FCE, 1994), p. 18.

40 *Ibid.*, pp. 34 and 37.

41 *Ibid.*, pp. 27–28. The Cristero rebellion took place between 1926 and 1929 when the church and its faithful declared war on the anticlerical state. The church hierarchy suspended religious services for three years.

42 Brown, "Why Foreign Oil Companies Shifted Their Production," pp. 362–385.

43 Ramón P. de Negri to Marte Gómez, New York, 28 September 1925, in Gómez, *Vida política*, p. 74.

44 R. P. de Negri to Marte Gómez, Berlin, 27 August 1927, *ibid.*, pp. 164–65.

45 Marte R. Gómez to Antonio Hidalgo, Ciudad Victoria, 4 May 1925, and Gómez to Calles, Ciudad Victoria, 5 June 1925, *ibid.*, pp. 59–62.

46 Gómez to de Negri, 28 September 1927, *ibid.*, pp. 168–169; Fowler Salamini, "Tamaulipas," p. 205.

47 "Mexico and Bolshevism," in Murray, *Mexico before the World*, p. 194.

48 "La desorientación de nuestra economía política," *El Universal*, 16 February 1927.

49 "Las lecciones del Bolshevismo para México," *El Universal*, 11 April 1927.

50 Pedro de Alba, "La contienda entre Rusia y los Estados Unidos," *Excélsior*, 31 March 1927.

51 Leonard Folgarait, *So Far from Heaven: David Alfaro Siqueiros' The March of*

Humanity *and Mexican Revolutionary Politics* (Cambridge, London, and New York: Cambridge University Press, 1987), pp. 4–13.

52 "Address of President Coolidge before United States Association in April 1927 and Comments of President Calles Thereon," in *Foreign Relations of the United States*, 1927 (Washington, D.C.: U.S. Government, 1942), vol. 3, pp. 209–25.

53 Victoriano Salado Alvarez, "México y la diplomacia norteamericana," and Manuel Pardo, "México cara a cara con Estados Unidos," *Excélsior*, 1 August 1927; "Conferencia dictada por Moisés Sáenz," *Excélsior*, 14 October 1927.

7 The United States as Good Neighbor

1 Walter Lippmann, "Vested Rights and Nationalism in Latin America," *Foreign Affairs* 5, no. 3 (April 1927), p. 355.

2 *Ibid.*, p. 353.

3 *Ibid.*, pp. 362–63.

4 Franklin D. Roosevelt, "Our Foreign Policy: A Democratic View," *Foreign Affairs* 6, no. 4 (July 1928), p. 583.

5 *Ibid.*, p. 584.

6 *Ibid.*, p. 585.

7 See Ogden L. Mills, "Our Foreign Policy: A Republican View," *Foreign Affairs* 6, no. 4 (July 1928), p. 555.

8 *Ibid.*, pp. 566–67.

9 *Ibid.*, p. 572.

10 Cited in Bryce Wood, *The Making of the Good Neighbor Policy* (New York and London: Columbia University Press, 1961), p. 126. Emphasis in the original.

11 *Ibid.*, pp. 118–26.

12 Melzer, "Dwight Morrow's Role," pp. 14–15 and 185; Seldes, *You Can't Print That*, p. 349; Nicholson, *Dwight Morrow*, p. 309.

13 Beals, *Glass Houses*, p. 264; Ferdinand Lundberg, *Imperial Hearst: A Social Biography* (New York: Equinox Cooperative, 1936), pp. 284–90.

14 U.S. Congress, Senate Special Committee to Investigate Propaganda, *Hearings before a Special Committee to Investigate Propaganda or Money Alleged to Have Been Used by Foreign Governments to Influence United States Senators* (Washington, D.C.: U.S. Government Printing Office, 1928), p. 193.

It could well be that after the Hearst scandal and Dwight Morrow's foray into public relations, newspapers became wary of publishing unverified rumors. Journalist Francis McCullagh discovered this for himself. McCullagh had been a correspondent for the *New York Herald* and the *Manchester Guardian* in Russia since 1904. After the revolution, he was jailed by the Bolsheviks and expelled from the country in 1922. Abhorred by the Soviet discrimination against religion, McCullagh set out on a crusade against the Mexican government headed by Calles, who had been waging a war on the Catholic Church. McCullagh tried to indict Calles as "the red czar of Mexico" in a number of daily newspapers. Not a single one was willing to publish blood-dripping sketches of Mexico in which McCullagh tried to demonstrate parallels between political developments in the Soviet Union and in Mexico. As he could not find a publisher for his thrilling stories, he concluded that both the U.S. press and President Calles were Communist; finally, he was forced to publish his articles in a book and thus reached a much more limited audience than he had hoped. See Captain Francis McCullagh, *Red Mexico: A Reign of Terror in America* (New York: Louis Carrier, 1928), pp. 26–27.

15 Nicholson, *Dwight Morrow*, p. 322; Melzer, "Dwight Morrow's Role," pp. 188–91 and 204.

16 The *New York Times*, 15 September 1930.

17 Cited by Stanley Robert Ross, "Dwight Morrow and the Mexican Revolution," *Hispanic American Historical Review* 38, no. 4 (November 1958), pp. 510–11.

18 Melzer, "Dwight Morrow's Role," 264–72.

19 Gaddis, *Russia, the Soviet Union and the United States*, pp. 106–18; Mills, "Our Foreign Policy," pp. 555–86; Hamilton Fish Armstrong, "After Ten Years: Europe and America," *Foreign Affairs* 7, no. 1 (October 1928), pp. 1–19; Little, "Anti-bolshevism," p. 378; Eduard Maximilian Mark, "The Interpretation of Soviet Foreign Policy in the United States, 1928–1947" (Ph.D. diss., University of Connecticut, 1978), pp. 1–4.

20 Filene, *Americans and the Soviet Experiment*, pp. 109–21; Manning, "Soviet-American Relations," p. 39; Wilson, *Ideology and Economics*, pp. 60 and 148.

21 Kellogg to Morrow, Washington, D.C., 6 November 1927, reel 6, file 711.12/1119a.

22 J. Reuben Clark Jr., "The Oil Settlement with Mexico," *Foreign Affairs*, no. 4 (July 1928), p. 605. As undersecretary of state in 1928, Clark published his well-known "Memorandum on the Monroe Doctrine." In the memorandum Clark declared that Roosevelt's Corollary of 1904 justifying interventions in Latin America had no validity under the Monroe Doctrine. Clark's memorandum, however, did not directly repudiate the practice of intervention. This repudiation occurred at the Montevideo and Buenos Aires conferences in 1933 and 1936, when Franklin D. Roosevelt subscribed to the principle that no state had the right to intervene in the internal or external affairs of another. See Robert Dallek, *The American Style of Foreign Policy: Cultural Politics and Foreign Affairs* (New York and Oxford: Oxford University Press, 1983), p. 105.

23 Robert Olds to Morrow, Washington, D.C., 29 November 1927, reel 89, file 812.6363/2438a.

24 Cited by Clark, "The Oil Settlement," p. 614.

25 Ross, "Dwight Morrow," pp. 514–15.

26 Smith, *The United States and Revolutionary Nationalism*, pp. 256–57; Kane, "Corporate Power," pp. 189–90; Melzer, "Dwight Morrow's Role," p. 202.

27 Colonel Alexander MacNab, cited by Jean Meyer, *La Cristiada: El conflicto entre la iglesia y el estado, 1926–1929* (Mexico City: Siglo XXI, 1976), p. 317.

28 Ethan Ellis, "Dwight Morrow and the Church-State Controversy in Mexico," *Hispanic American Historical Review* 38, no. 4 (November 1958), pp. 482–505.

29 Joseph Edmund Sterrett and Joseph Stancliffe Davis, "The Fiscal and Economic Condition of Mexico: Report Submitted to the International Committee of Bankers on Mexico," New York, 25 May 1928, p. 258. Hispanic Division, Library of Congress.

30 Melzer, "Dwight Morrow's Role," pp. 258–64.

31 Ernest Gruening, *Mexico and Its Heritage* (New York and London: Century, 1929), pp. 150–52; Melzer, "Dwight Morrow's Role," p. 296.

32 Edward Lowry to secretary of state, Guadalajara, 29 November 1927, reel 88, file 812.00/29234; Weddell to secretary of state, Mexico, 8 December 1927, reel 90, file 812.00B/196.

33 Harold Thompson, assistant military attaché, G-2 report, 14 and 17 August, and 7 September 1928, MID, reel 1, files 2220, 2249 and 2279; Abraham Rudy to secretary of state, Mexico, 4 December 1928, reel 89, file 812.00/29373.

34 Gruening, *Mexico and Its Heritage*, p. 322.

35 Morrow to secretary of state, Mexico City, 20 July 1928, reel 88, file 812.00/29218.

36 Tzvi Medin, *El minimato presidencial: Historia política del maximato, 1928–1935* (Mexico City: ERA, 1985), pp. 29–32.

37 Harold Thompson, G-2 report, Mexico City, 14 and 17 August 1928, MID, reel 1, files 2280 and 2249.

38 Melzer, "Dwight Morrow's Role," pp. 342–43 and 479.

39 Morrow to secretary of state, Mexico City, 6 September 1928 and 3 December 1928, reel 89, files 812.00/29317 and 29372.

40 Schoenfeld to secretary of state, Mexico, 29 January 1929, reel 90, file 812.00B/226; Morrow to secretary of state, Mexico, 8 March 1929, reel 90, file 812.00B/234.

41 Schoenfeld to secretary of state, Mexico City, 28 January 1929, reel 89, file 812.00/29393; the *Washington Post*, 20 February 1929, AGN, Fondo Legal Emilio Portes Gil, box 27, file 4.

42 Dulles, *Yesterday in Mexico*, p. 394; Lorenzo Meyer, Rafael Segovia, and Alejadra Lajous, *Historia de la Revolución Mexicana, 1928–1934: Los inicios de la institucionalización* (Mexico City: El Colegio de México, 1981), pp. 235–53; Melzer, "Dwight Morrow's Role," pp. 380–81.

43 Marte Gómez to Eduardo Villaseñor, Mexico, 12 April 1929; Fernando de la Fuente to Marte Gómez, Mexico, 13 May 1929; both in Gómez, *Vida política*, pp. 229–31.

44 Melzer, "Dwight Morrow's Role," pp. 381–84.

45 José Gonzalo Escobar to Herbert Hoover, n.p., 31 March 1929, AGN, Fondo Legal Emilio Portes Gil, box 27, file 4.

46 Meyer et al., *Los inicios*, pp. 202–6; Melzer, "Dwight Morrow's Role," p. 386.

47 Stevens to Stimson, New York, 25 March 1929, reel 89, file 812.00/29438.

48 Harnden to secretary of state, Tampico, 6 May 1929, reel 89, file 812.00/29446.

49 Kelley to J. Edgar Hoover, Washington, D.C., 8 June 1929, reel 90, file 812.00B/240A; Coleman to secretary of state, Riga, Latvia, 16 July 1929, reel 90, file 812.00B/242. Kelley referred to the foundation of the Communist Confederación Sindical Unitaria de Mexico (CSUM) in January 1929.

50 Melzer, "Dwight Morrow's Role," pp. 387–94.

51 John Skirius, *José Vasconcelos y la cruzada de 1929* (Mexico City: Siglo XXI, 1978), p. 130.

52 "Mexico Breaks Off with Soviet Russia," *New York Times*, 24 January 1930; "Rompimiento aplaudido," *El Nacional Revolucionario*, 28 January 1930. Arthur Bliss Lane to secretary of state, Mexico City, D.C., 17 October 1930, reel 1, file 812.00/29528; Dawson to Tanis, Washington, D.C., 22 December 1930, reel 1, file 812.00/29536; Gordon Johnston to secretary of state, Mexico City, 16 January 1931, reel 1, file 812.00/29538.

53 Wolfe, *The Fabulous Life of Diego Rivera*, pp. 271–75; Melzer, "Dwight Morrow's Role," pp. 596–97.

54 The total U.S. investments in Latin America were $5,802,776,450; in Cuba, $1,232,635,000; in Mexico in 1932, $887,360,200. See Melzer, "Dwight Morrow's Role," pp. 569–99.

55 Eyler N. Simpson, *The Ejido: Mexico's Way Out* (Chapel Hill: University of North Carolina Press, 1937), pp. 581–82.

56 Ross, "Dwight Morrow," p. 507.

57 Manuel Téllez to SRE, Washington, 17 October 1930, ASRE, 41-26-135; Anthony Troncoso, "Hamilton Fish Sr. and the Politics of American Nationalism, 1912–1945" (Ph.D. diss., State University of New Jersey, New Brunswick, 1993), ch. 9–11.

58 SRE to Téllez, Mexico City, 18 October 1930, ASRE, 41-26-135; *Washington Post*, 21 October 1930.

59 SRE to Téllez, Mexico City, 14 November 1930, ASRE, 41-26-135.

60 Arthur Bliss Lane to Genaro Estrada, Mexico City, 19 November 1930; Estrada to Bliss Lane, Mexico City, 19 November 1930; Secretaría de Gobernación to SRE, Mexico City, 11 February 1931, ASRE, 41-26-135. As will be examined in the next chapter, Secretaría de Gobernación knew more than what it was willing to share with the U.S. government.

8   The Ideological Excesses of the Comintern

1 Fitzpatrick, *The Russian Revolution*, pp. 104–5.

2 Michal Reiman, *The Birth of Stalinism: The USSR on the Eve of the "Second Revolution"* (Bloomington: Indiana University Press, 1987), pp. 12–14.

3 Fitzpatrick, "The Problem of Class Identity," in Fitzpatrick, Rabinovitch, and Stites, eds., *Russia in the Era of NEP*, p. 29; Ball, *Russia's Last Capitalists*, pp. 60–64; Siegelbaum, *Soviet State and Society*, p. 202; Gorodetsky, *The Precarious Peace*, pp. 211–40; Robert C. Tucker, *Stalin in Power: The Revolution from Above, 1928–1941* (New York: W. W. Norton, 1990), p. 70.

4 Theodore Draper, "The Strange Case of the Comintern," *Survey* 18, no. 3 (summer 1972), pp. 94–105; "Bukharin on Three Periods of Postwar Development and the Tasks of the Communist International," in Xenia J. Eudin and Robert M. Slusser, eds., *Soviet Foreign Policy, 1928–1934: Documents and Materials*, 2 vols. (University Park: Pennsylvania State University Press, 1966), vol. 1, pp. 106–20; Stephen Cohen, *Bukharin and the Bolshevik Revolution* (New York: Oxford University Press, 1973), pp. 415–16; Nicholas N. Kozlov and Eric D. Weitz, "Reflections on the Origins of the 'Third Period': Bukharin, the Comintern and the Political Economy of Weimar Germany," *Journal of Contemporary History* 24 (1989), pp. 387–410; Tucker, *Stalin in Power*, p. 79. The third period should have lasted until the downfall of capitalism itself. In fact, however, the Comintern abandoned this policy in 1934.

5 Lindley to Foreign Office, Oslo, 21 April 1926, PRO, FO 371, file 11756/472.

6 Beals, *Glass Houses*, p. 344.

7 Alexandr Makar, personal file, ASRE, 41-17-80; Makar to Torreblanca, Mexico, 16 May 1928, AGN, O/C, 205-R-44.

8 Jack Starr-Hunt, *Excélsior*, 2 March 1930.

9 Beals, *Glass Houses*, p. 345.

10 Desmond Ovey to Sir Austin Chamberlain, Mexico, 4 February 1929, PRO, FO 371, file 13501/1400; Foreign Office to Ogilvie Forbes, London, 31 October 1929, PRO, FO 371, file 14033/4916.

11 Ogilvie Forbes to Foreign Office, Mexico, 29 August 1929, PRO, FO 371, file 13502/5016; Beals, *Glass Houses*, p. 344.

12 *Ibid.*, pp. 346 and p. 354.

13 Kagan to Litvinov, Moscow, 23 September 1927, and Makar to the Soviet ambassador in Paris, Berlin, 31 December 1927, AVPRF, Office of Mexico, register 6, file 2, p. 102.

14 Beals, *Glass Houses*, p. 355; Bacelis to the chief of police, Mexico, 18 June 1931; "Versión taquigráfica de la investigación sobre Granovsky hecha con personas conectadas con él," "Declaración de Sergio Granovsky," and "Informe del agente 3 del Departamento Confidencial de la Secretaría de Gobernación," 10 August 1931 in AGN, ramo Gobernación, box 23, file 267.

15 Beals, *Glass Houses*, p. 355.

16 Carr, *Foundations of a Planned Economy*, vol. 3, part 1, pp. 166–177; Draper, "The Strange Case," p. 133.

17 The theory of social fascism dates back to 1922 when the fascists has risen to power in Italy. See Draper, "The Strange Case," p. 121; *Sexto Congreso de la Internacional Comunista* (Mexico City: Siglo XXI, 1977), pp. 150–52, 158–60, and 328–29; Joan Urban Barth, *Moscow and the Italian Communist Party: From Togliatti to Berlinguer* (London: I. B. Tauris, 1986), pp. 45–46.

18 It was, in fact, Trotsky who criticized the Comintern for neglecting to pay attention to the rising political and economic importance of the United States in the Western Hemisphere. See Trotsky, *The Third International after Lenin*, p. 6.

19 Leon Trotsky, *The First Five Years*, vol. 1, pp. 181–99; Kozlov and Weitz, "Reflections on the Origins of the 'Third Period,'" pp. 390–94. Whereas only British financial domination of Argentina figured in Lenin's *Imperialism, the Highest State of Capitalism*, Varga's updated version drew a new parallel between British and U.S. domination of capital in Latin America and quantified U.S. financial superiority over the British on the continent. See Varga and Mendelsohn, eds., *New Data for V. I. Lenin's Imperialism*, p. 191.

20 Eugen Varga, *The Decline of Capitalism* (1928), cited in Richard Day, *The 'Crisis' and the 'Crash': Soviet Studies of the West* (London: NLB), 1981, pp. 146–55.

21 A. Lozovsky, *El movimiento sindical latino americano: Sus virtudes y sus defectos* (Montevideo: Nuevos Rumbos, 1929), pp. 6–56; Carr, *Foundations*, vol. 3, part 3, pp. 975–76; Manuel Caballero, *Latin America and the Comintern, 1919–1943* (Cambridge, England, and New York: Cambridge University Press, 1986), pp. 65–96.

22 See chapters 2 and 5. Alfred Stirner, pseudonym of the Swiss Edgar Woog, was one of the founders of Juventudes Comunistas in Mexico and an intimate friend of most of the Mexican Communists during the 1920s.

23 Katayama to the political secretariat of the ECCI, Moscow, 14 January 1928; Banderas, "The Mexican Question," Minute no. 65 of the meeting of the PolitSecretariat of the ECCI, 14 January 1928. RTsKhIDNI, fond 495, register 3, file 52.

24 Interventions by Kuusinen, Bukharin, and Codovilla; *ibid.*

25 *Inprecorr* 8, no. 76 (30 October 1928), p. 1393, and no. 78 (November 1928), p. 1465.

26 Carr, *Foundations*, vol. 3, part 1, pp. 199–200.

27 Bertram Wolfe in *Inprecorr* 8, no. 46 (8 August 1928), p. 620; Carr, *Foundations*, vol. 3, part 3, pp. 978–79; *Sexto Congreso*, p. 85.

28 Comité de Defensa Proletaria to the Federación Obrera, Michoacán, Mexico, 8 December 1928; "Bases constitutivas del Comité de Defensa Proletaria," in Rodolfo Echeverría Collection, Hoover Institution Archive, box 15, file 15.7; "In the Camp of Our Enemies," *Inprecorr* 9, no. 1 (3 January 1929), p. 15; "Letter from Mexico: The Creation of Workers' and Peasants' Block in Mexico," *Inprecorr* 9, no. 6 (1 February 1929), pp. 1001–6.

29 Orestes to Alexander, Mexico, 9 March 1929, 23 March 1929, and 30 March 1929), RTsKhIDNI, fond 534, register 4, file 289.

30 Arnoldo Martínez Verdugo, ed., *Historia del Comunismo en México* (Mexico City: Grijalbo, 1985), pp. 92–96.

31 "In the Camp of Our Enemies," *Inprecorr* 9, no. 1 (3 January 1929), p. 15.

32 "ECCI Manifesto on Mexico," *Inprecorr* 9 (19 July 1929), p. 732.

33 Luis, "Conversaciones con los delegados de Mexico," Buenos Aires, 28 May 1929, RTsKhIDNI, fondo 495, register 79, file 9.

34 Heather Fowler Salamini, *Movilización campesina en Veracruz (1920–1938)* (Mexico City: Siglo XXI, 1978), pp. 84–90.

35 Villaseñor, *Memorias*, vol. 1, p. 294; Emilio Portes Gil, *Autobiografía de la Revolución Mexicana* (Mexico City: Instituto Mexicano de Cultura, 1964).

36 Falcón and García, *La semilla en el surco*, p. 187.

37 Orestes to Alexander, Mexico City, 9 March 1929, RTsKhIDNI, fond 534, register 4, file 289.

38 Vittorio Vidali, *Comandante Carlos* (Mexico City: Cultura Popular, 1986), pp. 63–64, and *Retrato de mujer, una vida con Tina Modotti* (Puebla, Mexico: Universidad Autónoma de Puebla, 1984), p. 16.

39 Bernardo Claraval, *Cuando fui Comunista* (Mexico City: Polis, 1944), p. 111. Communist militants, such as Vidali, took their stories with them when they died. In his autobiography, David Alfaro Siqueiros, a Communist miners' leader in Jalisco at the time of the Escobar rebellion, glosses over the months of the military uprising and the party's participation in it. The next thing he recounts, without giving any reason, is the intimate life in the Lecumberri prison in which he lands shortly thereafter. See David Alfaro Siqueiros, *Me llamaban el Coronelazo: Memorias de David Alfaro Siqueiros* (Mexico City: Grijalbo, 1977), ch. 12. See also Donald L. Herman, *The Comintern in Mexico* (Washington, D.C.: Public Affairs, 1974), pp. 96–97. For a different interpretation, see Martínez Verdugo, ed., *Historia del Comunismo en México*, pp. 114–15.

40 *Inprecorr*, vol. 9, no. 32, 19 July 1929, p. 732.

41 M.D.R. (Manuel Díaz Ramírez), "The White Terror in Mexico," *Inprecorr* 9, no. 32 (5 July 1929), p. 705; "Fascism," *Inprecorr* vol. 9, no. 34 (19 July 1929), p. 732.

42 See chapter 9.

43 John Barber, *Soviet Historians in Crisis, 1928–1932* (New York: Holmes and Neyer, 1981), pp. 7–8 and 53.

44 *Rabochaia Gazeta*, 28 January 1930, translation by Sir Esmond Ovey to Foreign Office, Moscow, 28 January 1930, PRO, FO 371, file 574/647.

45 *Ibid.*

46 M. Litvinov, *Vneshniaia politika SSSR: Rechi i zaiavlenia, 1927–1937* (Moscow: Gosudarstvennoe Social'no-ekonomicheskoe Izdatel'stvo, 1937), p. 344.

47 Esmond Ovey to Henderson, Moscow, 3 February 1930, PRO, FO 371, file 14875/574.

48 S. Sevin, "Meksika na puti k fashizmu," *Mezhdunarodnaia Zhizn'*, no. 2, 1930, pp. 86–101.

49 Harrison George, "Mexico Before and After the Break with the Soviet Union," *Inprecorr* 10, no. 12 (6 March 1930), pp. 203–4; Hernán Laborde, "The Political Situation in Mexico," *Inprecorr* 10, no. 41 (4 September 1930), pp. 859–60; Albert Moreau, "War Clouds on Mexican Horizon," *Inprecorr* 10, no. 43 (18 September 1930), pp. 904–5.

50 "Against Terror, Reaction and Betrayal in Mexico," *Inprecorr* 10, no. 4 (23 January 1930), p. 68.

51 M. Karpovskii, "K agrarnomu voprosu v Meksike," *Agrarnye Problemy*, nos. 3–4 (1932), pp. 44–75.

52 Emilio Portes Gil, *Quince años de política mexicana* (Mexico City: Olimpo, 1954), p. 406.

53 Krestinski to Alexandrov, Moscow, 17 January 1936, AVPRF, Office of Mexico, fond 110, register 13, file 1.

9 The Break in Relations between Mexico and the USSR

1 Dulles, *Yesterday in Mexico*, pp. 355–69.

2 Marte Gómez to Cosío Villegas, Mexico City, 31 July 1928, in *Vida política*, p. 203.

3 Marte Gómez to Alberto Pani, Mexico City, 18 September 1928, *ibid.*, pp. 208–9; Villaseñor, *Memorias*, vol. 1, p. 282.

4 Rodolfo Cerdas Cruz, *La hoz y el machete: La Internacional Comunista, América Central y la revolución en Centro América* (San José, Costa Rica: Universidad Estatal a Distancia, 1986); Piero Gleijeses, *Shattered Hope: The Guatemalan Revolution and the United States, 1944–1954* (Princeton, N.J.: Princeton University Press, 1991), p. 19.

5 Julio Madero to SRE, San Salvador, 10 October 1927; ASRE, 21-26-106.

6 Liss, *Marxist Thought in Latin America*; Harry E. Vanden, *National Marxism in Latin America: José Carlos Mariátegui's Thought and Politics* (Boulder, Colo.: Lynne Rienner, 1986); Roque Dalton, *Miguel Mármol: Los sucesos de 1932 en El Salvador* (San José, Costa Rica: EDUCA, 1972), pp. 143–162.

7 Mella became a legend even before he became a martyr. It was said that when the Cuban government refused to allow a Soviet ship to dock in Havana, Mella jumped into the shark-infested sea and swam to the ship to shake hands with the red sailors. See K. S. Karol, *Guerrillas in Power: The Course of the Cuban Revolution* (New York: Hill and Wang, 1970), p. 65. Mella's own account of the incident is less heroic: the ship *Vorovsky*, like all the other ships, was waiting to be loaded with Cuban sugar. Mella, with a group of Communists, covered the three miles from shore to ship in a motor boat. See "Una tarde bajo la bandera roja," in Fabio Grobart, ed., *Julio Antonio Mella: Escritos revolucionarios* (Mexico City: Siglo XXI, 1978), p. 77; Raquel Tibol, *Julio Antonio Mella en* El Machete: *Antología*

parcial de un luchador y su momento histórico (Mexico City: Fondo de Cultura Popular, 1968), pp. 39–53.

8 Trejo y Lerdo to General Aarón Sáenz, Havana, 26 April 1926; SRE to Trejo y Lerdo, Mexico City, 14 May 1926, ASRE, 45-4-45; Olga Cabrera, "Un crimen político que cobra actualidad," *Nueva Antropología* 7, no. 27 (July 1985), pp. 55–65.

9 Liss, *Marxist Thought in Latin America*, pp. 243–47.

10 Tibol, *Julio Antonio Mella*, pp. 62–63; Eudocio Ravines, *The Yenan Way* (New York: Scribner's, 1951), p. 57; Julio Antonio Mella, "Krest'ianskoe dvizhenie v Meksike," *Agrarnye Problemy* (1927): 183–85.

11 Vidali, *Retrato de mujer*, p. 12; Christiane Barckhausen-Canale, *Verdad y leyenda de Tina Modotti* (La Habana, Cuba: Casa de las Américas, 1989), pp. 141–46; Vidali dates Mella's departure for Veracruz in December 1928, Barckhausen-Canale puts it in September. Vidali writes that Mella confided the purpose of his mission to Tina Modotti, his companion. Barckhausen-Canale denies that Modotti knew about it.

12 Cabrera dates Machado's decision to assassinate Mella as October 1928. See Cabrera, "Un crimen político," p. 58. An alternative hypothesis could be that Machado's well-known concern with Mella's subversive activities in Mexico was exploited by U.S. intelligence, which might have engineered a way to slip the document to the Mexican consulate in Antwerp as if it had come from Cuba.

13 Dwight Morrow to the Department of State, Mexico City, 28 July 1928, reel 90, file 812.00B/205; enclosure no. 1: "Lista completa de los agentes de la III Internacional de la Comisión de Acción directa y de propaganda en el extranjero nombrados para la organización del Centro de Acción de la América Central," *ibid.*, file 812.OOB/216.

14 *Ibid.*

15 Morrow to the Department of State, Mexico City, 3 August 1928, reel 90, file 812.00B/207; Morrow to the Department of State, Mexico City, 9 August 1928, file 812.00B/206; Morrow to the Department of State, Mexico City, 9 October 1928, file 812.00B/210.

16 "Lista Completa," reel 90, file 812.00B/216. Probable forgeries such as this one neglected to respect correct spelling of names and of Soviet institutions. For instance, the document referred to the "central committee," although the Comintern had an executive committee. In addition, the document mentioned that the Central Committee of the Mexican Communist Party had thirteen members although in fact it had only five. The names mentioned did not coincide with the real names of its members except for one. For a comparison, see Vilém Kahan, ed., *Bibliography of the Communist International, 1919–1979*, vol. 1 (Leiden: E. J. Brill), 1990.

17 Cabrera, "Un crimen político," p. 60.

18 "Sírvase dar instrucciones para que se la trate con toda consideración y cuidado," Portes Gil to General Lucas González, Cuautla, 12 January 1929; J. Aguilar y Maya to Portes Gil, Mexico, 12 January 1929; Adolfo Roldán to Portes Gil, 12 January 1929; all in AGN, Fondo Legal Emilio Portes Gil, box 28, file 5.

19 Compare Alan Knight, "Mexico's Elite Settlement: Conjuncture and Consequences," in John Higley and Richard Gunther, eds., *Elites and Democratic Consolidation in Latin America and Southern Europe* (New York: Cambridge University Press, 1992), pp. 113–45.

20 Before delegating the presidency tasks to Emilio Portes Gil in December 1928, Calles presented a bill of amnesty to the Chamber of Deputies that was designed to bring back political exiles. Dwight Morrow commented on the proposed bill, viewing it as a healthy sign that the past was forgiven, even for political groups that had taken up arms against the government in the 1920s. Although the Obregonistas opposed the measure, it became law in December 1928, and throughout the following year individuals who applied for amnesty could return to Mexico. See Morrow to secretary of state, Mexico City, 18 October 1928, reel 90, 812.00B/0027.

   The history of the PNR has been examined in a number of studies. See Luis Javier Garrido, *El partido de la Revolución institucionalizada* (Mexico City: Siglo XXI, 1982); Medin, *El minimato presidencial.*

21 Herschel Johnson to secretary of state, Mexico City, 10 January 1930, reel 1, file 812.00/29488; Rafael Segovia and Alejandra Lajous, "La consolidación del poder," in Meyer et al., *Los inicios*, pp. 5–84; Dulles, *Yesterday in Mexico*, p. 435.

22 Villaseñor, *Memorias*, vol. 1, p. 282.

23 Dulles, *Yesterday in Mexico*, pp. 436–57.

24 Portes Gil, *Autobiografía*, pp. 417–24.

25 *El Universal*, 8 December 1928.

26 Clark, *La organización obrera*, pp. 214–60; Lorenzo Meyer, *Historia de la Revolución Mexicana, 1928–1934: El conflicto social y los gobiernos del maximato* (Mexico City: El Colegio de México, 1980), pp. 101–10.

27 Portes Gil, *Autobiografía*, p. 425; Gómez to Eduardo Villaseñor, Mexico City, 12 April 1929, in *Vida política*, pp. 229–31.

28 Fernando de la Fuente to Gómez, Mexico City, 13 May 1929, *ibid.*, pp. 231–32.

29 Villaseñor to Gómez, London, 16 December 1929, *ibid.*, pp. 249–250.

30 *Ibid.* Emphasis in original.

31 Cited in James W. Wilkie and Edna Monzón de Wilkie, *México visto en el siglo XX: Entrevistas de historia oral* (Mexico City: Instituto de Investigaciones Económicas, 1969), p. 654.

32 Gómez to Villaseñor, Mexico, 10 January 1930, in *Vida política*, p. 257. Gómez to Emilio Gutiérrez, 26 February 1930, *ibid.*, p. 262; Wilkie and Monzón, *México visto en el siglo XX*, p. 91.

33 Cited by Wilkie and Monzón, *ibid.*, pp. 98 and 104–7; Gómez to Calles, París, 13 November 1930, *Vida política*, p. 308.

34 Jesús Silva Herzog, *Una vida en la vida de México* (Mexico City: Siglo XXI, 1986), pp. 110–11.

35 Silva Herzog to SRE, Moscow, 15 February 1929, ASRE, 18-13-27 and ASRE, 30-29-252; Silva Herzog in *Pravda*, 7 March 1929, ASRE, L-E-815; Silva Herzog to Estrada, Moscow, 4 December 1929, AGN, Archivo Particular Emilio Portes Gil, box 28, file 6.

   The Mexican consul, Armendáriz del Castillo, who had reached the Russian capital ahead of Silva Herzog, wrote home that the Soviets ascribed little importance to relations with Mexico, "forgetting the difficult and critical circumstances which our Government had to face to grant recognition to the Soviets." Mariano Armendáriz del Castillo to undersecretary of foreign relations, Moscow, 24 December 1928, ASRE, 39-8-14; Mariano Armendáriz del Castillo, personal file, ASRE, 29-1-12.

36 "Informe confidencial," Jesús Silva Herzog to undersecretary of foreign relations, Moscow, 6 May 1929, ASRE, 39-8-14.

37 "Informe económico confidencial," Silva Herzog to undersecretary of foreign relations, Moscow, 4 July 1929, ASRE, 39-8-14.

38 As an adviser to the Liga Nacional Agraria, Silva Herzog had met Rodríguez shortly before leaving for the Soviet Union and knew that Rodríguez cherished the idea of insurrection. "The time was right to launch Communist revolution in Mexico," Rodríguez had reportedly said. But "I told him that was utopian because Mexico was not ready and that to launch a struggle with that end would be to fruitlessly sacrifice the peasants." See Silva Herzog, *Una vida*, pp. 113–114.

39 Litvinov to Silva Herzog, Moscow, 26 October 1929, ASRE, 14-25-2, and AVPRF, Office of Mexico, register 1-i, file 1.

40 Wilkie and Monzón, *México visto en el siglo XX*, p. 654; Silva Herzog, *Una vida*, p. 115.

41 "Informe político confidencial," Jesús Silva Herzog to SRE, Moscow, 4 July 1929, ASRE, 14-25-2.

42 "Informe," Silva Herzog to undersecretary of foreign relations, Moscow, 3 December 1929, ASRE, 39-8-14.

43 Named after coal miner Alexei Stakhanov, the "Stakhanov movement" was a drive for higher productivity by intensifying and rationalizing work processes. The government held up production records by emulation.

44 "Informe político confidencial," Silva Herzog to SRE, Moscow, 4 December 1929, ASRE, 14-25-2.

45 Silva Herzog, *Una vida*, p. 117.

46 Dr. Luis Lara Pardo, "México no puede ser comunista," *Excélsior*, 23 September 1929, in which the journalist translates the *Times* interview with Portes Gil and comments on it.

47 "México y el capitalismo," *Excélsior*, 24 September 1929.

48 "Los Comunistas no desfallecen," *Excélsior*, 13 October 1929.

49 "Una banda de terroristas internacionales ha caído en poder de la autoridad," *Excélsior*, 22 December 1929.

50 Villa Michel to SRE, Berlin, 11 January 1930, ASRE, 41-26-135; Portes Gil, *Quince años*, pp. 393–403.

51 Villa Michel to SRE, Berlin, 14 March 1930, ASRE, 41-26-135; See also Daniela Spenser, "El fin de la década de los años veinte y el extraño caso de Alf Caputo," *Historias*, no. 36 (1996); and Herschel Johnson to Genaro Estrada, Mexico City, 29 April 1930; Arthur Bliss Lane to Genaro Estrada, Mexico City, 19 November 1930, ASRE, 41-26-135.

52 Secretaría de Gobernación to SRE, Mexico City, 2 September 1929, ASRE, IV-135-42.

53 "No por Comunistas sino por explotadores de los obreros mexicanos fueron expulsados," *El Nacional Revolucionario*, 18 January 1930.

54 "Ruptura de relaciones con Rusia," *El Nacional Revolucionario*, 24 January 1930; "México tiene las pruebas en sus manos," *El Nacional Revolucionario*, 26 January 1930; Portes Gil, *Quince años*, pp. 388–89; Pascual Ortiz Rubio, "Informe presidencial," 1 September 1930, Archivo Histórico Diplomático Mexicano, *Un siglo de relaciones internacionales de México a través de los mensajes presidenciales* (Mexico: SRE, 1935), p. 326.

55 "La ruptura con Moscú," *El Nacional Revolucionario*, 25 January 1930.

56 *Ibid.*

57 Campos Ortiz to SRE, Washington, D.C., 3 February 1930, ASRE, 41-26-135; J. Pani to SRE, Hamburg, 14 February 1930, and Villa Michel to SRE, 27 February and 11 March 1930, ASRE, 41-26-135; Villa Michel to SRE, Berlin, 11 January 1930, ASRE, 41-26-135. The attempt on Ortiz Rubio's life was carried out by Daniel Flores, a follower of José Vasconcelos. See Dulles, *Yesterday in Mexico*, pp. 487–89.

58 Monzón to Foreign Office, Mexico City, 10 February 1930, PRO, FO 371, file 14875/574; *Hamburger Fremdenblatt*, 11 February 1930, in "Propaganda y acti-vidades de la URSS para implantar el Comunismo en México, Informes de las oficinas de México en el exterior," ASRE, 41-26-135. Beals, *Glass Houses*, p. 355; "Otra provocación contra la Unión Soviética," *El Machete*, no. 181 (May 1930).

59 "Por qué se detuvo a algunos individuos de ideas Comunistas," *El Nacional Revo-lucionario*, 21 February 1930.

60 *El Machete*, no. 179 (March 1930).

61 "La insolente actitud de los Comunistas," and "Los Comunistas en libertad," *El Nacional Revolucionario*, 21 March 1930.

62 *El Machete*, no. 185 (September 1930) and no. 189 (January 1931).

63 Luis Cabrera, preface to Fernando de la Fuente's *El Comunismo: Defensa mínima del ideal revolucionario mexicano sintetizado en la Carta de 1917* (Mexico City: Cultura, 1933), pp. iii–xii.

64 *El Nacional Revolucionario*, 31 May, 27 June, and 20 September 1929; Dulles, *Yesterday in Mexico*, p. 474; Meyer et al., *Los inicios*, pp. 67–84.

65 "La participación del Partido C. en la lucha electoral," *El Machete*, no. 178 (7 November 1929).

66 *Ibid.*

67 Gómez to Pani, Mexico City, 18 February 1929, in *Vida política*, p. 228; Juan Bustillo Oro, *Vientos de los veintes: Cronicón testimonial* (Mexico City: Sep/ Setentas, 1973), p. 114; Skirius, *José Vasconcelos y la cruzada de 1929*, pp. 140–41 and 180–82; *El Universal*, 22 November 1929.

BIBLIOGRAPHY

ARCHIVES

Mexico
Archivo de Vicente Lombardo Toledano
Archivo Diplomático de la Secretaría de Relaciones Exteriores
Archivo General de la Nación
    Ramo Gobernación
    Ramo Presidentes Obregón/Calles
    Fondo Particular de Emilio Portes Gil
Archivo Privado de Manuel Gómez Morín
Archivo Privado de Vito Alessio Robles
Centro de Estudios del Movimiento Obrero y Socialista
Hemeroteca Nacional
Historia de Mexico, Condumex
    Archivo de Venustiano Carranza

United States
Columbia University.
    Alexandra Kollontay Oral History Project
    The Bakhmetev Archive
Hoover Institution Archives, Stanford, California.
    Bertram D. Wolfe Collection
    Joseph Freeman Papers
    Rodolfo Echeverría Martínez Collection
National Archives and Records Service, Washington, D.C.
    Records of the Department of State Relating to the Internal Affairs of Mexico,
        1910–1929 and 1930–1939. RG 59.
    Records of the Department of State Relating to Political Relations between the
        United States and Mexico, 1910–1929. RG 59.
    Records of the Department of State Relating to Political Relations between
        Mexico and Other States, 1910–1929. RG 59.
    Records of the Federal Bureau of Investigation. FBI Investigative Case Files,
        1907–1923. RG 65.
    U.S. Military Intelligence Reports: Mexico 1919–1941. RG 165.

Europe
Arkhiv Vneshnei Politiki Rossiiskoi Federatsii, Moscow, Russian Federation.
International Institute of Social History, Amsterdam.
Public Record Office, Foreign Office, London.
Russian Center for Preservation and Study of Documents of Contemporary History
    (formerly the Central Party Archive), Russian Federation.

PUBLISHED SOURCES

Archivo Histórico de la Diplomacia Mexicana. *Un siglo de relaciones internacio-
   nales de México a través de los mensajes presidenciales.* Mexico City: SRE,
   1995.
Los cuatro primeros congresos de la Internacional Comunista. Mexico City: Siglo
   XXI, 1981.
Discursos del General Alvaro Obregón. Mexico City: Dirección General de Educa-
   ción Militar, 1932.
Dokumenty vneshnei politiki SSSR. 20 vols. Moscow: Gosudarstennoe Izdatel'stvo
   Politicheskoi Literatury, 1917–1936, 1962.
Executive Committee of International Red Aid. *Ten Years of International Red Aid
   in Resolutions and Documents, 1922–1932.* n.p., 1932.
Foreign Relations of the United States, 1927, vol. 3. Washington, D.C.: U.S. Govern-
   ment, 1941.
Ministerstvo Innostrannykh del SSSR.
Ministerstvo Vneshnei Torgovli SSSR. *Vneshniaia Torgovlia SSSR za 1918–1940
   goda.* Moscow: Vneshtorgizdat, 1960.
Representación Comercial de la U.R.S.S. *U.R.S.S.: Annario para 1927.* Mexico City:
   Representación Comercial de las U.R.S.S., 1927.
Second Congress of the Communist International: Minutes and Proceedings. 2 vols.
   London: New Park Publications, 1977.
Sexto Congreso de la Internacional Comunista. Mexico City: Siglo XXI, 1977.
Stationary Office, Great Britain. *Documents Illustrating the Hostile Activities of
   the Soviet Government and Third International against Great Britain.* London:
   HMSO, 1927.
U.S. Congress. Senate Special Committee to Investigate Propaganda. *Hearings be-
   fore a Special Committee to Investigate Propaganda or Money Alleged to Have
   Been Used by Foreign Governments to Influence United States Senators.* Wash-
   ington, D.C.: U.S. Government Printing Office, 1978.

PERIODICALS

Latin America
La Correspondencia Sudamericana

Mexico
El Demócrata
Excélsior
El Machete
El Nacional Revolucionario
El Universal
Nuestros Ideales

United States
New York American
New York Times
New York Times Current History

Europe
Agrarnye Problemy
Communist International
Ezhegodnik Kominterna
International Press Correspondence (Inprekorr)
Krasnyi Internatsional Profsoiuzov
Krestianskii Internatsional
Mezhdunarodnaia Zhizn'
Mezhdunarodnoe Rabochee Dvizhenie
Na Agrarnom Fronte
Planovoie Khoziaistvo
Rabochaia Gazeta

BOOKS

Abel, Christopher, and Colin M. Lewis. *Latin America, Economic Imperialism and the State: The Political Economy of the External Connection from Independence to the Present.* London: Athlon, 1985.

Alessio Robles, Vito. *Mis andanzas con nuestro Ulises.* Mexico City: Botas, 1938.

Alexander, Robert J. *Communism in Latin America.* New Brunswick, N.J.: Rutgers University Press, 1957.

Alvarez del Castillo, Juan Manuel. *Memorias.* Mexico City: n.p., 1960.

Arriola Woog, Enrique, ed. *Sobre Rusos y Rusia: Antología documental.* Mexico City: Lotería Nacional para la Asistencia Pública, 1994.

Ball, Alan M. *Russia's Last Capitalists: The Nepmen, 1921–1929.* Berkeley and London: University of California Press, 1987.

Barber, John. *Soviet Historians in Crisis, 1928–1932.* New York: Holmes and Neyer, 1981.

Barckhausen-Canale, Christiane. *Verdad y leyenda de Tina Modotti.* La Habana: Casa de las Américas, 1989.

Barrios, Elías. *El escuadrón de hierro.* Mexico City: Cultura Popular, 1978.

Barth Urban, Joan. *Moscow and the Italian Communist Party: From Togliatti to Berlinguer.* London: I. B. Tauris, 1986.

Bartley, Russell H. *Imperial Russia and the Struggle for Latin American Independence, 1808–1828.* Austin: University of Texas Press, 1978.

Beals, Carleton. *Glass Houses: Ten Years of Free-Lancing.* New York: J. B. Lippincott, 1938.

Benjamin, Thomas. *A Rich Land, a Poor People: Politics and Society in Modern Chiapas.* Albuquerque: University of New Mexico Press, 1989.

Benjamin, Thomas, and Mark Wasserman, eds. *Provinces of the Revolution: Essays on Regional Mexican History, 1910–1929.* Albuquerque: University of New Mexico Press, 1990.

Bent, Silas. *Strange Bedfellows: A Review of Politics, Personalities, and the Press.* New York: Horace Liveright, 1928.

Besedovsky, Grigory. *Revelations of a Soviet Diplomat.* Westport, Conn.: Hyperion, 1931.

Blasier, Cole. *The Hovering Giant: U.S. Responses to Revolutionary Change in Latin America, 1910–1985.* Pittsburgh: University of Pittsburgh Press, 1985.

Bojórquez, Juan de Dios. *Obregón: Aspectos de su vida*. Mexico City: Editorial Cultura, 1935.

Bottomore, Tom B. *Elites and Society*. New York: Basic Books, 1964.

Boudon, Raymond. *The Analysis of Ideology*. Chicago: University of Chicago Press, 1989.

Britton, John A. *Carleton Beals: A Radical Journalist in Latin America*. Albuquerque: University of New Mexico Press, 1987.

Brook-Shepherd, Gordon. *The Storm Petrels: The Fight of the First Soviet Defectors*. New York and London: Harcourt Brace Jovanovitch, 1977.

Buchenau, Jürgen. *In the Shadow of the Giant: The Making of Mexico's Central American Policy, 1876–1930*. Tuscaloosa: University of Alabama Press, 1996.

Buckingham, Peter H. *America Sees Red: Anti-Communism in America, 1870s to 1980s: A Guide to Issues and References*. Claremont, Calif.: Regina Books, 1988.

Bustillo Oro, Juan. *Vientos de los veintes: Cronicón testimonial*. Mexico City: Sep-Setentas, 1973.

Caballero, Manuel. *Latin America and the Comintern, 1919–1943*. Cambridge, England: Cambridge University Press, 1986.

Cabrera, Luis. *La Revolución es la Revolución*. Mexico City: Gobierno de Guanajuato, 1977.

Campa, Valentín. *Mi testimonio: Memorias de un Comunista mexicano*. Mexico City: Cultura Popular, 1978.

Cárdenas, Enrique. *La hacienda pública y la política económica, 1929–1958*. Mexico City: El Colegio de México, Fideicomiso Historia de las Américas, and FCE, 1994.

Cárdenas, Héctor. *Las relaciones mexicano-soviéticas: Antecedentes y primeros contactos diplomáticos, 1789–1927*. Mexico City: SRE, 1974.

——. *Historia de las relaciones entre México y Rusia*. Mexico City: SRE and FCE, 1993.

Cárdenas, Héctor, and Alexander Sizonenko. *Relaciones mexicano-soviéticas, 1917–1980*. Mexico City and Moscow: SRE and Academy of Sciences, 1981.

Carr, Barry. *Marxism and Communism in Twentieth-Century Mexico*. Lincoln and London: University of Nebraska Press, 1992.

Carr, E. H. *The Bolshevik Revolution, 1917–1923*. 3 vols. London: Macmillan, 1950.

——. *The Interregnum, 1923–1924*. New York: Macmillan, 1954.

——. *Socialism in One Country, 1924–1926*. New York: Macmillan, 1964.

——. *Foundations of a Planned Economy, 1926–1929*. 3 vols. New York: Macmillan, 1976.

Carroll, Malcolm. *Soviet Communism and Western Opinion, 1919–1921*. Edited by Frederic B. M. Hollyday. Chapel Hill: University of North Carolina Press, 1985.

Cerdas Cruz, Rodolfo. *La hoz y el machete: La Internacional Comunista, América Central y la revolución en Centro América*. San José, Costa Rica: Universidad Estatal a Distancia, 1986.

Challener, Richard D., ed. *From Isolation to Containment, 1921–1952: Three Decades of American Foreign Policy from Harding to Truman*. New York: St. Martin's Press, 1970.

Chentalinski, Vitali. *De los archivos literarios del KGB*. Barcelona: Anaya & Mario Muchnik, 1994.

Claraval, Bernardo. *Cuando fui Comunista*. Mexico City: Polis, 1944.

Clark, Marjorie Ruth. *La organización obrera en México*. Mexico City: ERA, 1984; reprint, Chapel Hill: University of North Carolina Press, 1934.

Clements, Barbara Evans. *Bolshevik Feminist: The Life of Alexandra Kollontai*. Bloomington and London: Indiana University Press, 1979.

Clissold, Stephen, ed. *Soviet Relations with Latin America, 1918–1968: A Documentary History*. London: Oxford University Press, 1970.

Cohen, Stephen F. *Bukharin and the Bolshevik Revolution*. New York: Oxford University Press, 1973.

Collotti-Pischel, Enrica, and Chiara Robertazzi. *L'Internazionale Communiste et les problèmes coloniaux, 1919–1935*. Paris: Mouton, 1968.

Conger, Amy. *Edward Weston in Mexico, 1923–1926*. Albuquerque: University of New Mexico Press, 1983.

Conquest, Robert. *Stalin: Breaker of Nations*. London: Weidenfeld, 1993.

Córdoba, Arnaldo. *La ideología de la Revolución Mexicana: La formación del nuevo régimen*. Mexico City: ERA, 1973.

Corzo Ramírez, Ricardo, José G. González Sierra, and David A. Skerritt. *Nunca un desleal: Cándido Aguilar, 1889–1960*. Mexico City: El Colegio de México and Gobierno del Estado de Veracruz, 1986.

Craig, Gordon, and Felix Gilbert, eds. *The Diplomats, 1919–1939*. Princeton: Princeton University Press, 1953.

Dallek, Robert. *The American Style of Foreign Policy: Cultural Politics and Foreign Affairs*. New York and Oxford: Oxford University Press, 1983.

Dalton, Roque. *Miguel Mármol: Los sucesos de 1932 en El Salvador*. San José, Costa Rica: EDUCA, 1972.

Daniels, Josephus. *The Wilson Era: Years of War and After, 1917–1923*. Chapel Hill: University of North Carolina Press, 1946.

———. *Shirt-Sleeve Diplomat*. Chapel Hill: University of North Carolina Press, 1947.

Daniels, Robert Vincent. *The Conscience of the Revolution: Communist Opposition in Soviet Russia*. Cambridge, Mass.: Harvard University Press, 1960.

———. *A Documentary History of Communism*. New York: Random House, 1960.

Davis, David Brion, ed. *The Fear of Conspiracy: Images of Un-American Subversion from the Revolution to the Present*. Ithaca, N.Y., and London: Cornell University Press, 1971.

Day, Richard B. *Leon Trotsky and the Politics of Economic Isolation*. Cambridge, England: Cambridge University Press, 1973.

———. *The 'Crisis' and the 'Crash': Soviet Studies of the West*. London: NLB, 1981.

De la Fuente, Fernando. *El Comunismo: Defensa mínima del ideal revolucionario mexicano sintetizado en la Carta de 1917*. Mexico City: Cultura, 1933.

Debo, Richard. *Revolution and Survival: The Foreign Policy of Soviet Russia, 1917–1918*. Toronto and Buffalo: University of Toronto Press, 1979.

Degras, Jane, ed. *The Communist International, 1919–1943*. London: Royal Institute, 1956.

———. *Soviet Documents on Foreign Policy*. 3 vols. London and New York: Oxford University Press, 1952.

Desmond, Robert W. *Crisis and Conflict: World News Reporting between Two Wars, 1920–1940*. Iowa City: University of Iowa Press, 1982.

Deutscher, Isaac. *The Prophet Unarmed: Trotsky, 1921–1929*. London: Oxford University Press, 1959.

Dillon, Emile J. *Mexico on the Verge*. New York: George H. Doran, 1921.

——. *President Obregón: A World Reformer*. Boston: Small, Maynard, 1923.

Draper, Theodore. *American Communism and Soviet Russia: The Formative Years*. reprint; New York: Vintage Books, 1986; New York: Viking, 1960.

——. *The Roots of American Communism*. New York: Viking Press, 1957.

Dulles, John W. F. *Yesterday in Mexico: A Chronicle of the Revolution, 1919–1936*. Austin: University of Texas Press, 1967.

Duranty, Walter. *I Write as I Please*. New York: Simon and Schuster, 1935.

Ellis, Ethan L. *Frank B. Kellogg and American Foreign Relations, 1925–1929*. New Brunswick, N.J.: Rutgers University Press, 1961.

Eran, Oded. *Mezhdunarodniki: An Assessment of Professional Expertise in the Making of Soviet Foreign Policy*. Israel: Turtlegove, 1979.

Eudin, Xenia J., and Robert M. Slusser. *Soviet Foreign Policy, 1928–1934: Documents and Materials*. 2 vols. University Park: Pennsylvania State University Press, 1966.

Executive Committee of the Communist International. *Strategy of the Communists: A Letter from the Communist International to the Mexican Communist Party*. Chicago, Ill.: Workers Party of America, 1923.

Falcón, Romana, and Soledad García. *La semilla en el surco: Adalberto Tejeda y el radicalismo en Veracruz, 1883–1960*. Mexico City: El Colegio de México and Gobierno del Estado de Veracruz, 1986.

Ferrell, Robert H., ed. *American Secretaries of State and Their Diplomacy*. New York: Cooper Square, 1963.

Filene, Peter. *Americans and the Soviet Experiment, 1917–1933*. Cambridge, Mass.: Harvard University Press, 1967.

——. *American Views of Soviet Russia, 1917–1965*. Homewood, Ill.: Dorset, 1968.

Fischer, Louis. *The Soviets in World Affairs: A History of the Relations between the Soviet Union and the Rest of the World, 1917–1929*. 2 vols. London and New York: Jonathan Cape, 1930.

Fitzpatrick, Sheila. *The Russian Revolution, 1917–1932*. New York and Oxford: Oxford University Press, 1982; reprint, Oxford University Press, 1992.

Fitzpatrick, Sheila, Alexander Rabinovitch, and Richard Stites, eds. *Russia in the Era of NEP: Explorations in Soviet Society and Culture*. Bloomington: Indiana University Press, 1991.

Florescano, Enrique. *El nuevo pasado mexicano*. Mexico City: Cal y Arena, 1992.

Freymond, Jacques, ed. *Contributions a l'histoire du Comintern*. Geneva: Librairie Droz, 1965.

Folgarait, Leonard. *So Far from Heaven: David Alfaro Siqueiros' The March of Humanity and Mexican Revolutionary Politics*. Cambridge, London, and New York: Cambridge University Press, 1987.

Foner, Eric, and John A. Garraty, eds. *The Reader's Companion to American History*. Boston: Houghton Mifflin, 1991.

Foner, Philip S. *U.S. Labor Movement and Latin America: A History of Workers' Response to Internvention*, vol. 1, 1846–1919. Mass.: Bergin and Garvey, 1988.

Fowler Salamini, Heather. *Movilización campesina en Veracruz (1920–1938)*. Mexico City: Siglo XXI, 1978.

Frankenhalter, Marilyn. *José Revueltas: El solitario solidario*. Miami: Universal, 1979.

Fried, Richard M. *Nightmare in Red: The McCarthy Era in Perspective*. New York and Oxford: Oxford University Press, 1990.

Frost, Elsa Cecilia, Michael C. Meyer, and Josephina Vásquez, eds. *El trabajo y los trabajadores en la historia de México*. Mexico City and Tucson: El Colegio de Mexico and University of Arizona Press, 1979.

Gaddis, John Lewis. *Russia, the Soviet Union and the United States: An Interpretative History*. 2d ed. New York: McGraw-Hill, 1990.

Galindo, Hermila. *La Doctrina Carranza y el acercamiento indolatino*. Mexico City: SRE, 1919.

Gall, Olivia. *Trotsky en México y la vida política en el periodo de Cárdenas, 1937–1940*. Mexico City: ERA, 1991.

García de León, Antonio. *Resistencia y utopía*. 2 vols. Mexico City: ERA, 1985.

Gardner, Lloyd. *Safe for Democracy: The Anglo-American Response to Revolution, 1913–1923*. New York: Oxford University Press, 1984.

Garrido, Luis Javier. *El partido de la Revolución institucionalizada: Medio siglo de poder político en México. La formación del nuevo estado (1928–1945)*. Mexico City: Siglo XXI, 1982.

Garrison Villard, Oswald. *Prophets True and False*. New York and London: Alfred A. Knopf, 1928.

Gellman, Irwin F. *Good Neighbor Diplomacy: United States Policies in Latin America, 1933–1945*. Baltimore and London: Johns Hopkins University Press, 1979.

Gilderhus, Mark T. *Diplomacy and Revolution: U.S.-Mexican Relations under Wilson and Carranza*. Tucson: University of Arizona Press, 1977.

Gill, Mario. *México y la Revolución de Octubre*. Mexico City: Cultura Popular, 1975.

Glad Betty. *Charles Evans Hughes and the Illusion of Innocence: A Study in American Diplomacy*. Urbana: University of Illinois Press, 1966.

Gleijeses, Piero. *Shattered Hope: The Guatemalan Revolution and the United States, 1944–1954*. Princeton, N.J.: Princeton University Press, 1991.

Gómez, Marte R. *La reforma agraria de México: Su crisis durante el período, 1928–1934*. Mexico City: Porrúa, 1964.

——. *Vida política contemporánea: Cartas de Marte R. Gómez*. Mexico City: Fondo de Cultura Económica, 1978.

Gorodetsky, Gabriel. *The Precarious Truce: Anglo-Soviet Relations, 1924–1927*. Cambridge, England: Cambridge University Press, 1977.

Grew, Joseph C. *Turbulent Era: A Diplomatic Record of Forty Years, 1904–1945*. London: Hammond, 1953.

Grobart, Fabio, ed. *Julio Antonio Mella: Escritos revolucionarios*. Mexico City: Siglo XXI, 1978.

Gruening, Ernest. *Mexico and Its Heritage*. New York and London: Century, 1929.

Guerra, François-Xavier. *México: Del Antiguo Régimen a la Revolución*. 2 vols. Translated by Sergio Fernández Bravo. Mexico City: Fondo de Cultura Económica, 1988.

Guzmán Esparza, R., ed. *Memorias de don Adolfo de la Huerta según su propio dictado*. Mexico City: Guzmán, 1957.

Haber, Stephen H. *Industry and Underdevelopment: Industrialization of Mexico, 1890–1940*. Stanford: Stanford University Press, 1989.

Hájek, Miloš. *La Tercera Internacional: La política de frente único, 1921–1935*. Barcelona: Grijalbo, 1984.

Hall, Linda B. *Alvaro Obregón: Power and Revolution in Mexico, 1911–1920*. El Paso: Texas A&M University Press, 1981.

Hammond, John Hays. *The Autobiography of John Hays Hammond*. 2 vols. New York: Farrar and Rinehart, 1935.

Heale, M. J. *American Anticommunism: Combating the Enemy Within, 1830–1970*. Baltimore and London: Johns Hopkins University Press, 1990.

Heinrichs, Waldo H. Jr. *American Ambassador: Joseph C. Grew and the Development of the United States Diplomatic Tradition*. Boston: Little, Brown and Company, 1966; reprint, New York and Oxford: Oxford University Press, 1986.

Heller, Mikhail, and Alexander Nekrich. *Utopia in Power: The History of the Soviet Union from 1917 to the Present*. New York: Summit Books, 1985.

Herman, Donald. *The Comintern in Mexico*. Washington, D.C.: Public Affairs, 1974.

Herman, Edward, and Noam Chomsky. *Manufacturing Consent: The Political Economy of the Mass Media*. New York: Pantheon Books, 1988.

Herrera, Hayden. *Frida: A Biography of Frida Kahlo*. New York: Harper and Row, 1985.

Hicks, John D. *Republican Ascendancy, 1921–1933*. New York: Harper and Brothers, 1960.

Higley, John, and Richard Gunther, eds. *Elites and Democratic Consolidation in Latin America and Southern Europe*. New York: Cambridge University Press, 1992.

Hilton, Stanley E. *Brazil and the Soviet Challenge, 1917–1947*. Austin: University of Texas Press, 1991.

Hobsbawm, Eric. *Age of Extremes: The Short Twentieth Century, 1914–1991*. London: Michael Joseph, 1994.

Hodges, Donald, and Ross Gaudy. *Mexico, 1910–1982: Reform or Revolution*. London: Zed, 1983.

Hofstadter, Richard. *The Paranoid Style in American Politics and Other Essays*. New York: Alfred A. Knopf, 1965.

Hogan, Michael, and Thomas G. Paterson. *Explaining the History of American Foreign Relations*. Cambridge and New York: Cambridge University Press, 1991.

Hohenberg, John. *Foreign Correspondence: The Great Reporters and Their Times*. New York and London: Columbia University Press, 1964.

Hooks, Margaret. *Tina Modotti: Photographer and Revolutionary*. London, England: Pandora, 1993.

Hopkins, Mark W. *Mass Media in the Soviet Union*. New York: Pegasus, 1970.

Howland, Hewitt H. *Dwight Whitney Morrow: A Sketch in Admiration*. Introduction by Calvin Coolidge. New York and London: The Century, 1930.

Hull, Cordell. *The Memoirs of Cordell Hull*. 2 vols. New York: Macmillan, 1948.

Hunt, Lynn, ed. *The New Cultural History*. Berkeley and London: University of California Press, 1989.

Hunt, Michael H. *Ideology and U.S. Foreign Policy*. New Haven and London: Yale University Press, 1987.

Jacobs, Dan N. *Borodin: Stalin's Man in China*. Cambridge, Mass.: Harvard University Press, 1981.

Jasny, Naum. *Soviet Economists of the Twenties*. London and Cambridge, England: Cambridge University Press, 1972.

Jeffreys-Jones, Rhodri. *American Espionage: From Secret Service to CIA*. New York: Free Press, 1977.

Johnson, Chalmers, ed. *Ideology and Politics in Contemporary China*. Seattle and London: University of Washington Press, 1973.

Johnston, Robert H. and Alan Cassels, eds. *Soviet Foreign Policy, 1918–1945: A Guide to Research and Research Materials*. Wilmington, Del.: Scholarly Resources, 1991.

Joseph, Gilbert M. *Revolution from Without: Yucatán, Mexico, and the United States, 1880–1924*. Cambridge, England: Cambridge University Press, 1982.

Karol, K. S. *Guerillas in Power: The Course of the Cuban Revolution*. New York: Hill and Wang, 1970.

Katkov, George. *Russia 1917: The February Revolution*. New York: Harper and Row, 1967.

Katz, Friedrich. *The Secret War in Mexico: Europe, the United States and the Mexican Revolution*. Chicago and London: University of Chicago Press, 1981.

Keeble, Curtis. *Britain and the Soviet Union, 1917–1989*. London: Macmillan, 1990.

Kenez, Peter. *The Birth of the Propaganda State: Soviet Methods of Mass Mobilization, 1917–1929*. Cambridge, England: Cambridge University Press, 1985.

Kerensky, Alexander. *The Catastrophe: Kerensky's Own Story of the Russian Revolution*. New York and London: D. Appleton, 1927.

King, Rosa E. *Tempest over Mexico: A Personal Chronicle*. Boston: Little, Brown and Company, 1938.

Knight, Alan. *The Mexican Revolution*. 2 vols. Cambridge, England: Cambridge University Press, 1986; reprint, Lincoln: University of Nebraska Press, 1990.

——. *U.S.-Mexican Relations 1910–1940: An Interpretation*. San Diego, Calif.: Center for U.S.-Mexican Studies, 1987.

Knightley, Phillip. *The Second Oldest Profession: Spies and Spying in the Twentieth Century*. New York: W. W. Norton, 1986.

Knei-Paz, Baruch. *The Social and Political Thought of Leon Trotsky*. Oxford: Clarendon Press, 1978.

Koenker, Diane P., William G. Rosenberg, and Ronald Grigor Suny, eds. *Party, State, and Society in the Russian Civil War: Explorations in Social History*. Bloomington and Indianapolis: Indiana University Press, 1989.

Kolakowski, Leszek. *Main Currents of Marxism*. 3 vols. Oxford: Oxford University Press, 1982.

Krauze, Enrique. *Caudillos culturales en la Revolución Mexicana*. Mexico City: Siglo XXI, 1976.

——. *El vértigo de la victoria: Alvaro Obregón*. Mexico City: Fondo de Cultura Económica, 1987.

——. *Reformar desde el origen: Plutarco Elías Calles*. Mexico City: Fondo de Cultura Económica, 1987.

Krauze, Enrique, Jean Meyer, and Cayetano Reyes. *Historia de la Revolución Mexicana, 1924–1928: La reconstrucción económica.* Mexico City: El Colegio de México, 1981.

Krenn, Michael L. *U.S. Policy toward Economic Nationalism in Latin America, 1917–1929.* Wilmington, Del.: Scholarly Resources, 1990.

Krivitsky, W. G. *In Stalin's Secret Service: An Exposé of Russia's Secret Police by the Former Chief of the Soviet Intelligence in Western Europe.* New York: Harper and Brothers, 1934.

Kruglak, Theodore E. *The Two Faces of Tass.* Minneapolis: University of Minneapolis Press, 1962.

Kublin, Hyman. *Asian Revolutionary: The Life of Sen Katayama.* Princeton, N.J.: Princeton University Press, 1964.

Kuusinen, Aino. *The Rings of Destiny: Inside Soviet Russia from Lenin to Brezhnev.* New York: William Morrow, 1974.

Lasch, Christopher. *American Liberals and the Russian Revolution.* New York, 1962.

Lazitch, Branko, and Milorad M. Drachkovitch. *Lenin and the Comintern.* Stanford: Hoover Institution Press, 1972.

———. *Biographical Dictionary of the Comintern.* Stanford: Hoover Institution Press, 1986.

León, Luis. *Crónica del poder en los recuerdos de un político en el México revolucionario.* Mexico City: Fondo de Cultura Económica, 1987.

Leuchtenberg, William E. *The Perils of Prosperity, 1914–1932.* Chicago and London: University of Chicago Press, 1958.

———, ed. *The Unfinished Century: America Since 1900.* Boston: Little, Brown and Company, 1973.

Levenstein, Harvey A. *Labor Organizations in the United States and Mexico: A History of Their Relations.* Westport, Conn.: Greenwood, 1971.

Lewin, Moshe. *Political Undercurrents in Soviet Economic Debates.* Princeton: Princeton University Press, 1974.

———. *The Making of the Soviet Union: Essays in the Social History of Interwar Russia.* New York: Pantheon Books, 1985.

Link, Arthur, ed. *Woodrow Wilson and a Revolutionary World, 1913–1921.* Chapel Hill: University of North Carolina Press, 1982.

Lippmann, Walter. *Liberty and the News.* New York: Harcourt, Brace and Howe, 1920.

Liss, Sheldon B. *Marxist Thought in Latin America.* Berkeley: University of California Press, 1984.

Litvinov, Maxim M. *Vneshniaia politika SSSR: Rechi i zaiavlenia, 1927–1937.* Moscow: Gosudarstvennoe Social'no-ekonomicheskoe Izdatelstvo, 1937.

Lovenstein, Meno. *American Opinion of Soviet Russia.* Washington, D.C.: American Council on Public Affairs, 1941.

Lowenthal, Abraham F., ed., *Exporting Democracy: The United States and Latin America.* Baltimore and London: Johns Hopkins University Press, 1991.

Loyola Díaz, Rafael. *La crisis Obregón-Calles y el estado mexicano.* Mexico City: Siglo XXI, 1980.

Lozovsky, A. *El movimiento sindical latino americano: Sus virtudes y sus defectos.* Montevideo: Nuevos Rumbos, 1929.

Lundberg, Ferdinand. *Imperial Hearst: A Social Biography.* New York: Equinox Cooperative, 1936.

Lyons, Eugene. *Assignment to Utopia.* New York: Harcourt, Brace and Company,
1937.

Macías, Carlos, ed. *Plutarco Elías Calles: Correspondencia personal (1919–1945).*
Mexico City: Gobierno del Estado Sonora, Instituto Sonorense de Cultura,
Fideicomiso Archivos Plutarco Elías Calles y Fernando Torreblanca, and FCE,
1991.

Markham, James W. *Voices of the Red Giants: Communications in Russia and
China.* Iowa: Iowa University Press, 1967.

Martínez Verdugo, Arnoldo, ed. *Historia del Comunismo en México.* Mexico City:
Grijalbo, 1985.

McCauley, Martin, ed. *The Russian Revolution and the Soviet State, 1917–1921:
Documents.* London and Basingstoke: Macmillan, 1975.

———. *The Soviet Union Since 1917.* London and New York: Longman, 1981.

McCullagh, Francis. *Red Mexico: A Reign of Terror in America.* New York: Louis
Carrier, 1928.

Medin, Tzvi. *El minimato presidencial: Historia política del maximato, 1928–1935.*
Mexico City: ERA, 1985.

Mejía González, Adolfo. *México y la Unión Soviética en la defensa de la paz.* Mexico
City: Novosti, 1986.

Mella, Julio Antonio. *Escritos revolucionarios.* Mexico City: Siglo XXI, 1978.

Mena Brito, Bernardino. *Bolshevismo y democracia en México.* 2 vols. Mexico City:
Botas, 1933.

Meyer, Jean. *La Cristiada: El conflicto entre la iglesia y el estado, 1926–1929.* Mexico City: Siglo XXI, 1976.

Meyer, Jean, Enrique Krauze, and Cayetano Reyes. *Historia de la Revolución Mexicana, 1924–1928: Estado y sociedad con Calles.* Mexico City: El Colegio de
México, 1981.

Meyer, Lorenzo. *México y los Estados Unidos en el conflicto petrolero (1917–1942).*
Mexico City: El Colegio de México, 1972.

———. *Historia de la Revolución Mexicana, 1928–1934: El conflicto social y los
gobiernos del maximato.* Mexico City: El Colegio de México, 1980.

———. *Su Majestad Británica contra la Revolución Mexicana, 1900–1950: El fin de un
imperio informal.* Mexico City: El Colegio de México, 1991.

———. *La segunda muerte de la Revolución Mexicana.* Mexico City: Cal y Arena,
1992.

Meyer, Lorenzo, Rafael Segovia, and Alejandra Lajous. *Historia de la Revolución
Mexicana, 1928–1934: Los inicios de la institucionalización. La política del
maximato.* Mexico City: El Colegio de México, 1981.

Mommsen, Wolfgang J., and Jürgen Osterhammel. *Imperialism and After: Con-
tinuities and Discontinuities.* London: Allen and Unwin, 1986.

Mondragón, Magdaleno. *Cuando la Revolución se cortó las alas: Intento de una
biografía del General Francisco J. Múgica.* Mexico City: B. Costa Amic, 1966.

Montgomery, David. *The Fall of the House of Labor: The Workplace, the State, and
American Labor Activism, 1865–1925.* Cambridge and Paris: Cambridge University Press and Editions de la Maison des Sciences de l'Homme, 1987.

Monzón, Luis. *Algunos puntos sobre el Comunismo*. Mexico City: Soria, 1924.

Murray, Robert Hammond. *Mexico before the World: Public Documents and Addresses of Plutarco Elías Calles*. New York: Academy, 1927.

Murray, Robert K. *Red Scare: A Study in National Hysteria, 1919–1920*. Minneapolis: University of Minnesota Press, 1955.

——. *The Harding Era: Warren G. Harding and His Administration*. Minneapolis: University of Minnesota Press, 1969.

——. *The Politics of Normalcy: Governmental Theory and Practice in the Harding-Coolidge Era*. New York: W. W. Norton, 1973.

Newhall, Nancy, ed. *The Day Books of Edward Weston*. 2 vols. New York: George Eastman House, 1973.

New York State Legislative Joint Committee Investigating Seditious Activities. Vols. 1 and 2. New York: n.p., 1920.

Nicholson, Harold. *Dwight Morrow*. New York: Harcourt, Brace and Company, 1930.

Obregón, Alvaro. *Discursos del General Alvaro Obregón*. Mexico City: Dirección General de Educación Militar, 1932.

O'Connor, Timothy Edward. *Diplomacy and Revolution: G. V. Chicherin and Soviet Foreign Affairs, 1918–1930*. Ames: Iowa University Press, 1988.

Olveda, Jaime, José María Muriá, and Agustín Vaca. *Aporte diplomático de Jalisco: Cañedo, Corona y Vadillo*. Mexico City: SRE and Gobierno del Estado de Jalisco, 1988.

Ortiz Rubio, Pascual. *Discursos políticos (1929)*. Mexico City: n.p. 1930.

Oswald, Gregory J., and Anthony J. Strover, eds. *The Soviet Union and Latin America*. New York: Praeger, 1968.

Painter, Nell Irvin. *Standing at Armageddon: The United States, 1877–1919*. New York and London: W. W. Norton, 1987.

Palavicini, Félix. *Mi vida revolucionaria*. Mexico City: Botas, 1937.

Pani, Alberto J. *Apuntes autobiográficos*. 2 vols. Mexico City: Porrúa, 1950.

Pearce, Brian, ed. *Congress of the Peoples of the East: Baku, September 1920*. Petrograd: House of the Communist International, 1920; reprint, London: New Park, 1977.

Pestkowski, Stanislaw. *Wspomnienia revolucjonisty*. Lodz, Poland: Wydawnictwo Lodzkie, 1961.

Poniatowska, Elena. *Tinísima*. Mexico City: ERA, 1992.

Poppino, Rollie E. *International Communism in Latin America: A History of the Movement, 1917–1963*. New York: Free Press, 1964.

Porter, Roy, and Mikulás Teich, eds. *Revolution in History*. Cambridge, England: Cambridge University Press, 1986.

Portes Gil, Emilio. *Quince años de política mexicana*. Mexico City: Olimpo, 1954.

——. *Autobiografía de la Revolución Mexicana: Un tratado de interpretación histórica*. Mexico City: Instituto Mexicano de Cultura, 1964.

Power, Richard Gid. *Secrecy and Power: The Life of J. Edgar Hoover*. New York and London: Macmillan, 1987.

Quirk, Robert E. *The Mexican Revolution, 1914–1915*. New York: W. W. Norton, 1960.

Raat, W. Dirk. *Los Revoltosos: Mexico's Rebels in the United States, 1903–1923*. College Station: Texas A&M University Press, 1981.

Raat, W. Dirk, and William H. Beezley, eds. *Twentieth-Century Mexico.* Lincoln and London: University of Nebraska Press, 1986.

Rabinovitch, Alexander. *The Bolsheviks Come to Power: The Revolution of 1917 in Petrograd.* New York: W. W. Norton, 1976.

Radosh, Ronald. *American Labor and United States Foreign Policy.* New York: Random House, 1969.

Ramos Pedrueza, Rafael. *La estrella roja: Doce años de vida soviética.* Mexico City: n.p., 1929.

Ravines, Eudocio. *The Yenan Way.* New York: Scribner's, 1951.

Reed, John. *Insurgent Mexico.* London: Penguin, 1983.

Reiman, Michael. *The Birth of Stalinism: The USSR on the Eve of the "Second Revolution."* Bloomington: Indiana University Press, 1987.

Richardson, William H. *Mexico through Russian Eyes, 1806–1940.* Pittsburgh: University of Pittsburgh Press, 1988.

Richmond, Douglas W. *Venustiano Carranza's Nationalist Struggle, 1893–1920.* Lincoln and London: University of Nebraska Press, 1983.

Rivera, Diego. *My Art, My Life.* New York: Citadel Press, 1960.

Rivera, Diego. *Arte y política.* Edited by Raquel Tibol. Mexico City: Grijalbo, 1979.

Rodríguez, Jaime, ed. *The Revolutionary Process in Mexico: Essays on Political and Social Change, 1880–1940.* Los Angeles: University of California Press, 1990.

Rojahn, Jürgen, ed. *The Communist International and Its National Sections.* Leiden: Peter Lang, 1998.

Rosenberg, Emily S. *Spreading the American Dream: American Economic and Cultural Expansion: 1880–1945.* New York: Hill and Wung, 1982.

Rosenberg, William G., ed. *Bolshevik Visions: First Phase of the Cultural Revolution in Soviet Russia.* Ann Arbor, Mich.: Ardis, 1984.

Ross, Stanley R., ed. *Fuentes de la historia contemporánea de México: Periódicos y revistas.* Mexico City: El Colegio de México, 1965.

Roy, M. N. *Memoirs.* Bombay: Allied, 1964.

Ruiz, Ramón Eduardo. *The Great Rebellion: Mexico, 1905–1924.* New York: W. W. Norton, 1980.

Ruiz Abreu, Alvaro. *José Revueltas: Los muros de la utopía.* Mexico City: Cal y Arena, 1992.

Saénz, Aaron. *La política internacional de la Revolución: Estudios y Documentos.* Mexico City: FCE, 1961.

Salazar, Rosendo, and José G. Escobedo. *Las pugnas de la gleba.* 2 vols. Mexico City: Editorial Avante, 1923.

Salisbury, Richard V. *Anti-Imperialism and International Competition, 1920–1929.* Wilmington, Del.: Scholarly Resources, 1988.

Santos, Gonzalo N. *Memorias.* Mexico City: Grijalbo, 1986.

Seldes, George. *You Can't Print That: The Truth behind the News, 1918–1928.* New York: Payson and Clark, 1929.

Service, Robert. *The Russian Revolution, 1900–1927.* Atlantic Highlands, N.J.: Humanities, 1986.

——. *Lenin: A Political Life.* 2 vols. Bloomington and Indianapolis: Indiana University Press, 1991.

Schmitt, Karl M. *Communism in Mexico: A Study in Political Frustration.* Austin: University of Texas Press, 1965.

Schoultz, Lars. *National Security and United States Policy toward Latin America.* Princeton, N.J.: Princeton University Press, 1987.

Shapiro, Leonard. *The Communist Party of the Soviet Union.* New York: Random House, 1959; reprint, London: Methuen, 1978.

Shipman, Charles. *It Had to Be Revolution: Memoirs of an American Radical.* Ithaca, N.Y.: Cornell University Press, 1993.

Siegelbaum, Lewis H. *Soviet State and Society Between Revolutions, 1918–1929.* Cambridge, England: Cambridge University Press, 1992.

Silva Herzog, Jesús. *Una vida en la vida de México.* Mexico City: Siglo XXI, 1972.

Simpson, Eyler N. *The Ejido: Mexico's Way Out.* Chapel Hill: University of North Carolina Press, 1937.

Siqueiros, David Alfaro. *Me llamaban el Coronelazo: Memorias de David Alfaro Siqueiros.* Mexico City: Grijalbo, 1977.

Skirius, John. *José Vasconcelos y la cruzada de 1929.* Mexico City: Siglo XXI, 1978.

Skocpol, Theda. *States and Social Revolutions: A Comparative Analysis of France, Russia and China.* Cambridge, England, and New York: Cambridge University Press, 1979.

Smith, Cornelius C. *Emilio Kosterlitzky: Eagle of Sonora and the Southwest Border.* Glendale, Calif.: Arthur H. Clark, 1970.

Smith, Robert Freeman. *The United States and Revolutionary Nationalism in Mexico, 1916–1932.* Chicago and London: University of Chicago Press, 1972.

Spenser, Daniela. *El Partido Socialista Chiapaneco: Rescate y reconstrucción de su historia.* Mexico City: Casa Chata, 1988.

Spolansky, Jacob. *The Communist Trail in America.* New York: Macmillan, 1951.

Steel, Ronald. *Walter Lippmann and the American Century.* Boston: Little, Brown and Company, 1980.

Steffens, Lincoln. *The Autobiography of Lincoln Steffens.* New York: Harcourt, Brace and Company, 1931.

Stern, Geoffrey. *The Rise and Decline of International Communism.* Aldershot: Edward Elgar, 1990.

Stites, Richard. *Revolutionary Dreams: Utopian Vision and Experimental Life in the Russian Revolution.* New York and Oxford: Oxford University Press, 1989.

Sudoplatov, Pavel, and Anatoli Sudoplatov. *Special Tasks: The Memoirs of an Unwanted Witness—A Soviet Spymaster.* Boston: Little Brown, 1994.

Sworakowski, Witold S. *The Communist International and Its Front Organizations.* Stanford: Hoover Institution Press, 1965.

Taibo, Paco Ignacio II. *Bolshevikis: Historia narrativa de los orígenes del Comunismo en México (1919–1925).* Mexico City: Joaquín Mortiz, 1986.

Tannenbaum, Frank. *Mexico: The Struggle for Peace and Bread.* New York: Alfred A. Knopf, 1950.

Taracena, Alfonso. *Historia extraoficial de la Revolución Mexicana desde las postrimerías del Porfirismo hasta los sucesos de nuestros días.* Mexico City: Jus, 1972.

Thomson, Arthur. *The Conspiracy against Mexico.* Oakland, Calif.: International, 1919.

Tibol, Raquel. *Julio Antonio Mella en* El Machete: *Antología parcial de un luchador y su momento histórico.* Mexico City: Fondo de Cultura Popular, 1968.

——. *Diego Rivera: Arte y política.* Mexico City: Grijalbo, 1979.

Trotsky, Leon. *The First Five Years of the Communist International.* 2 vols. New York and London: Pioneer, 1945.

——. *The Third International after Lenin.* New York: Pioneer, 1957.

——. *The Permanent Revolution and Results and Prospects.* New York: Merit, 1969.

——. *The History of the Russian Revolution.* London: Pluto, 1977.

Tucker, Robert C. *Stalin in Power: The Revolution from Above, 1928–1941.* New York and London: W. W. Norton, 1990.

Tulchin, Joseph S. *The Aftermath of War: World War I and U.S. Policy toward Latin America.* New York: New York University Press, 1971.

Tuñón Pablos, Esperanza. *Mujeres que se organizan: El Frente Unico pro Derechos de la Mujer, 1935–1938.* Mexico City: UNAM and Porrúa, 1992.

Turner, Frederick C. *The Dynamic of Mexican Nationalism.* Chapel Hill: University of North Carolina Press, 1968.

Ulam, Adam B. *Expansion and Coexistence: The History of Soviet Foreign Policy, 1917–1973.* New York: Praeger, 1968.

Uldricks, Teddy J. *Diplomacy and Ideology: The Origins of Soviet Foreign Policy.* London and Beverly Hills: Sage, 1979.

Vacs, Aldo César. *Discreet Partners: Argentina and the USSR Since 1917.* Pittsburgh: University of Pittsburgh Press, 1984.

Valadés, José C. *Memorias de un joven rebelde.* 2 vols. Mexico City: Universidad Autónoma de Sinaloa, 1986.

Vanden, Harry E. *National Marxism in Latin America: José Carlos Mariátegui's Thought and Politics.* Boulder, Colo.: Lynne Rienner, 1986.

——. *Latin American Marxism: A Bibliography.* New York and London: Garland, 1991.

Varga, E., and L. Mendelsohn, eds., *New Data for V. I. Lenin's Imperialism, the Highest Stage of Capitalism.* London: Lawrence and Wishart, n.d.

Vasconcelos, José. *Memorias: El desastre.* Mexico City: Fondo de Cultura Económica, 1958 (originally published in 1938).

Vaughan, Mary Kay. *The State, Education and Social Class in Mexico, 1880–1928.* DeKalb, Ill.: Northern Illinois University Press, 1982.

Vázquez, Josefina Zoraida, and Lorenzo Meyer. *México frente a Estados Unidos: Un ensayo histórico, 1776–1980.* Mexico City: El Colegio de México, 1982.

Vera-Estañol, Jorge. *Carranza and His Bolshevik Regime.* Los Angeles: Wayside Press, 1920.

Vidali, Vittorio. *Retrato de mujer, una vida con Tina Modotti.* Puebla, Mexico City: Universidad Autónoma de Puebla, 1984.

——. *Comandante Carlos.* Mexico City: Cultura Popular, 1986.

Villaseñor, Victor Manuel. *Memorias de un hombre de izquierda.* Mexico City: Biografías Gandesa, 1976.

Voline (pseudonym for Vsevolod Eichenbaum). *The Unknown Revolution, 1917–1921.* New York: Free Life Editions, 1975.

Volkogonov, Dmitri. *Stalin: Triumph and Tragedy.* Translated by Harold Shukman. London: Weidenfeld and Nicholson, 1991.

Vovelle, Michel. *Ideologies and Mentalities.* Translated by Eamon O'Flaherty. Chicago: Chicago University Press, 1990.

Walsh, Thomas F. *Katherine Anne Porter and Mexico: The Illusion of Eden.* Austin: University of Texas Press, 1992.

Werner, M. R., and John Starr. *Teapot Dome*. New York: Viking, 1959.

Wieczynski, Joseph L. *The Modern Encyclopedia of Russian and Soviet History*. Gulf Breeze, Fl.: Academic International, 1976.

Wilkie, James W., amd Edna Monzón de Wilkie. *México visto en el siglo XX: Entrevistas de historia oral*. Mexico City: Instituto de Investigaciones Económicas, 1969.

Williams, William Appleman. *Empire as a Way of Life*. Oxford: Oxford University Press, 1980.

Wilson, Joan Hoff. *Ideology and Economics: U.S. Relations with the Soviet Union, 1918–1933*. Colombia: University of Colombia Press, 1974.

Wolfe, Bertram D. *The Fabulous Life of Diego Rivera*. New York: Stein and Day, 1963.

———. *A Life in Two Centuries: An Autobiography*. New York: Stein and Day, 1981.

Womack, John. *Zapata and the Mexican Revolution*. New York: Alfred A. Knopf, 1970.

Wood, Bryce. *The Making of the Good Neighbor Policy*. New York and London: Columbia University Press, 1961.

Woroszylski, Wiktor. *Vida de Mayakovsky*. Mexico City: ERA, 1980.

Zebadúa, Emilio. *Banqueros y revolucionarios: La soberanía financiera de México, 1914–1929*. Mexico City: El Colegio de México and Fondo de Cultura Económica, 1994.

ARTICLES

Adleson, Leif. "Coyuntura y conciencia: Factores convergentes en la fundación de los sindicatos petroleros de Tampico durante la década de los 20." In *El trabajo y los trabajadores en la historia de México*, ed. Elsa Cecilia Frost, Michael Meyer, and Josefina Zoraida Vázquez, 632–661. Mexico City and Tucson: El Colegio de México and University of Arizona Press, 1979.

Anderson, Bo, and James Cockroft. "Control and Cooptation in Mexican Politics." *International Journal of Comparative Sociology* 7 (March 1966): 11–28.

Armstrong, Hamilton Fish. "After Ten Years: Europe and America." *Foreign Affairs* 7, no. 1 (October 1928): 1–19.

Bailey, David. "Revisionism and the Present Historiography of the Mexican Revolution." *Hispanic American Historical Review* 58, no. 1 (February 1978): 62–79.

Beelen, George D. "The Harding Administration and Mexico: Diplomacy by Economic Persuasion." *The Americas* 41, no. 2 (October 1984): 177–89.

Blackwell, Russell. "Julio Antonio Mella." *The Militant*, 15 (January 1931), p. 3.

Brody, Marcel. "Alexandra Kollontay." *Preuves*, no. 14 (April 1952): 21–32.

Brooks, Jeffrey. "Public and Private Values in the Soviet Press, 1921–1928." *Slavic Review* 48, no. 1 (spring 1989): 16–35.

Brown, Jonathan C. "Why Foreign Oil Companies Shifted Their Production from Mexico to Venezuela during the 1920s." *American Historical Review* 90, no. 2 (April 1985): 362–85.

Cabrera, Olga. "Un crimen político que cobra actualidad." *Nueva Antropología* 7, no. 27 (July 1985): 55–65.

Calles, Plutarco E. "The Policies of Mexico Today." *Foreign Affairs* 5, no. 1 (October 1926): 320–28.

Chicherin, Georgi. "La politique exterieure des Deux Internationales." *L'Internationales Communiste*, no. 6 (October 1919), pp. 11–13.

——. "Address by USSR People's Commissar of Foreign Affairs G. V. Chicherin at the Fourteenth Congress of the VKP (b) (1925)." *Russian Studies in History* 31 (spring 1993), pp. 62–64.

Clark, J. Reuben, "The Oil Settlement with Mexico." *Foreign Affairs*, no. 4 (July 1928): 605–17.

Corey, Esther. "Passage to Russia: A Personal Reminiscence." *Survey*, no. 53 (October 1964): 23–32.

——. "Passage to Russia, II." *Survey*, no. 55 (April 1965): 103–15.

Danilov, Victor. "We are Starting to Learn about Trotsky." *History Workshop*, no. 29 (spring 1990): 136–46.

Draper, Theodore. "The Ghost of Socialfascism." *Commentary* (February 1969): 34–45.

——. "The Strange Case of the Comintern." *Survey* 18, no. 3 (summer 1972): 122–153.

Ellis, Ethan L. "Dwight Morrow and the Church-State Controversy in Mexico." *Hispanic American Historical Review* 38, no. 4 (November 1958): 482–505.

Gálvez, Alejandro. "La sección mexicana de la Internacional Comunista y el movimiento obrero, 1919–1943." *Iztapalapa* 3, no. 6 (January–June 1982): 236–51.

——. "Julio Antonio Mella: Un Marxista revolucionario. Debate en torno a su vida y su muerte." *Crítica de la Economía Política* 30 (1986): 2–38.

Gilderhus, Mark T. "Senator Albert B. Fall and 'The Plot against Mexico.' " *New Mexico Historical Review* 48, no. 4 (October 1973): 299–311.

Gilly, Adolfo. "La larga travesía." *Nexos* 91 (July 1985): 15–29.

Gómez, Manuel. "From Mexico to Moscow." *Survey* 53 (October 1964): 33–46.

——. "From Mexico to Moscow, II." *Survey* 55 (April 1965): 116–25.

Haber, Stephen H. "Assessing the Obstacles to Industrialization: The Mexican Economy, 1830–1940." *Journal of Latin American Studies* 24, part 1 (February 1992): 1–32.

Hall, Linda. "Alvaro Obregón and the Politics of Mexican Land Reform, 1920–1924." *Hispanic American Historical Review* 60, no. 2 (1980): 213–38.

Horn, James. "El embajador Sheffield contra el presidente Calles." *Historia Mexicana* 78, no. 2 (October–December 1970): 265–84.

——. "U.S. Diplomacy and the Specter of Bolshevism in Mexico, 1924–1927." *The Americas* 32, no. 1 (July 1975): 31–45.

Hunt, Michael H. "The Long Crisis in U.S. Diplomatic History: Coming to Closure." *Diplomatic History* 16, no. 1 (winter 1992): 115–40.

Ingemanson, Brigitta. "The Political Function of Domestic Objects in the Fiction of Aleksandra Kollontai." *Slavic Review* 48, no. 1 (spring 1989): 71–82.

Judt, Tony. "A Clown in Regal Purple: Social History and the Historians." *History Workshop*, no. 7 (spring 1979): 67–94.

Kane, Stephen N. "Corporate Power and Foreign Policy: Efforts of American Oil Companies to Influence United States Relations with Mexico, 1921–1928." *Diplomatic History* 1, no. 2 (spring 1977): 170–98.

Katz, Friedrich. "El gran espía de Mexico." *Boletín del Fideicomiso Archivos Plutarco Elías Calles y Fernando Torreblanca*, no. 20 (September–December 1995): 1–31.

Kennan, George. "The Sisson Documents." *The Journal of Modern History* 28, no. 2 (June 1956): 130–54.

Killen, Linda. "The Search for a Democratic Russia: Bakhmetev and the United States." *Diplomatic History* 2, no. 3 (summer 1978): 237–56.

Knight, Alan. "The Mexican Revolution: Bourgeois? Nationalist? Or Just a Great Rebellion?" *Bulletin of Latin American Research* 4 (1985): 1–37.

Kochanski, Aleksander. "El sindicalismo latinoamericano: Materiales del archivo moscovita de la Internacional Sindical Roja." *Estudios Latinoamericanos* 11 (1988): 249–95.

Kozlov, Nicholas N., and Eric D. Weitz. "Reflections on the Origins of the 'Third Period': Bukharin, the Comintern and the Political Economy of Weimar Germany." *Journal of Contemporary History* 24 (1989): 387–410.

Lachmann, Richard. "Class Formation without Class Struggle: An Elite Conflict Theory of the Transition to Capitalism." *American Sociological Review* 55, no. 3 (June 1990): 398–414.

Levenstein, Harvey. "The AFL and Mexican Immigration in the 1920s: An Experiment in Labor Diplomacy." *Hispanic American Historical Review* 48 (May 1968): 206–19.

Leuchtenberg, William E. "The Pertinence of Political History: Reflections on the Significance of the State in America." *The Journal of American History* 3, no. 3 (December 1986): 585–600.

Lippmann, Walter. "Vested Rights and Nationalism in Latin America." *Foreign Affairs* 5, no. 3 (April 1927): 333–42.

Little, Douglas. "Antibolshevism and American Foreign Policy, 1919–1939: The Diplomacy of Self-Delusion." *American Quarterly* 35 (fall 1983): 376–89.

Mella, Julio Antonio. "Krest'ianskoe dvizhenie v Meksike." *Agrarnye Problemy* (1927): 183–85.

Mills, Ogden L. "Our Foreign Policy: A Republican View." *Foreign Affairs* 6, no. 4 (July 1928): 555–86.

Oswald, Gregory. "México en la historiografía soviética." *Historia Mexicana* 14, no. 3 (January–March 1965): 691–706.

Pantsov, Aleksandr Vadimovich. "Lev Davidovich Trotskii." *Soviet Studies in History* 30, no. 1 (summer 1991): 7–43.

Quintanilla, Susana. "Los intelectuales y la política mexicana: Estudio de caso." *Secuencia*, no. 24 (September–December 1992): 47–73.

Rabe, Stephen G. "Marching Ahead (Slowly): The Historiography of Inter-American Relations." *Diplomatic History* 13, no. 3 (summer 1989): 297–316.

Rapoport, Mario. "Argentina and the Soviet Union: History of Political and Commercial Relations (1917–1955)." *Hispanic American Historical Review* 66, no. 2 (1986): 239–85.

Richardson, William H. "Maiakovskii en México." *Historia Mexicana* 29, no. 4 (April–June 1980): 623–39.

Riguzzi, Paolo. "México, Estados Unidos y Gran Bretaña, 1867–1910: Una difícil relación triangular." *Historia Mexicana* 41, no. 3 (January–March, 1992): 365–436.

Roosevelt, Franklin D. "Our Foreign Policy: A Democratic View." *Foreign Affairs* 6, no. 4 (July 1928): 573–586.

Ross, Stanley Robert. "Dwight Morrow and the Mexican Revolution." *Hispanic American Historical Review* 38, no. 4 (November 1958): 506–28.

Ross, Steven J. "Struggle for the Screen: Workers, Radicals, and the Political Uses of Silent Film." *American Historical Review* 96, no. 2 (April 1991): 333–67.

Scarzanella, Eugenia. "La imagen de América Latina en la prensa y en los debates de la III Internacional, 1929–1935." *Estudios Latinoamericanos* 6 (1980): 193–206.

Singer, Alan. "Communists and Coal Miners: Rank-and-File Organizing in the United Mine Workers of America during the 1920s." *Science and Society* 55, no. 2 (summer 1991): 102–157.

Spenser, Daniela. "El fin de la década de los años veinte en México y el extraño caso de Alf Caputo." *Historias*, no. 36 (1996): 73–83.

Stimson, Henry L. "The United States and the Other American Republics," *Foreign Affairs*, no. 3 (1931): 1–14.

Stratton, David H., ed. "The Memoirs of Albert Fall." *Southwestern Studies* 4, no. 3 (1966): 1–67.

Szlajfer, Henryk. "Review Essay: *Latin America and the Comintern:* An Interesting Book with Many Mistakes." *Boletín de Estudios Latinoamericanos y del Caribe*, no. 46 (June 1989): 111–18.

Tardanico, Richard. "State Dependency and Nationalism: Revolutionary Mexico, 1924–1928." *Comparative Studies in Society and History* 24, no. 3 (July 1982): 23–46.

Tobler, Hans-Werner. "Las paradojas del ejército revolucionario: Su papel social en la reforma agraria mexicana, 1920–1935." *Historia Mexicana* 21, no. 81 (July–September 1971): 38–79.

"United States Inquiry into Bolshevism: Lenine-Trotzky Regime in Russia Described by Eye Witnesses—Views of Sympathizers," *New York Times Current History* 10 (April–September 1919), pp. 128–144.

Vizcaino, Rogelio, and Paco Ignacio Taibo II. "El camarada José Allen: Informe sobre el primer secretario general del PCM y agente norteamericano." *Nexos* 61 (January 1983): 6–12.

Womack, John. "The Mexican Economy during the Revolution, 1910–1920: Historiography and Analysis." *Marxist Perspective* 1, no. 4 (winter 1978): 80–123.

THESIS, DISSERTATIONS, AND UNPUBLISHED WORKS

Agosti, Aldo. "World Revolution and World Party of the Revolution: The Evolution of Two Concepts." Paper presented at the International Scientific Conference, *History of the Comintern in the Light of New Documents*, Moscow, 20–22 October 1994.

Andrews, Gregory Alan. "American Labor and the Mexican Revolution, 1910–1924." Ph.D. diss., Northern Illinois University, 1988.

——. "Toward a Consensus on U.S. Hegemony in Latin America: American Labor and U.S. Officials View the Mexican Revolution." Paper presented at Southeastern Social Science Association, Austin, Texas, 1991.

Christopulos, Diana K. "American Radicals and the Mexican Revolution, 1900–1925." Ph.D. diss., State University of New York at Binghamton, 1980.

Coogan, Peter F. "Geopolitics and the Intellectual Origins of Containment." Ph.D. diss., University of North Carolina at Chapel Hill, 1991.

García Marsh, Alma María. "Ideology and Power: A Study of the Mexican State under Porfirio Díaz (1876–1911) and Lázaro Cárdenas (1934–1940)." Ph.D. diss., Harvard University, 1982.

Haynes, Keith A. "Order and Progress: The Revolutionary Ideology of Alberto J. Pani." Ph.D. diss., Northern Illinois University, 1981.

Holubnychy, Lydia. "Michael Borodin and the Chinese Revolution, 1923–1925," Ph.D. diss., Columbia University, 1979.

Manning, Donald James. "Soviet-American Relations, 1929–1941: The Impact of Domestic Considerations on Foreign Policy Decision-Making." Ph.D. diss., Michigan State University, 1978.

Mark, Eduard Maximilian. "The Interpretation of Soviet Foreign Policy in the United States, 1928–1947." Ph.D. diss., University of Connecticut, 1978.

Melzer, Richard. "Dwight Morrow's Role in the Mexican Revolution: Good Neighbor or Meddling Yankee?" Ph.D. diss., University of New Mexico, 1979.

Propas, Frederic Lewis. "The State Department, Bureaucratic Politics and Soviet-American Relations, 1918–1938." Ph.D. diss., University of California at Los Angeles, 1982.

Shero, Olga P. "Soviet Activities in Central America: The Historical Antecedents." 2 vols. Ph.D. diss., Georgetown University, 1985.

Shirinia, Kirill. "The Comintern: A World Party and Its National Sections." Paper presented at the International Scientific Conference, *History of the Comintern in the Light of New Documents*, Moscow, 20–22 October 1994.

Sterett, Joseph E., and Joseph S. Davis. "The Fiscal and Economic Condition of Mexico: Report Submitted to the International Committee of Bankers on Mexico." New York, 25 May 1928, Hispanic Division, Library of Congress.

Troncoso, Anthony. "Hamilton Fish Sr. and the Politics of American Nationalism, 1912–1945." Ph.D. diss., State University of New Jersey, New Brunswick, 1993.

INDEX

Daniela Spenser is a Fellow at Centro de
Investigaciones y Estudios Superiores en
Antropología Social in Mexico City. This
is her first book in English.

Library of Congress Cataloging-in-
Publication Data
Spenser, Daniela.
The impossible triangle : Mexico, Soviet
Russia, and the United States in the 1920s /
Daniela Spenser ; foreword by Friedrich
Katz.
  p.   cm. — (American encounters/global
interactions)
Includes bibliographical references and
index.
ISBN 0-8223-2256-0 (cloth : alk. paper). —
ISBN 0-8223-2289-7 (paper : alk. paper)
1. Mexico—Foreign relations—Soviet
Union. 2. Soviet Union—Foreign relations—
Mexico. 3. Mexico—Foreign relations—
1910–1946. 4. Soviet Union—Foreign
relations—1917–1945. 5. Mexico—Foreign
relations—United States. 6. United States—
Foreign relations—Mexico. I. Title.
II. Series.
F1228.5.S65S64   1999
327.72047—DC21   98-23653